Ultimate Salesforce LWC Developers' Handbook

Build Dynamic Experiences, Custom User Interfaces, and Interact with Salesforce data using Lightning Web Components (LWC) for Salesforce Cloud

Cihan Fethi Hizar

www.orangeava.com

First published: December 2023

Published by: Orange Education Pvt Ltd, AVA™

Address: 9, Daryaganj, Delhi, 110002

ISBN: 978-81-96801-94-6

www.orangeava.com

Dedicated To

My Wife, My Son

and

My beloved Parents

About the Author

Cihan Fethi Hizar, a highly skilled computer engineer, holds a degree in Computer Engineering from Galatasaray University, an MBA from Maltepe University, and a Master's degree in Engineering and Technology Management from Bogazici University. With a career spanning over a decade, he has been actively involved in software development projects since 2006.

Serving as a Salesforce Consultant for global-end clients since 2013, he has delivered numerous projects for renowned brands such as Coca-Cola, Thermo King, Cision, Medtronic, Absa, and more.

Cihan's expertise spans various technical areas, encompassing Salesforce Core Platform Development (LWC, Apex, Declarative Tools, Flows, Aura Components, VF Pages), Salesforce DevOps (Microsoft Azure, GitHub, GitLab, Flosum, Gearset, OwnBackup, SFDX CLI), Web Application Development (JavaScript, PHP), Cloud Server Management (Amazon Web Services), REST-Based/SOAP-Based Integrations, and Database Design and Management.

As a certified Salesforce professional, he holds a range of certifications, including Salesforce Administrator, Salesforce Advanced Administrator, Salesforce Platform App Builder, Salesforce Sales Cloud Consultant, Salesforce Service Cloud Consultant, Salesforce Experience Cloud Consultant, Salesforce Platform Developer 1, Salesforce Platform Developer 2, and Salesforce JavaScript Developer 1. Affiliated with Salesforce as an ISV Partner and serving as the Owner of ABC Cloud Services, Cihan remains at the forefront of the industry, contributing to the growth and development of the Salesforce community.

About the Technical Reviewer

Pranav Sudhakar is a Salesforce Professional with extensive experience in Salesforce implementations. Currently working as a Lead Consultant and Salesforce Practice Leader for CG Infinity, he has worked in the past with other popular names like Saleforce.com and Tata Consultancy Services. A multi-cloud certified consultant, he has worked on designing and building solutions across Sales Cloud, Service Cloud, Experience Cloud, and Industries Cloud and possesses working knowledge of a ton of other Salesforce projects.

Pranav is also a Four Star Ranger and an active member of the Trailblazer Community. He has been a keen contributor to the Salesforce Fundamentals program for a long time and loves to participate in other Salesforce webinars as a guest speaker.

Acknowledgements

There are a few people I want to thank for the continued and ongoing support they have given me during the writing of this book. First and foremost, I would like to thank my wife for continuously encouraging me to write the book. I could have never completed this book without her support.

I gratefully acknowledge Mr. Pranav Sudhakar Dixit for his kind technical scrutiny of this book. My gratitude also goes to the Orange Education - AVA team (especially to Sonali Biswas, Shubha Murthy, Sreeja Nair, and Priyanka Arora) for being supportive enough to provide me with quite a long time to finish the book.

Preface

This book is a complete guide for Salesforce Lightning Web Component (LWC) Framework, the recent frontend framework of Salesforce which will (most probably) replace Aura components and Visualforce pages completely in the future. Salesforce LWC Framework is also an open-source project of Salesforce Inc. From this perspective, we can say it is somehow similar to Meta's (Facebook's) React.js or Google's Angular.js.

LWC Framework is using modern browsers' features and it will continue to evolve with browsers, with ECMAScript (JavaScript). That's why we can confidently see that it is the present and the future of the Salesforce development environment. Companies and Salesforce partners are currently focusing on migrating old-school Aura components and Visualforce pages into Lightning Web Components. New projects are planned to be developed by using LWC. So, if you're a developer in the Salesforce ecosystem, nowadays, learning LWC already becomes a must.

This book is divided into 10 chapters. They will cover all aspects of Salesforce LWC Framework, starting from the very basics to Lightning Data Service, Lightning Message Service, Lightning Out, Lightning Design System, how to use LWC with Flows, how to test and debug LWCs, etc. Each chapter has practical code examples. Therefore, the reader will have the chance to see different LWC features in action. The reader can download these code examples and use them in her/his Salesforce orgs. We have also 2 appendices at the end of the book where the reader will consolidate her/his know-how about Aura-LWC co-existence and how to migrate from Aura to LWC.

Chapter 1 will do an introduction to the LWC Framework to clarify why it was needed by Salesforce despite the fact that there are already Aura components (and Visualforce pages) around. In this chapter, we'll also present the open-source aspect of the LWC Framework.

Chapter 2 With this chapter, things will start to get warmer as we build our first Lightning Web Component. By using this very first LWC, we'll see how lightning web components are structured, which files in LWC bundles have what purposes, and so on. Moreover, we'll also touch on JavaScript modules to have a good ground to build our LWC know-how upon.

Chapter 3 is where we learn all the LWC basic programming details as data binding, properties, conditional rendering, iterators, rendering lists, decorators, composition and slots, lifecycle hooks, static resources, and so on. In addition to this chapter, we see how to implement navigation in LWC, how to display notifications and how to work with Apex backend.

Chapter 4 is all about data services, specifically about Lightning Data Service. This chapter shows us all the aspects of Lightning Data Service, starting with base components, continuing with the famous "@wire" decorator and finally how to obtain data from backend Apex classes.

Chapter 5 enlightens the secrets of event management in LWC. We see how to define custom events and the ways of their propagation. Then we jump to how to publish and subscribe events using the pubsub module to show one way to enable non-hierarchical communication between independent Lightning web components. But of course, we crown this topic by learning the famous Lightning Message Service, which is a great feature allowing communication not only between Lightning web components but also with Aura components and even with Visualforce pages.

Chapter 6 Like LWC is the future and the present of front-end development for Salesforce, Flows is the new king for non-coded application development. In this chapter, we learn how to use LWC with Flows, which also opens the doors to a new world where someday we may even see these two technologies make obsolete the usage of Apex classes.

Chapter 7 Until this chapter, all we learn is about the development of Salesforce. But when it comes to Salesforce, there is no limit: with Lightning Out it is even possible to develop applications outside of Salesforce, which continues to easily communicate with Salesforce orgs. During the writing of this book (Winter '24 release), Lightning Out continues to be in the "Beta" version, but it promises so much and we learn it in this chapter.

Chapter 8 When it comes to front-end development, styling, design, and user experience are the topics as important as JavaScript programming. Luckily for us, Salesforce built an entire design system for Lightning development: Lightning Design System. In this chapter, we learn all its features and how to use them effectively in our projects.

Chapter 9 Good programming which provides excellent user experience is nothing if there are security flaws in the application. In this chapter, we learn how to develop secure Lightning Web Component applications by first understanding the popular threats (like XSS, CSRF attacks and so on.) because as the saying goes "without knowing your enemy, you cannot build a strong fortress". Fortunately, the security responsibility is not solely on the developers' shoulders as Salesforce already provides very important easy-to-configure, easy-to-use security platforms like Lightning Locker, Lightning Web Security and CSP (Content Security Policy) configurations. Taking into account all of them, we can say that we learn all about LWC security in this chapter.

Chapter 10 While finalizing the book, with this chapter, we learn the last missing pieces of Lightning Web Component development: the testing and the debugging. Therefore, we complete our journey to master LWC development without missing anything.

Get a Free eBook

We hope you are enjoying your recently purchased book! Your feedback is incredibly valuable to us, and to all other readers looking for great books.

If you found this book helpful or enjoyable, we would truly appreciate it, if you could take a moment to leave a short review with a 5 star rating on Amazon. It helps us grow, and lets other readers discover our books.

As a thank you, we would love to send you a free digital copy of this book, and a **30%** discount code on your next cart value on our official websites:

www.orangeava.com

www.orangeava.in (For Indian Subcontinent)

☑ **Here's how:**

Leave a review for the book on Amazon.

Take a screenshot of your review, and send an email to **info@orangeava.com** (it can be just the confirmation screen).

Once, we receive your screenshot, we will send you the digital file, within 24 hours.

Thank you so much for your support – it means a lot to us!

Downloading the code bundles and colored images

Please follow the link or scan the QR code to download the **Code Bundles** of the book:

https://github.com/ava-orange-education/Ultimate-Salesforce-LWC-Developers-Handbook

The code bundles and images of the book are also hosted on ***https://rebrand.ly/c038e7***

In case there's an update to the code, it will be updated on the existing GitHub repository.

Errata

We take immense pride in our work at **Orange Education Pvt Ltd,** and follow best practices to ensure the accuracy of our content to provide an indulging reading experience to our subscribers. Our readers are our mirrors, and we use their inputs to reflect and improve upon human errors, if any, that may have occurred during the publishing processes involved. To let us maintain the quality and help us reach out to any readers who might be having difficulties due to any unforeseen errors, please write to us at :

errata@orangeava.com

Your support, suggestions, and feedback are highly appreciated.

DID YOU KNOW

Did you know that Orange Education Pvt Ltd offers eBook versions of every book published, with PDF and ePub files available? You can upgrade to the eBook version at **www.orangeava.com** and as a print book customer, you are entitled to a discount on the eBook copy. Get in touch with us at: **info@orangeava.com** for more details.

At **www.orangeava.com**, you can also read a collection of free technical articles, sign up for a range of free newsletters, and receive exclusive discounts and offers on AVA™ Books and eBooks.

PIRACY

If you come across any illegal copies of our works in any form on the internet, we would be grateful if you would provide us with the location address or website name. Please contact us at **info@orangeava.com** with a link to the material.

ARE YOU INTERESTED IN AUTHORING WITH US?

If there is a topic that you have expertise in, and you are interested in either writing or contributing to a book, please write to us at **business@orangeava.com**. We are on a journey to help developers and tech professionals to gain insights on the present technological advancements and innovations happening across the globe and build a community that believes Knowledge is best acquired by sharing and learning with others. Please reach out to us to learn what our audience demands and how you can be part of this educational reform. We also welcome ideas from tech experts and help them build learning and development content for their domains.

REVIEWS

Please leave a review. Once you have read and used this book, why not leave a review on the site that you purchased it from? Potential readers can then see and use your unbiased opinion to make purchase decisions. We at Orange Education would love to know what you think about our products, and our authors can learn from your feedback. Thank you!

For more information about Orange Education, please visit **www.orangeava.com**.

Table of Contents

Chapter 1
Introduction

Introduction

Welcome, Salesforce Developer!

Here, we are ready to sail for a new adventure!

We will start by looking very briefly at what are **Lightning Web Components** and why they are the present and the future for Salesforce Lightning developments, while we already have old trusted Visualforce Pages and brand new very capable Aura Components.

You need to have a good understanding of JavaScript to become a successful LWC Developer because LWC means more JavaScript than Salesforce.

Structure

In this chapter, we will discuss the following topics:

- Lightning Web Components (LWC)
- Problem with Visualforce pages
- Aura components getting outdated
- LWC as an open-source JavaScript framework
- Problem-solving with small reusable components

Lightning Web Components (LWC)

In one sentence, Lightning Web Components is an open-source UI framework developed in Salesforce. Basically, we can use LWC not solely for customizing Salesforce but also to develop a third-party web application which can be run independently, not related to any Salesforce org implementation. However, if we aim to use LWC for customizing a Salesforce org implementation, it is good to know that LWC is supported only for Enterprise, Performance, Unlimited and Developer editions. For anything below, you cannot use LWC.

Salesforce Inc. is a member of the World Wide Web Consortium (W3C) and constantly contributes to the development of open web standards and it is in the Ecma International Technical Committee 39 (TC39), which is the committee responsible for JavaScript Language development. So it won't be inaccurate to say that LWC is one of the biggest achievements of the company's continuous contributions to the open web standards.

LWC is built upon core web components standards which consist of code that runs natively in browsers; thus it is possible to have an extremely lightweight framework which delivers exceptional performance. After all, most of the code we are going to write, while working with LWC, will be standard JavaScript and HTML along with CSS.

Note: If you are not sure what are Web Components standards and you are curious to learn them, you can visit their GitHub Repo page: https://github.com/WICG/webcomponents

---

Briefly, we can see LWC as the intersection of the Salesforce Platform development tools and the open web standards. With this framework, **Salesforce Inc.** is now able to take advantage of the evolving standards that are constantly improving what browsers can present to a user. So as developers, we'll also take advantage of doing standard web developments while working with LWC because it would be easier to:

- Use existing solutions in our development efforts, even if those solutions are presented on other platforms.
- Take advantage of all other developers' experiences, even if those developers are not providing solutions directly for the Salesforce Platform.
- Develop faster by enjoying the latest JavaScript enhancements (when we improve our JavaScript skills, we can already be halfway to becoming LWC experts).

However, as stated above, LWC is at the intersection; so not only is it possible to get the advantage of the outside world but in addition, we can also enjoy all the standard components we may need for a Salesforce org customization, developed by Salesforce for the developers. They are listed on the Component Reference page of the LWC Documentation:

https://developer.salesforce.com/docs/component-library/overview/components.

On this page, when we filter for Lightning Web Components, it is possible to list all the 100+ standard LWCs, ready to use, by simply copy-pasting them into our IDE (Integrated Development Environment, example: Visual Studio Code). These standard components are very well documented, giving the developer the ability to customize them according to the specific needs of a task, almost instantly.

So, now it is time to visualize it. A simple LWC will consist of only three files: a JavaScript file as the controller, an HTML file as the view and a CSS file for styling the HTML. Here is a simple example that displays the famous **`Hello World`** message:

```
HTML:
<template>
      <input value={message}></input>
</template>

CSS:
input {
      color: blue;
}

JavaScript:
import {LightningElement} from ‘lwc’;
export default class HelloWorld extends LightningElement {
      message = ‘Hello World’;
}
```

At a minimum, all we need is to create those 3 files (1 JavaScript file, 1 HTML file and 1 CSS file (optional)) which all have the same name, for example, **helloworld.js, helloworld.html, helloworld.css**.

We will learn how to prepare a local development environment for developing LWC by using Visual Studio Code and its Salesforce DX extension in the next chapter but for now, to give a quick try for the preceding example, log in to LWC. Studio (https://app.lwc.studio/) by using your GitHub account:

Figure 1.1: *LWC.Studio Home Page*

Then, click on the **`New`** button to create a simple LWC Project in this playground as shown in *Figure* 1.2:

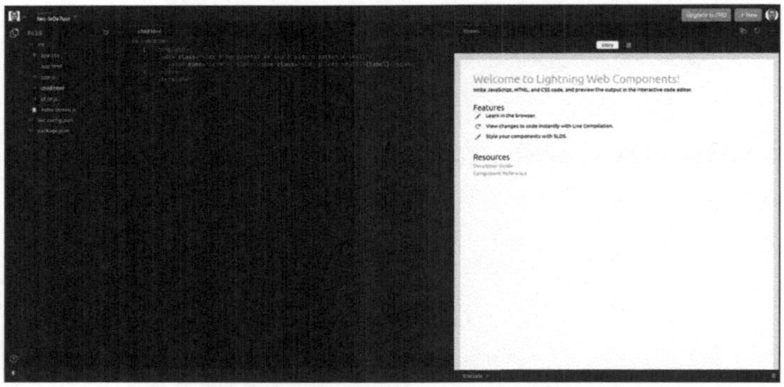

Figure 1.2: *New Empty LWC Project*

Here, we can delete all the existing files, initially created for us, and add our files by using the **+** button which appears when we mouse over the **`src`** folder as shown in *Figure* 1.3:

Figure 1.3: *We Added Our Files*

Tip: When we copy paste the code, if it is not working, check the **`index.stories.js`** file (which is a specific file for this LWC.Studio, not related to LWC development) and update all the **`app`** expressions by replacing them with **`helloworld`** as follows:

```
        import HelloWorld from "./helloworld";
    export const story = () => createElement("c-helloworld",
{ is: HelloWorld });
```

Problem with Visualforce pages

Now we have a basic understanding of what LWC is, and how it is developed by Salesforce and we even ran a simple example! We're definitely on a good track :) But being a Salesforce developer, one can wonder what's the need for a new framework like LWC, as we can already do whatever we need by writing good old reliable Visualforce pages!

This may seem a fair question if the Internet World stayed in its place where everyone was happy loading the entire page whenever the user does something on the web page; those were the good old days before mobile phones conquered our daily lives. So let's see why Visualforce pages are already a declining technology, and how they are currently being replaced by the Lightning Experience's new development tools like Aura Components and LWC.

Execution of the page

As you may already know, when a Visualforce page is initially loaded, all the page's data and actions are calculated and prepared in the backend by the Apex controller. Basically, the Visualforce page technological design is based on 1 server backend controller (Apex class) + 1 frontend view (which is the Visualforce page itself). As a result of this, whenever a user interacts with the page, for all the **`View State`** updates resulting from those interactions, the entire new updated **`View State`** is sent back to the backend controller expecting that it re-calculates a new page view and re-sends it to the frontend.

This lack of the frontend controller (which is expected to be a JavaScript file) makes the page's execution unnecessarily slow as with every change on the page, the browser needs to send not only the specific updates but everything again in a redundant manner. Briefly, each change on the page is a new page refresh in the Visualforce page's world.

However, the capable Visualforce page developers, in order to overcome this issue, started to add inline JavaScript scripts. But this comes with problems like the hacking of Salesforce records (in a manner where sometimes it is even possible to show records to users who don't have permission to see them) or other more serious security flaws.

That's why Salesforce needed to drop providing patches for Visualforce pages to overcome those problems and turned the wheel into a brand new experience- Lightning Experience.

Note: If you are curious to learn more about the `View State`, please consult the Salesforce documentation:

https://developer.salesforce.com/docs/atlas.en-us.pages.meta/pages/vf_dev_best_practices_optimizing_performance.html

---

Mobile-first world

While working with Visualforce pages, the developer is responsible for all page design and page responsiveness for different devices. That means even for a page which is expected to do a small job, it needs to have tons of inline CSS (and JavaScript) add-ons just to provide this responsiveness.

This cannot be simply acceptable in a forward-moving world in which salespeople are constantly dependent more and more on their mobile phones or different size devices like laptops and tablets.

In addition, mobile-first development techniques put the final nail on the need for one-page web applications in which the users can interact with the page without needing to leave it by having the ability to partially load it. Yes, this can also be done via Visualforce pages by adding inline JavaScript scripts but all of those attempts are just temporary patches for the new constantly evolving demands of the market, meaning it is not possible to consider them as state-of-the-art solutions.

Component-based design needs

The rise of the one-page applications also brings out the need for component-based designs in which when a developer creates (let's say) a hamburger menu for a page. This functionality should be able to be used by other pages as well without needing to copy-paste redundantly the same code for each page.

Again, for this purpose, another patch-like solution was once provided - Visualforce components. However, we can also consider this one as having been done in order to gain additional time before the new mobile-first experience (Lightning Experience) overruled the old world.

Security issues

Visualforce pages are by nature HTML pages in which a developer can put any mumbo-jumbo code including but not limited to inline redirects to third-party JavaScript libraries and any DOM updating code along with global Salesforce variables.

In addition to all of the above, most of the Visualforce pages are also dynamically updated according to the values given in the query string values defined in the URL of the page.

Here are some examples to demonstrate how easy it is to write insecure codes:

Example 1:

```
<script>
    var urlvalues = location.search;
    document.write(urlvalues);
</script>
```

In the preceding code snippet, as we can see, it is easily possible to realize a Cross Site Scripting (XSS) attack by basically adding any malicious script in the page URL's search string `(=query string)` as it will be run directly in the page itself.

Example 2:

```
<img src="http://www.yoursalesforceorg.com/yourvfpage/createuser?
email=attacker@attacker.com&type=admin....." height=1 width=1 />
```

Here, the **`img`** tag is a good example of a **Cross-Site Request Forgery (CSRF)** attack. If the user is already logged in to his/her Salesforce org and while having this Visualforce page opened in a separate tab, if he/she opens the attacker's web page which contains a direct link via a 1x1 **`img`** tag to this Salesforce org's Visualforce page, it is possible for the attacker to capture all the cookies or hijack the user's session or as seen in this example create a brand-new user for himself/herself in the Salesforce org.

Of course, there are many means, methods, and design patterns to write secure code in Visualforce pages despite those dangers and many built-in standard secure tags, properties being already provided by Salesforce that can be used to prevent those kinds of attacks. However, as security is not built-in on the platform, all depend on the skills of the Salesforce developer to take care of all of those potentialities. And everyone knows that most of the time the projects are highly time-restricted which doesn't give enough time to the developers to carefully handle all of those potential security flaws even if the developers are sufficiently experienced to be aware of those kinds of issues.

As we're going to discuss in the upcoming chapters, LWC already has built-in security - **Lightning Web Security** which enforces the developer to write secure code by default, even if he is not a fan of losing time to write secure code.

Aura components getting outdated

Visualforce page is an old technology from the old days of web application development where the needs are more basic than today's world but Salesforce already has Aura components which are modern, secure, 100% compatible with the Salesforce platform, and so on. So why do we need LWC?

In the previous section, we've learned about the proliferation (in a very short period of time) of different size devices like mobile phones, tablets, and laptops which are always connected, by having different needs for securities and applications.

World Wide Web Consortium (W3C) is a very big organization, having contributions from many big tech giants like Apple, Google, Amazon, Microsoft, IBM, Oracle, Mozilla, and more. and it is responsible for the development of the **Open Web Platform** to provide standards for everything which (will) run on the Web/Internet.

So all the browsers like Google Chrome, Mozilla Firefox, Opera, Chromium, Microsoft Edge, Apple Safari, and so on. are being standardized after the standards are finalized in W3C.

However, W3C is big and so it is slow by definition. This means tech companies cannot just wait for this consortium to finalize the standards. So every company, while waiting for the maturation of the standards, pushes their solutions to the market because the new devices are already there and the users are always expecting the best applications, and experiences with their devices. And the customers are always right!

Briefly, Aura components are the answer to those evolving needs of the users: it is basically a framework that fills the gaps of the browsers (which were depending on the ECMAScript 5 core language, via 2014 Web Stack) in order to provide cutting-edge reusable component-based web applications, screens to the users in the Salesforce Platform Lightning Experience.

So while in 2014 Web Stack with ECMAScript 5 language was being widely used, the web standards were only consisting of:

- ECMAScript 5
- Events
- Standard Elements
- Rendering

That's why the companies (like Salesforce) had to develop the below features under their frameworks:

- Data services
- UI components
- Component model
- Templates
- Rendering optimization
- Modules
- Language extensions

Consequently, Aura Components Framework had been developed to ensure the above solutions. We can see it as a **browser patch** which provides those additional features to the browsers. Aura components were not the only solution, Facebook's React.js, Google's Angular.js or Vue.js were all developed by the companies and organizations for this high level of abstraction.

However, when the 2019 Web Stack with ECMAScript 7 was published, things changed heavily because the web standards now started to cover the following:

- Web components
- Templates
- Custom elements
- Shadow DOM
- Modules
- ECMAScript 7
- Events
- Standard elements
- Rendering

So now, only the remaining features should be supported by the companies' private frameworks:

- Specialized services
- Data services
- UI components

This gives companies and organizations the chance to have lighter frameworks, which are just for providing specific solutions to the specific needs of their specific platforms: So this is not a coincidence that LWC also entered our life in 2019! It is a lighter and yet more secure Lightning Component Framework which resides in the **2019 Web Stack** along with **ECMAScript 7** core language.

That's why when you use Aura components with modern browsers, unintentionally you activate duplicate features, which means similar features which are already supported natively by the browsers. This is the reason Aura components are slower than LWC and this is the reason why Salesforce now continues to invest only in LWC.

So having this book is a good start to stay current because the future won't have Visualforce pages and (probably) won't have Aura components. The future is on LWC.

LWC as an open-source JavaScript framework

We now have a good understanding of why Salesforce needed to come up with this LWC Framework despite Visualforce pages and Aura components being around for some time. In this section, let us learn a little more about the **open-source** aspect of the LWC Framework and how to use it in the outside world like Vue.js or Angular.js etc.

The open-source project site's address is https://lwc.dev (Refer to *Figure* 1.4):

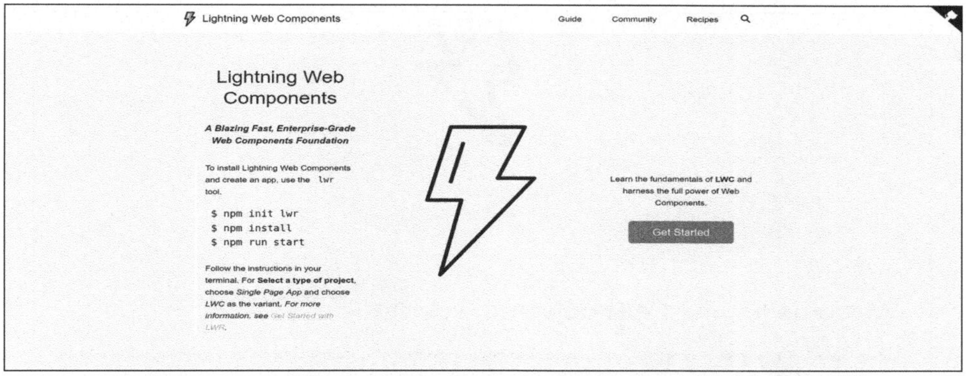

Figure 1.4: *LWC Open-source official site*

Installing and getting started

In order to install Lightning Web Components and start coding locally, we need the **Lightning Web Runtime (lwr)** tool. This can be installed via Node.js.

Note: Node.js is out of the scope of this book but as this is highly popular topic in JavaScript world, they are plenty of learning content in the Internet.

So follow these steps to run the first project:

1. In the terminal program, run **`npm init lwr.`**
2. Enter a project name like **`StaticSite`**.
3. Accept the default generated package name (**`staticsite`**), the default type of the project (**`Static  Site`**) and the default variant (**`Markdown Static Site`**).
4. Change the directory for the new project folder, **`cd StaticSite`**.
5. In the terminal, run **`npm install`**.
6. Finally, run **`npm run dev.`**

And voilà! The following figure shows what the site looks like:

Figure 1.5: *First LWR Powered Website Project*

It is possible to use any code editor to develop LWC, even a simple Notepad.

Simple LWC open-source application

We'll dive into the details of developing LWC for the Salesforce Lightning Platform in the next chapters but here let us see how to develop a simple application by using the LWC open-source tools.

In the previous section, we created a **`StaticSite`** which was using **`Markdown`** markup language for templating. So to be honest, this was not a good example of the LWC we would normally create for Salesforce. Now, by using the following commands in the command line, let's create a proper LWC (which can also be used in the Salesforce Platform):

- In the terminal program, run **`npm init lwr`**
- Enter the project name **`lwr-test-project`**
- Accept the default generated package name (**`lwr-test-project`**)
- Select the **`Single Page App`** type for the project (**`Static Site`**) and as a template choose **`LWC`**.
- Change the directory for the new project folder, **`cd lwr-test-project`**
- In the terminal, run **`npm install`**.
- Finally, run **`npm run dev`**.

Here is the screenshot for the commands (refer to *Figure* 1.6):

Figure 1.6: *We create and run the project by using the terminal program*

Now when we hit **`http://localhost:3000`**, here is how our LWC-based site is running (Refer to *Figure 1.7*):

Figure 1.7: *Our LWC-based site*

Yes, there is nothing much to see but at least we now have something to play with.

Tip: If you encounter an error similar to **`node vm module not found`** while trying to run the `npm run dev` command, in the project folder go to this subfolder:

`node_modules → @locker → near-membrane-node → dist`

And here update the **`index.cjs.js`** file by changing the 7th line into

`"var node_vm = require('vm');"`

So, our files to customize are under the **lwr-test-project → src → modules → example → app** folder. Here we can see and update the three bundle files:

- app.js
- app.html
- app.css

Here, let's first update the **app.js** as follows:

```
import { LightningElement } from 'lwc';
export default class HelloWorldApp extends LightningElement {
    name = "Robert Junior";
}
```

And let's update the **app.html** as:

```
<template>
    <main>
        <img src="/public/assets/recipes-logo.png" alt="logo" />
        <h1>Hello {name}!</h1>
    </main>
</template>
```

So basically, we did a simple data binding exercise. Here is the result (as expected) when we refresh the page (refer to *Figure 1.8*):

Figure 1.8: *The site after we're done with the data binding update*

Ok, this simple example is a good demonstration that we can develop entirely third-party independent web applications by using LWC Open Source, without depending on the Salesforce Platform. However, just to mention, LWC Open Source may have some **Beta** or **Generally Available for Open-source development but not for the Salesforce Platform** features. In addition, Salesforce doesn't promise to use every feature of LWC Open-source in the Salesforce Platform. So if something is working with LWC Open-source, that doesn't mean that this would also work as it is on the Salesforce Platform.

For LWC features that exist in the Salesforce Platform, always keep an eye on the LWC Developer Guide

(https://developer.salesforce.com/docs/component-library/documentation/en/lwc).

Problem-solving with small reusable components

So before concluding this chapter, let us discuss a little bit about the component-based application design: after all, all of those development tools, we've talked about so far, were created mainly to resolve this kind of web application design.

LWC (and Aura components) are designed to be either a container for other components or to be a standalone independent component that resolves one issue for us. For example, a **calendar** component is a very good example of a simple component that handles showing the date/time for the user.

Let's say we need to build a listing page for an e-commerce portal. One way (the bad way) to do this is to think of the page as a whole and implement a big LWC that has **`img`** tags, **`table`** with **`row`** and **`columns`** including conditions either a product exists in the stocks and showing the product actions (**`add to cart`** or **`add to wish list`**) accordingly. As this is an e-commerce portal, there will be **`reviews`** for the products, and **`product detail`** popups for each product, and so on.

If you design it as one big LWC without any child component, maintenance will be also more difficult than expected, consider this example: the customer asks to have a **`border`** around the **`images`** of the products, and at the same time he/she asks for a design update for the **`product details`** popups which are shown when a mouse-over is done by the user. As all of the controller methods are in the same LWC, the project manager may not even give those two simple tasks to two different developers in parallel as this would cause merging problems while both developers are working on the same LWC.

A basic solution to the above maintenance problems is to see the entire listing page as a sum of small re-usable components as follows:

- An image component responsible for showing the image of the product.
- A popup component responsible for showing the **`product detail`** and **`product reviews`** popup contents.
- A table component responsible for creating the main table for the page.
- A search component.
- A pagination component.
- A container component responsible for having all of the above components in order to build the page for the user.

The following figure shows how the component-based design would look:

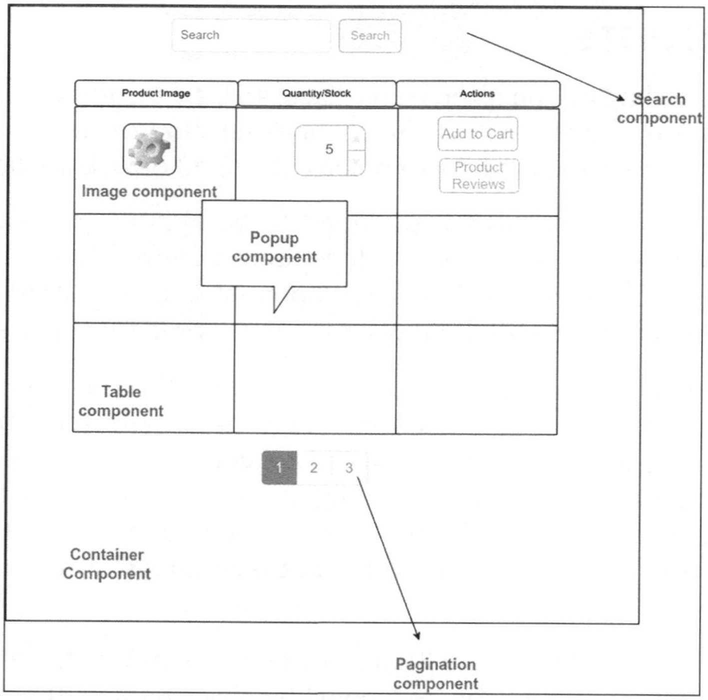

Figure 1.9: *Component-based Design For Our e-Commerce Portal Listing Page*

Now besides being able to maintain the page with multiple developers, it is also possible to use some components (like pagination, search, table, popup, and image) in another part of the application.

Conclusion

In this chapter, we made a good introduction to what basically LWC is and why it is the future despite having the good old Visualforce Pages and relatively new Aura Components. We also saw that LWC is not a private technology which is working solely in the Salesforce Platform but instead it was released as an open-source framework. We also mentioned what is component-based design and how LWC is fitting just as it should for any problem that requires component-based design. Throughout the chapter, we also had the chance to run some basic code in the cloud which warms us a little more for the next chapters.

In the next chapter, we're going to prepare our local development environment for starting to write our own LWC, and we'll become more familiar with the LWC bundle.

References

- World Wide Web Consortium (W3C) - https://www.w3.org
- World Wide Web Consortium (W3C) Member List - https://www.w3.org/Consortium/Member/List
- Ecma International Technical Committee 39, ECMAScript Language Specification - https://tc39.github.io/ecma262/
- Web components standards Github - https://github.com/WICG/webcomponents
- LWC Component Reference - https://developer.salesforce.com/docs/component-library/overview/components
- LWC.Studio - https://app.lwc.studio/
- Visualforce Pages View State - https://developer.salesforce.com/docs/atlas.en-us.pages.meta/pages/vf_dev_best_practices_optimizing_performance.htm
- Introducing Lightning Web Components - https://developer.salesforce.com/blogs/2018/12/introducing-lightning-web-components

CHAPTER 2
Creating Your First LWC

Introduction

With this chapter, things will start to get warmer. Firstly, we're going to prepare our development environment with Visual Studio Code and Salesforce DX Extensions. Before directly jumping into LWC, we'll look into JavaScript modules to obtain some background.

We continue our journey onwards by defining a simple LWC to examine the folder structure: HTML File, JavaScript File, Configuration File, CSS File, and SVG Icon. We'll also see how to use additional JavaScript files in one LWC bundle. After we show how to prepare our environment to write tests for a component, we're going to finish the chapter by showing how to work with LWCs entirely locally without needing to publish them to a Salesforce org.

Structure

In this chapter, we will discuss the following topics:

- Preparing Our Development Environment
- JavaScript Background: Modules
- LWC Folder Structure and Namespaces
- LWC Testing Prerequisites
- LWC Local Development

Preparing Our Development Environment

There are different alternatives for doing development on the Salesforce Platform, the best-known ones are:

- Salesforce CLI + Visual Studio Code + VS Code Salesforce Extension Pack
    - **Salesforce CLI** is the command-line tool for the Salesforce Platform and all **Salesforce Developer Experience (SFDX)** features.
    - **Visual Studio Code (VS Code)** is a general integrated development environment (IDE) in which the developers can develop code using many different programming languages (to be honest almost any language is supported). It is the currently officially supported IDE by Salesforce.
    - **VS Code Salesforce Extension Pack**, offered by Salesforce, includes tools that provide features for working with Salesforce development orgs (like scratch orgs, sandboxes and Developer Edition orgs). Here is the list of the tools included in this standard extension pack: Apex, Apex Interactive Debugger, Apex Replay Debugger, Salesforce CLI Integration, Aura Components, Visualforce, Lightning Web Components, SOQL, Salesforce Lightning Design System (SLDS) Validator.
        - There is also a second expanded version: **VS Code Salesforce Extension Pack (Expanded)**. This extension pack includes all the standard pack's tools but in addition, there are some other third-party tools for better code formatting and analyzing.
- **Force.com IDE:** This was a popular IDE before VS Code but it has been in a maintenance-only state now, since October 2019. It will become obsolete.
- **Illuminated Cloud:** This IDE is mostly for developers who are coming into the Salesforce world from other development experiences. It has a different taste but accomplishes exactly the same IDE tasks.

There are also web-based development environments:

- **Developer Console:** This is a standard in-house web-based development environment tool which exists in every Salesforce org by default. This is excellent for doing quick updates on Salesforce orgs but unfortunately, it doesn't support LWC development.
- **Code Builder**: Developed by Salesforce Labs, it can be installed from Salesforce AppExchange. It is currently in the Beta version. It supports LWC development.

In this book, we're going to use the **VS Code + VS Code Salesforce Extension Pack** along with **Salesforce CLI**, which is currently the de facto standard for Salesforce development.

Before we start with the tool downloads and installs, it may be a good idea to say a few words about the Salesforce CLI command-line tool:

- It is an extremely powerful, lightweight and fast tool which can be used to realize almost any task on the Salesforce Platform by using as simple as one-line commands.
- It can create and manage scratch orgs and sandboxes, including authorizations for orgs.
- It can create and execute tests.
- It can create and manage packages.
- It can be used for importing and exporting data.
- It can deploy metadata, read the metadata of an org, can be used to build DevOps automation, etc.

It may be really worth it to spare time to examine its commands and its capabilities via SFDX Developer Guide and SFDX Command Reference.

Ok, let's start with installing development tools. First, we install Salesforce CLI command-line tool from its official website (https://developer.salesforce.com/tools/sfdxcli):

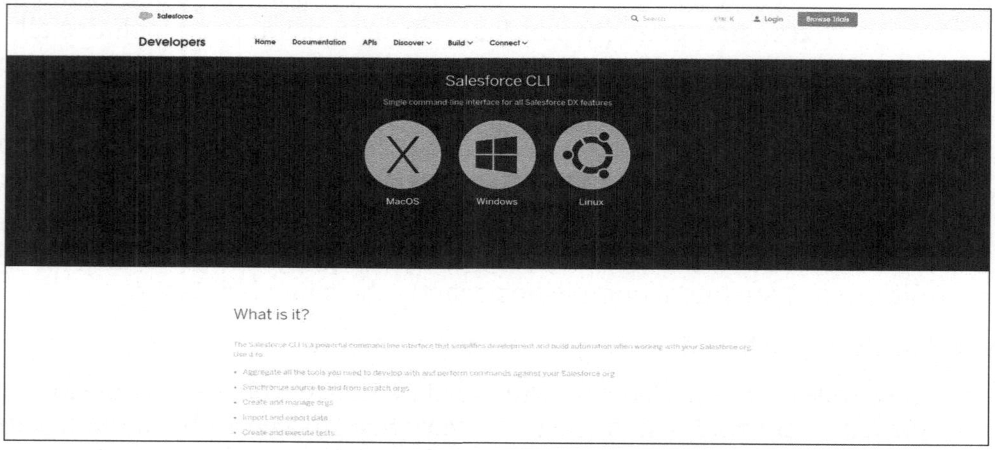

***Figure 2.1**: Salesforce CLI Official Website*

VS Code can be downloaded and installed from its official download page.

(https://code.visualstudio.com/download):

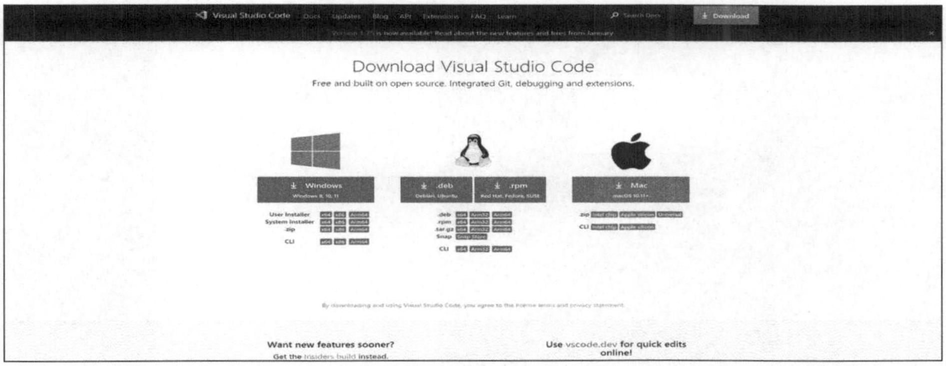

Figure 2.2: *VS Code download page*

After you install the VS Code into your computer, you can easily add the **`Salesforce Extension Pack`** by using the VS Code Extensions Marketplace:

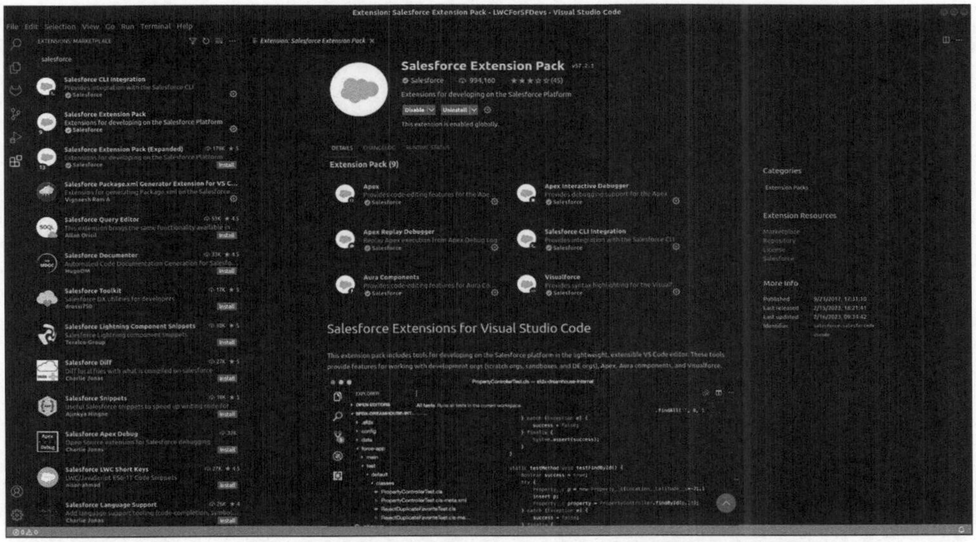

Figure 2.3*: Salesforce Extension Pack*

When we're done installing the VS Code and the VS Code Salesforce Extension Pack, the next step is to obtain a **Salesforce Developer Edition (DE) org**. These DE orgs are a full-featured copy of the Salesforce Platform, which are being offered for free by Salesforce. To obtain one, in the browser, open its sign-up page (https://developer.salesforce.com/signup) and fill out the form:

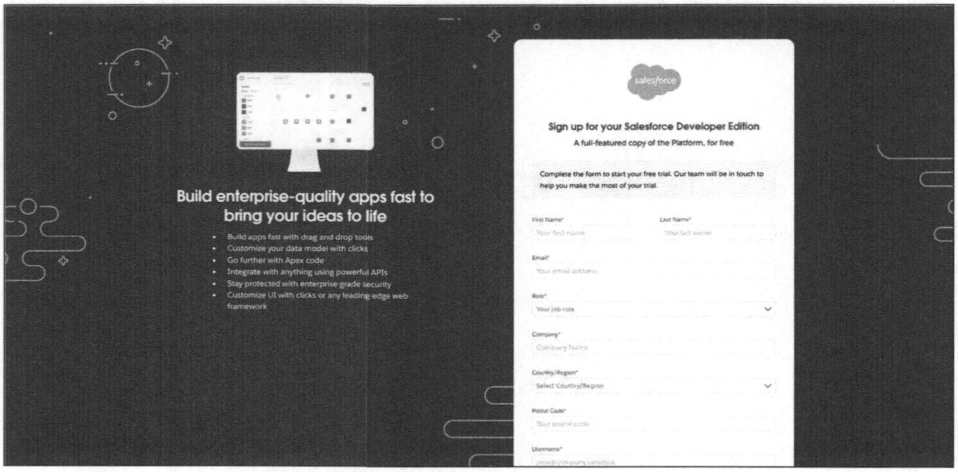

Figure 2.4: *Sign-up page for Salesforce DE org*

After we get a Salesforce DE org, now let's create a Salesforce SFDX Project by using **`VS Code Command Palette:`**

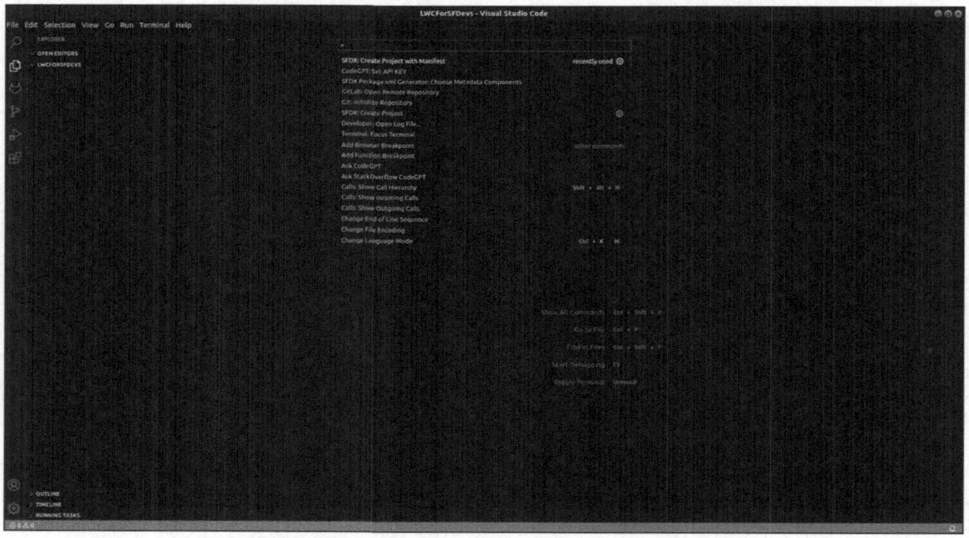

Figure 2.5: *Using Command Palette for creating our first SFDX Project*

While creating the project, select the **`Standard`** template and we can select any name we like as the project name. Here, we're using **`LWCForSFDevelopers.`**

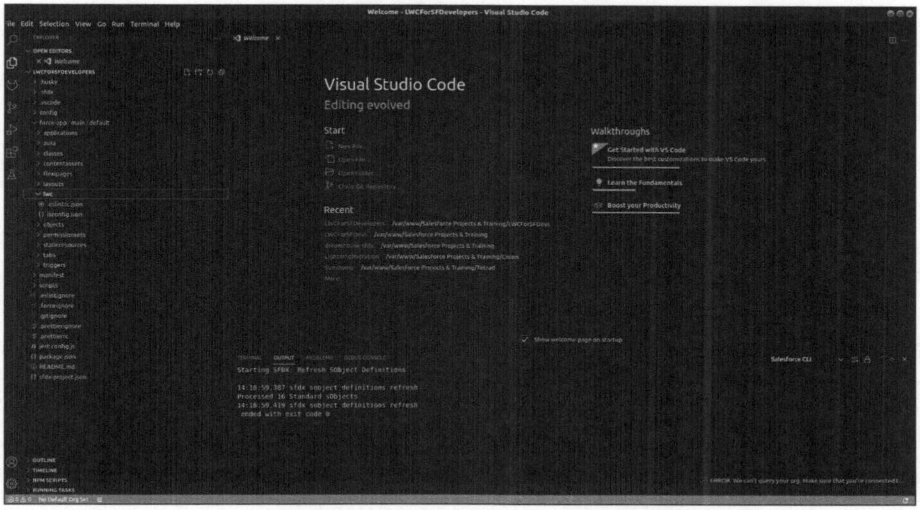

Figure 2.6: *SFDX Project is created*

Now let's set our Salesforce DE org as the default org for our SFDX project. For this one, we're using the **`SFDX: Authorize`** an Org command:

Figure 2.7: *Authorizing our DE org*

While authorizing the DE org, select **`Custom Login URL`** and enter the **`login URL`** of the Salesforce DE org. And we can surely determine any org alias we want, here we use **`LWC4SFDevelopersOrg.`**

Congratulations! We now have our development environment ready.

JavaScript Background: Modules

Before diving into the LWC world, we want to mention its JavaScript roots. In the previous chapter, we mentioned about the constant developments done in W3C ECMA International Technical Committee 39 (TC39): So, one of the important improvements to the ECMAScript language was the **new module system** of the ECMAScript6 (ES6). **`Modules`** were existing prior to ES6 but it is not wrong to say that with ES6 they achieve their ideal structure.

Note: While this book is being written, the current version of the ECMAScript was 14 (ES14), which was released in June 2023. The committee aims to make a major release every year in June.

A **module** is nothing but a JavaScript file which includes classes, standalone functions, and properties that can be exported to be used by other JavaScript files or as an inline HTML script. Thus, we can see a **module** as a JavaScript file in which we can specify which sections of the module can (or cannot) be accessed outside the module. A **module** can also load other modules so it is possible to have a modular structure in our JavaScript-based application by defining different functionalities of the application in different JavaScript modules. **Modules** are the basic technology to have a component-based design in our applications. As we're going to see in the following sections, LWC's main structure is based on the modules.

So let's define a simple module by writing the following code into a JS file (**`module1.js`**), under the folder **`jssamples`**(which we create under the **`force-app → main → default`** folder) in our SFDX Project:

```
class House {
      constructor() {
            this.numberOfBedrooms = 3;
            this.type = 'flat';
      }
}


function getBedrooms(house) {
```

```
  return  `The number of the bedrooms in the house is $(house.
numberOfBedrooms)`;
}


function getType(house) {
  return  `The house is a $(house.type)`;
}

const someConstant = 'LWC For Salesforce Developers';
```

There are 2 types of exports: **Named exports** and **Default exports**.

Each module can only have one default export. When a section is **`default exported`**, the importing file can use any name for calling it, but if a section is named **`exported`** then the importing file should use the exact name for using it. (Or if we want to use our names, we can also define aliases for the **`named imported`** sections in the importing file).

For doing the exports, please add the following lines at the end of the **`module1.js`** file:

```
export default House; // This is default export
export {getBedrooms, getType, someConstant}; // This is named export
```

Now let's create another module, called "**module2.js**" - again under the same "**jssamples**" folder, which will use those "**module1.js**" exported functionalities and properties:

```
import xyz from './module1.js';
import {getBedrooms, getType, someConstant} from './module1.js';

const house = new xyz();
console.log(house);
console.log(getBedrooms(house));
console.log(getType(house));
```

```
console.log(someConstant);
```

And finally, let's define a simple HTML file (called **`index.html`**) to run our work in the browser:

```
<!doctype html>
    <head>
        <title>JavaScript Modules</title>
    </head>
    <body>
        <script type=”module” src=”module2.js”></script>
    </body>
</html>
```

Here is the result:

Figure 2.8: *Module2 is using Module1 functionalities, properties*

As we may notice, in the **`index.html`**, **`module2.js`** is called by using **`script type = ‘module’`** not the usual common way **`script type = ‘text/javascript’`**. Moreover, it is good to note that we can run JavaScript modules in a proper web server via **`http(s)://`** protocol, they cannot be run as **`file://`** in the browsers.

Another thing to notice is, in **`module2.js`** we give **`xyz`** name for using the **`House`** class of the **`module1.js.`** As mentioned before, for **default export** the importing module can use any name (and also no need to use {..}) but for **named exports** we need to use the exact names of the functionalities, properties. However, if one really needs to use different names, even for **named exports,** this is possible to add an **alias**. Here is the updated **`module2.js`** which uses aliases for the named imports:

```
import xyz from ‘./module1.js’;
import {getBedrooms as gBeds, getType as gType, someConstant as myCons}
from ‘./module1.js’;
```

```
const house = new xyz();
console.log(house);
console.log(gBeds(house));
console.log(gType(house));
console.log(myCons);
```

As you can see despite using aliases, the result didn't change:

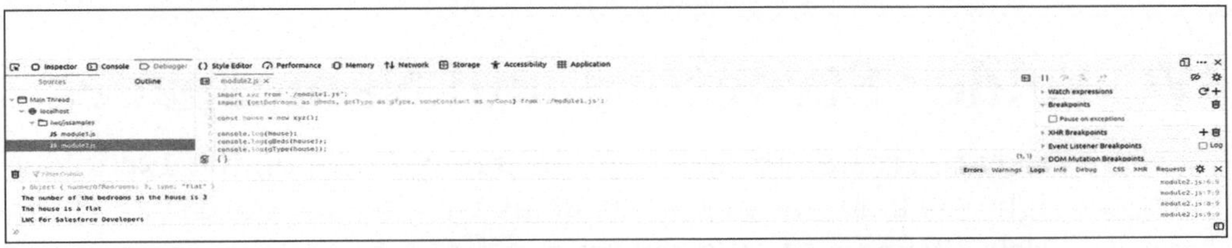

Figure 2.9: *Module2 is using Aliases for Named Imports*

Now, before closing this section, let's improve **`module1.js`** by doing the exports inline:

```
export default class House {
        constructor() {
                this.numberOfBedrooms = 3;
                this.type = 'flat';
        }
}

export function getBedrooms(house) {
  return  `The number of bedrooms in the house is ${house.numberOf
Bedrooms}`;
}

export function getType(house) {
  return  `The house is a ${house.type}`;
}

export const someConstant = 'LWC For Salesforce Developers';
```

As we can see, we don't need to put separate **export** expressions in the module but we can do the **export** declarations directly while defining the functionality, property etc.

Note: A script tag of `type = module` is loaded in parallel by the browser, that means it is deferred by the browser. So once loaded, it waits for the DOM to get ready and then it is executed. Thus, the page does not suffer performance penalty.

LWC Folder Structure and Namespaces

Now, we're ready to create our first LWC. In the VS Code, on the **`lwc`** folder of the project right-click and in the menu items we click on the **`SFDX: Create Lightning Web Component`**. We determine the name of the component as **`firstLWC`**, and use the default directory (Refer to *Figure* 2.10).

By default, Salesforce Extension Pack creates the JavaScript controller **`firstLWC.js`**, the template (view) file **`firstLWC.html`** and the configuration file **`firstLWC.js-meta.xml`** files. In addition, it also put the **`__test__`** folder along with the **`firstLWC.test.js`** testing template file for us (refer to *Figure* 2.11).

In this section, we're going to examine each of those files and discuss in addition **CSS** and **SVG** files which can also be added to the LWC bundle. Finally, we'll also talk about the namespacing in the LWCs.

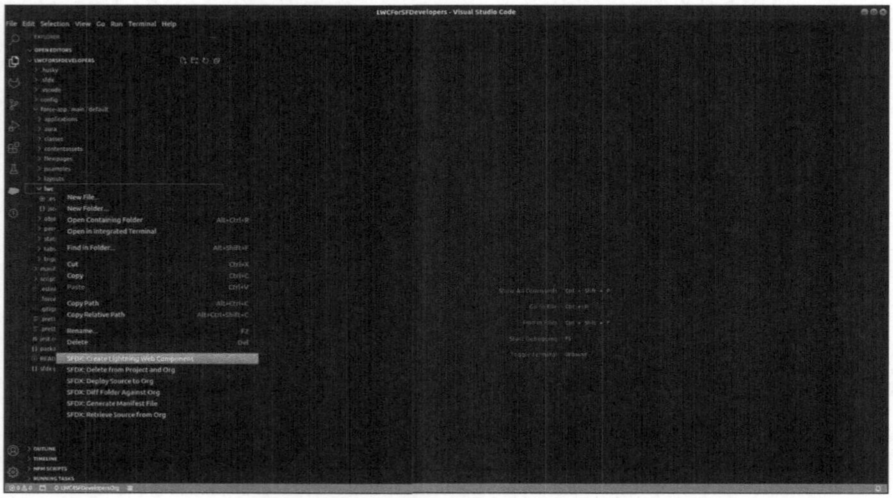

Figure 2.10: *Creating our first LWC*

Figure 2.11: *LWC Default Folder Structure*

Tip: There are some naming rules to be careful while creating a new LWC:

- The name should begin with a lowercase letter.
- Only the alphanumeric or underscore characters can be used.
    - However, as a best practice, we shouldn't use underscore character but instead we use **camelCase** (= first letter lowercase, then each other word in the name should be uppercase) while naming the component, example: **myFirstComponent.**
- No whitespace in the name and no underscore at the end.
- The name cannot contain two consecutive underscores.
- The name cannot contain a hyphen (dash).

While naming the component **camelCasing** is particularly important because when we **camelCase** the name of the LWC, it can be called directly in the HTML view file according to the HTML standard by having hyphens between the words (which is called kebab-casing), example: **<c-my-first-component></c-my-first-component>**

Component JavaScript File

Let's examine the general structure of the JavaScript file in our component:

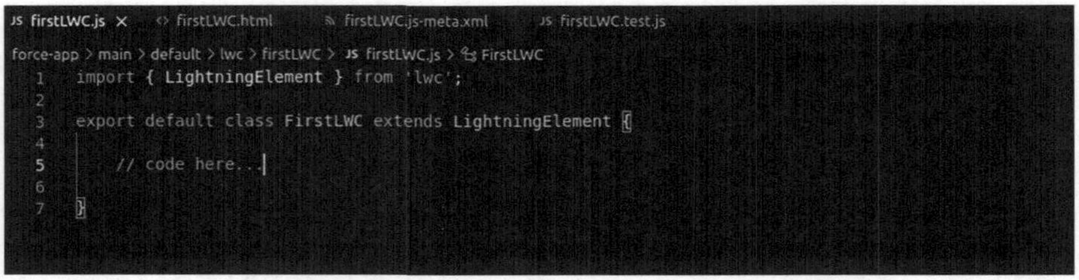

***Figure 2.12:** Component JavaScript File*

This is an example of a **UI component** which is used as a controller for the template (view) HTML file. Apart from UI components, we can also define LWCs as **service components (libraries)**. We'll discuss about the service components in the next section.

Here in our UI component, initially, we do a named import for `LightningElement` from the Salesforce standard module `lwc`:

```
import { LightningElement } from 'lwc';
```

`LightningElement` is a Salesforce Platform standard JavaScript class that gives your LWC the ability to use standard methods like `connectedCallback()`, `renderedCallback()`, `errorCallback (error, stack),` etc. Moreover, it is needed that our JavaScript class (here in this example `FirstLWC`) in the component should extend `LightningElement` in order to be the controller for the HTML template(view) file.

```
export default class FirstLWC extends LightningElement { … }
```

In a UI component, there can be only one `export default` which is the main class of our LWC. Currently, exporting other variables or functions in a UI component is not supported.

The class name should always be Pascal Case where the first letter of each word is capitalized. As our LWC is called `firstLWC`, our class name is determined as `FirstLWC`.

Adding Additional JavaScript Files into the LWC

We mentioned that every LWC (of type UI) should have one main JavaScript file which holds the main class of the component. However, this doesn't mean that the developer should add all the controller functionalities into this single file. It is possible to have a modular structure in which the developer can move different sets of functionalities under different JavaScript files in the same LWC.

To demonstrate how it is working, let's add a new JavaScript file (**`utils.js`**) in our **`firstLWC`** LWC bundle:

***Figure 2.13:** New JavaScript file in the LWC Bundle*

Let's copy-paste the code of **`module1.js`** that we've developed in the previous section into this new JavaScript file:

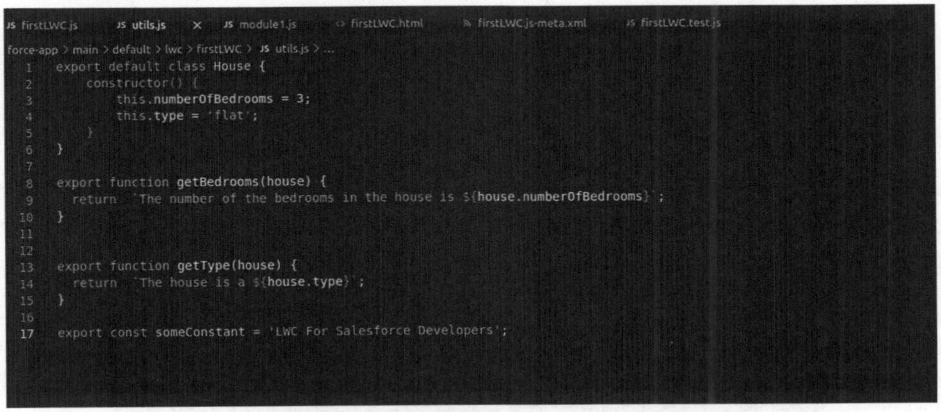

***Figure 2.14:** Our helper JavaScript file utils.js*

In order to use these functionalities and properties in our main JavaScript file, let's import them:

```
import { LightningElement } from 'lwc';
import xyz from './utils';
import {getBedrooms as gBeds, getType as gType, someConstant as myCons}
from './utils';

export default class FirstLWC extends LightningElement {
```

```
    house = new xyz();
    numberOfBeds = gBeds(this.house);
    houseType = gType(this.house);
    cons = myCons;
}
```

Careful readers will notice one difference here: while importing the functionalities and properties from **utils.js** (unlike what we've done in the previous JavaScript Background: Modules section) we're not using the **.js** file extension. No need to use it in Salesforce LWC Framework. We can simply use the filename as from **'./utils'**. One other thing to notice is that we're using a relative directory **(./)** while doing the imports from the additional JavaScript file, **utils.js.**

So, by using the **utils.js** functionalities and properties we're defining **house, numberOfBeds**, **houseType** and **cons** properties for our main JavaScript file **firstLWC.js.**

Service Component (Library)

Apart from UI components, we've mentioned that it is also possible to define pure JavaScript-based LWCs in order to use them as general libraries for the entire LWC application.

For this purpose, let's create a second LWC in our SFDX project, called **serviceComponentExample**:

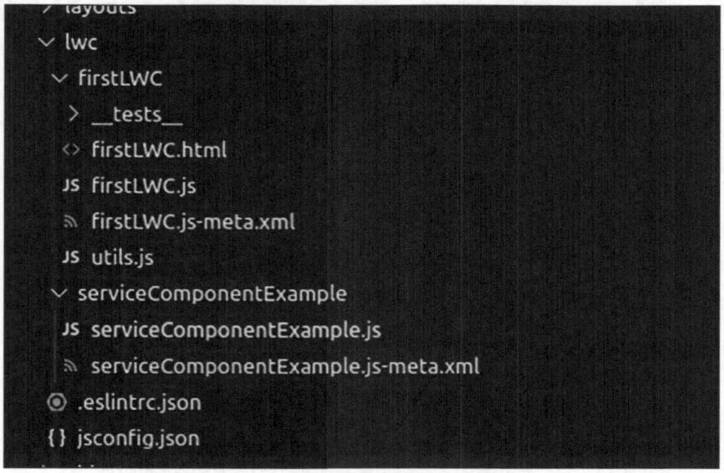

***Figure 2.15:** serviceComponentExample LWC is created*

As we can notice, there is no HTML template (view) file in this LWC because this is not a UI component but a service component which will be used as an in-house library for the LWC application.

So, let's add one basic method in order to demonstrate how it is working:

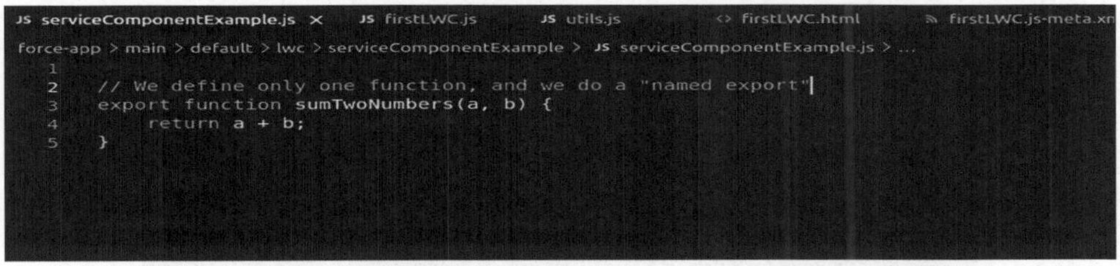

Figure 2.16: *We add one basic function in our service component*

We can use this **`sumTwoNumbers`** function of the **`serviceComponentExample`** service component by importing it to our main **`firstLWC`** UI component:

```
import { LightningElement } from 'lwc';
import xyz from './utils';
import {getBedrooms as gBeds, getType as gType, someConstant as myCons}
from './utils';
import {sumTwoNumbers} from 'c/serviceComponentExample';

export default class FirstLWC extends LightningElement {
    house = new xyz();
    numberOfBeds = gBeds(this.house);
    houseType = gType(this.house);
    cons = myCons;
    total = sumTwoNumbers(5,3);
}
```

There is only one difference from the previous **`utils.js`** example: As this **`serviceComponentExample`** is a separate component, we're importing it by using **`c/serviceComponentExample`**, not by using a relative directory **`./`**.

What if we have a complex service component in which there are many different JavaScript files for different functionalities, how can we import them to other UI components? Well, one thing to note is that exporting to other components can only be done via the main JavaScript file of the component. So, in our example, we can export the functionalities and properties only by using the **`serviceComponentExample.js`** file. So, the answer to this question is: firstly, we need to import those functionalities from other internal JavaScript files and then export them via the main **`serviceComponentExample.js`** file.

To see how this is working, let's create a second JavaScript file in the service component:

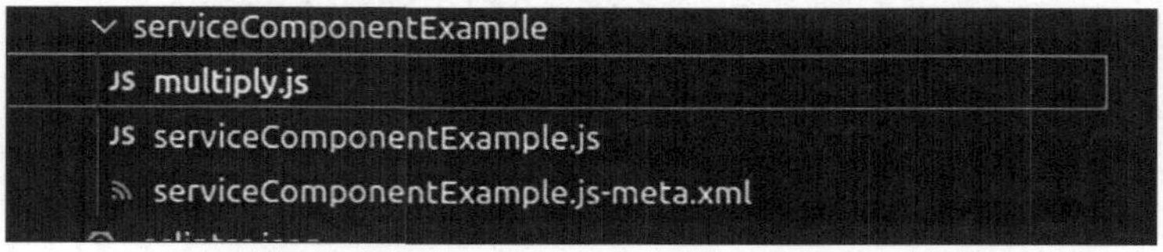

Figure 2.17: *New JavaScript file in the service component*

And here is the content of the **`multiply.js`**:

```
export function multiplyTwoNumbers(a, b) {
    return a * b;
}
```

As it is seen, we just put a simple multiplication function and export it.

In order to export this **`multiplyTwoNumbers`** method globally to other LWCs in the project, we use the **`export from`** syntax to import it and re-export it in the main **`serviceComponentExample.js`** JavaScript file:

```
export { multiplyTwoNumbers } from './multiply';
```

Let's see its updated version:

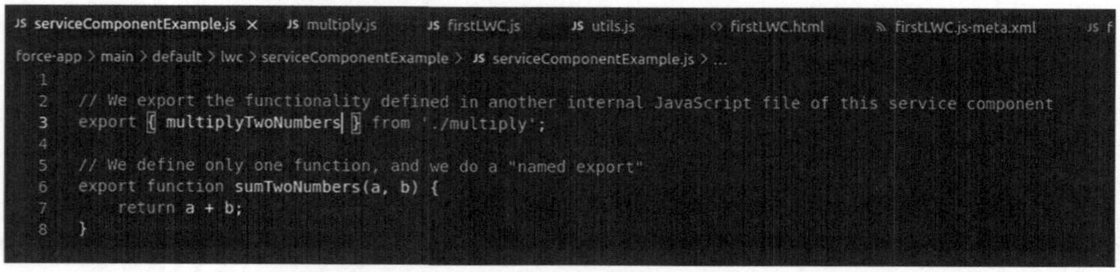

Figure 2.18: *serviceComponentExample is exporting functionality of its other internal JavaScript file*

Now let's use it in our main **firstLWC** UI component:

```
import { LightningElement } from 'lwc';
import xyz from './utils';
import {getBedrooms as gBeds, getType as gType, someConstant as myCons}
from './utils';
import {sumTwoNumbers, multiplyTwoNumbers} from 'c/serviceComponentExam-
ple';

export default class FirstLWC extends LightningElement {
    house = new xyz();
    numberOfBeds = gBeds(this.house);
    houseType = gType(this.house);
    cons = myCons;
    total = sumTwoNumbers(5,3);
    result = multiplyTwoNumbers(5,3);
}
```

Note: Exporting the functionalities, properties of other additional JavaScript files in a LWC bundle is possible only for service components. For UI components, there can be only one export, which is export default of the main class.

In our previous examples, we've defined an additional JavaScript file **utils.js** inside the **firstLWC** UI component bundle. So this is not possible to export the functionalities, properties of this **utils.js**, by using a syntax like **export { getBedrooms, getType, someConstant } from './utils'**. This kind of syntax is valid only for the service components.

Component HTML File

HTML files are only used in UI components, they are not needed in service components. They build actual screen output for the LWC. There is one rule for those files: everything should be between **<template>** … **</template>** tags.

Here's how our **firstLWC** LWC's HTML file looks when we first create this LWC:

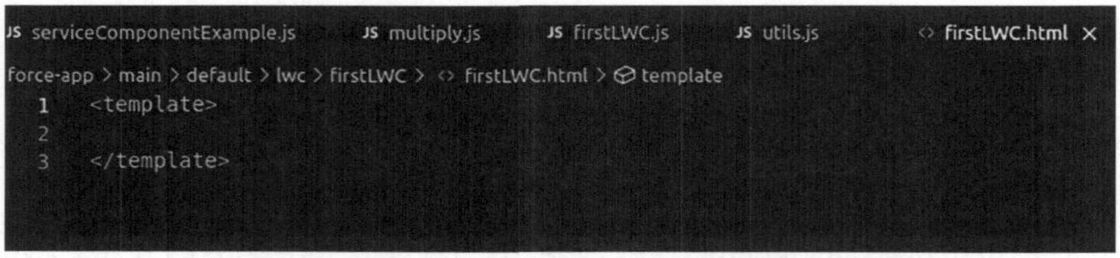

Figure 2.19: *For newly created LWCs the HTML file is almost empty*

In the previous section, in our **`firstLWC.js`** controller JavaScript file, we've already defined many properties:

```
house = new xyz();
numberOfBeds = gBeds(this.house);
houseType = gType(this.house);
cons = myCons;
total = sumTwoNumbers(5,3);
result = multiplyTwoNumbers(5,3);
```

Let's use them for printing out some results via the HTML file:

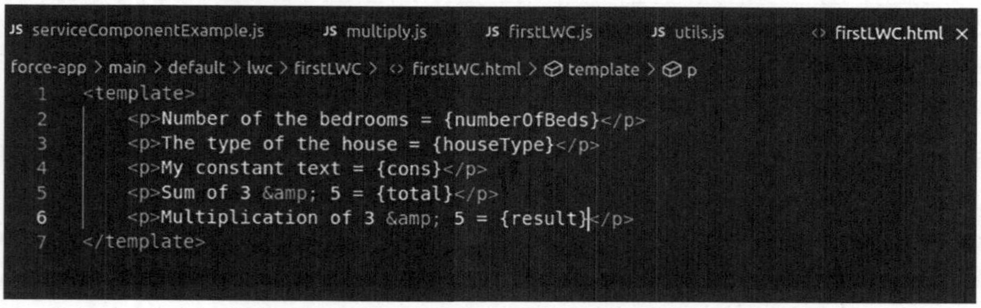

Figure 2.20: *HTML file has been updated with the values of the JavaScript controller file*

Now it is time to see how it is seen on the screen. For achieving this, we need to first update the component configuration file (**`firstLWC.js-meta.xml`**), then deploy the **`firstLWC`** LWC into our DE org and put it on a Lightning page.

For now, let's update **`firstLWC.js-meta.xml`** like the following (we're going to discuss this file's properties in the next section):

Tip: As our **firstLWC** LWC is dependent on the service component **serviceComponentExample** LWC, we need to first deploy this service component, then we can deploy **firstLWC.**

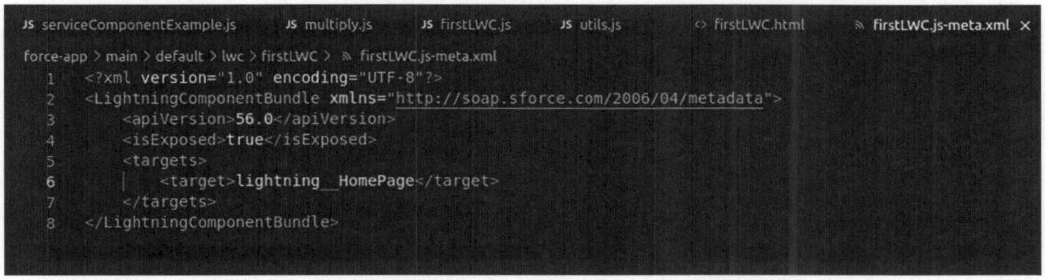

Figure 2.21: *Component Configuration File*

In order to deploy the components, we just need to right-click on any file in the **LWC** bundle and select the **SFDX: Deploy Source to Org** command.

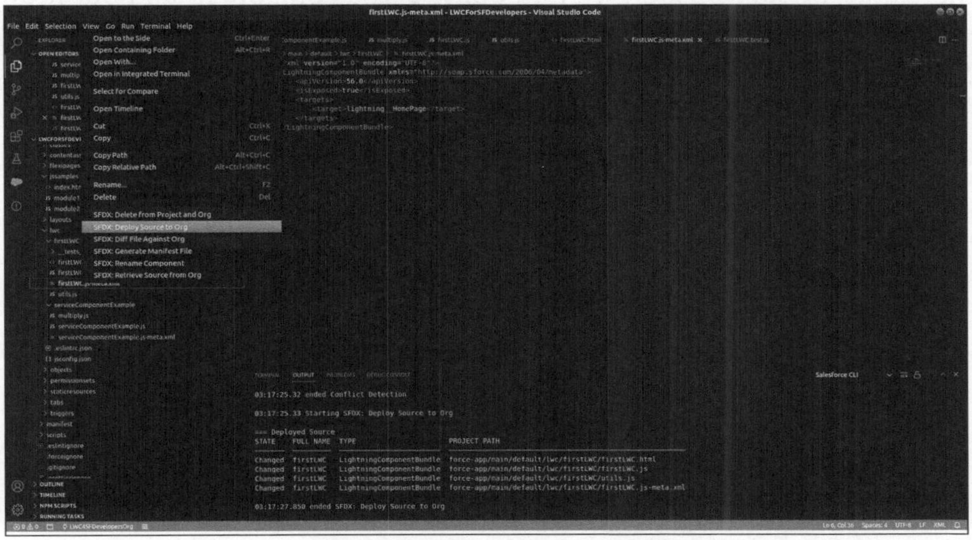

Figure 2.22: *Deploying the LWC*

Now in our Salesforce DE org, let's open any **Home** page and click on the **Edit Page** menu:

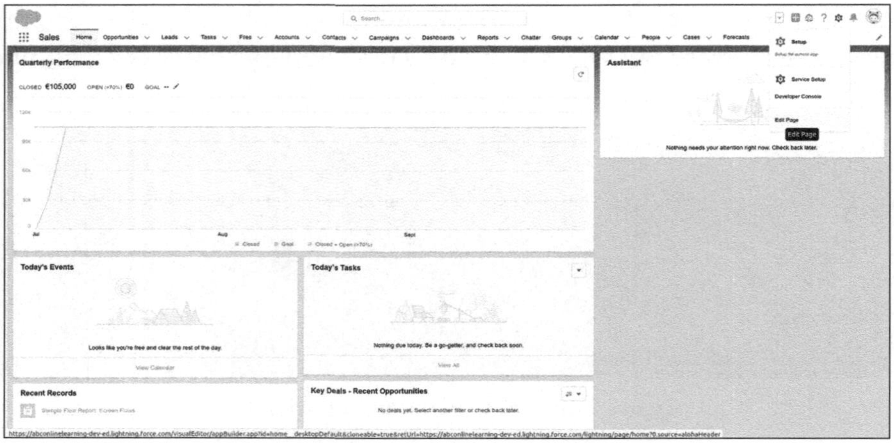

Figure 2.23: *For editing a Home page with Lightning App Builder*

In the Lightning App Builder, we find our **firstLWC** component and put it under the Assistant standard component, on the right section of the page. Then we save and activate the page as **Org Default**:

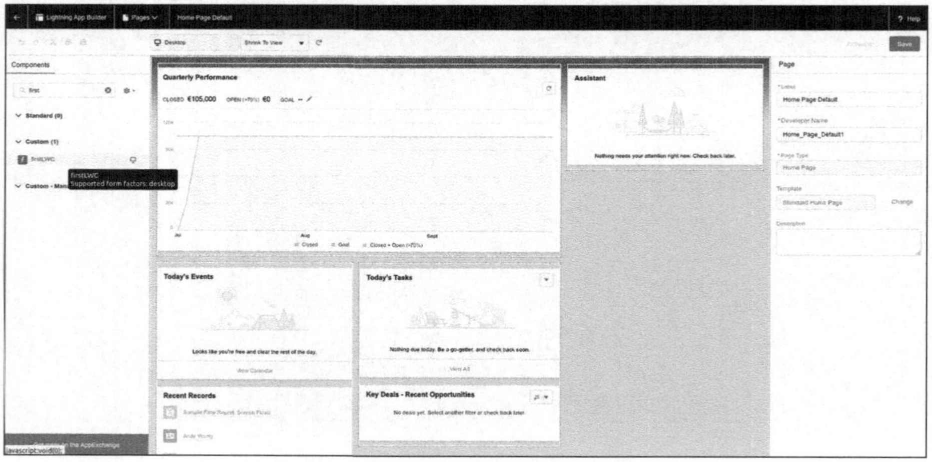

Figure 2.24: *Publishing our firstLWC LWC using Lightning App Builder*

Here, our first LWC is live in the right section, under the Assistant component:

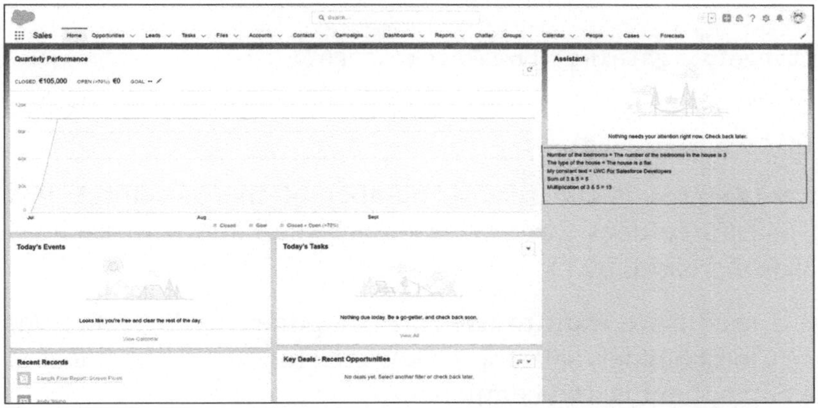

Figure 2.25: *firstLWC is live with the correct values as expected*

Tip: This is also possible to define multiple HTML template files in a single LWC bundle, similar to the JavaScript files. By using the standard **`render()`** method, we can define the conditions to guide the LWC when to render what template. We'll be showing an example related to this feature in the next chapter.

Component Configuration File

Each component (either this is a UI component or a service component) should have a configuration file. This configuration file defines the metadata values including:

- supported targets and supported devices
- whether or not the component is exposed to the Lightning App Builder or to the Experience Cloud
- label and description of the component
- properties (according to different targets) that we want to set values while we're placing the component in a target, etc.

Let's return to our current configuration file in the **`firstLWC`** LWC:

```
<?xml version=”1.0” encoding=”UTF-8”?>
<LightningComponentBundle xmlns=”http://soap.sforce.com/2006/04/
metadata”>
    <apiVersion>56.0</apiVersion>
    <isExposed>true</isExposed>
```

```
    <targets>
        <target>lightning__HomePage</target>
    </targets>
</LightningComponentBundle>
```

Here the **apiVersion** is the release number of the Salesforce Platform. (As we know, Salesforce does three releases per year, and with each release, this **apiVersion** is increased by 1.)

isExposed is used if we want to use this component in Lightning App Builder, Experience Cloud Builder, Salesforce Flow etc.: this should be (most of the time) **true** if the component is a UI component.

In the **targets** section, we define where to put this component in the Salesforce org: for different options, we can visit the documentation page. However, if we want to mention the main target options we can note that

- targets starting with **lightningCommunity__** are for the Experience Cloud,
- targets starting with **lightning__** are for the Lightning App Builder, Flows and other Salesforce internal org screens,
- targets starting with **lightningSnapin__** are for the Chatter.

For our **firstLWC** component's configuration, it is seen that the component can be put only on a Lightning Experience Home Page.

Now let's examine a more complete configuration file to improve our understanding:

```
<?xml version="1.0" encoding="UTF-8"?>
<LightningComponentBundle xmlns="http://soap.sforce.com/2006/04/
metadata">
    <apiVersion>56.0</apiVersion>
    <isExposed>true</isExposed>
    <masterLabel>Complex Component Example</masterLabel>
    <description>Shows different possible configuration options.</
description>
    <targets>
        <target>lightning__HomePage</target>
        <target>lightning__AppPage</target>
        <target>lightning__RecordPage</target>
```

```
    </targets>
    <targetConfigs>
        <targetConfig targets=”lightning__RecordPage”>
            <property name=”prop1” type=”String” />
            <objects>
                <object>Account</object>
                <object>Opportunity</object>
            </objects>
            <supportedFormFactors>
                <supportedFormFactor type=”Large” />
                <supportedFormFactor type=”Small” />
            </supportedFormFactors>
        </targetConfig>
        <targetConfig targets=”lightning__AppPage, lightning__HomePage”>
            <property name=”prop2” type=”Boolean” />
            <supportedFormFactors>
                <supportedFormFactor type=”Large” />
            </supportedFormFactors>
        </targetConfig>
    </targetConfigs>
</LightningComponentBundle>
```

Here as you can see the **apiVersion** is 56, the component is **exposed**, and there is a **label** and **description** for the component.

Under the **targets** section, we see that this component is exposed for Lightning Home Page, Lightning Record Pages and any Lightning App Builder Page.

From the **targetConfigs**, we understand that this component is exposed only for the **Account** and **Opportunity** record pages: There is also a property **prop1** that should be determined while putting this component into one of those record pages.

However, when we look at the **targetConfig** of the **Lightning Home Page** and **Lightning App Builder Page**, we see that there is this **prop2** property that should be determined.

supportedFormFactors are used to define whether the component supports desktop format (**`large`**), phone format (**`small`**) or both. By default, components on **`Home pages`** support only desktop formats (**large**) and components on app and record pages support both formats (**large** and **small**). In our example configuration, it is seen that the component is supporting both formats for record pages but the only desktop format (**`large`**) for home and app pages. That means, when we use the component in a small device (phone) it will not render for home and app pages as it supports only the **`large`** form factor.

Tip: In order to determine those **`prop1`** and **`prop2`** properties while putting the component into the relevant screens, we need to be sure that those properties are existing in our main JavaScript file by having **`@api`** decorator. We'll discuss more on decorators in the next chapter.

Component CSS File

For styling our components, we can add CSS files to the LWC bundle. The name of the CSS file should be the same as the component.

To demonstrate how it is functioning, let's add **`firstLWC.css`** to our component and make the <p> contents bold.

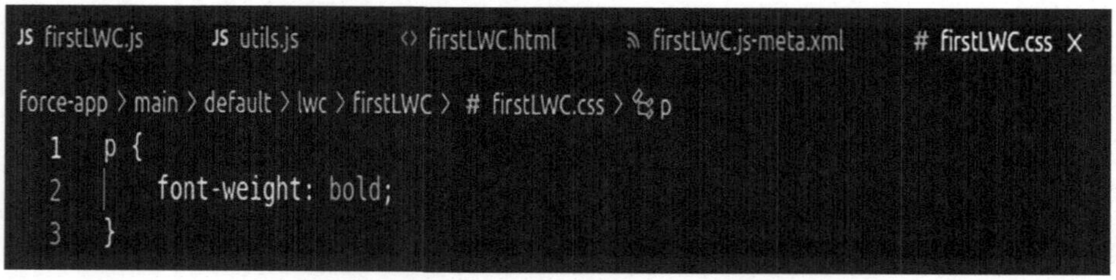

Figure 2.26: *We make the paragraphs bold*

After we re-deploy the component, here is the updated look:

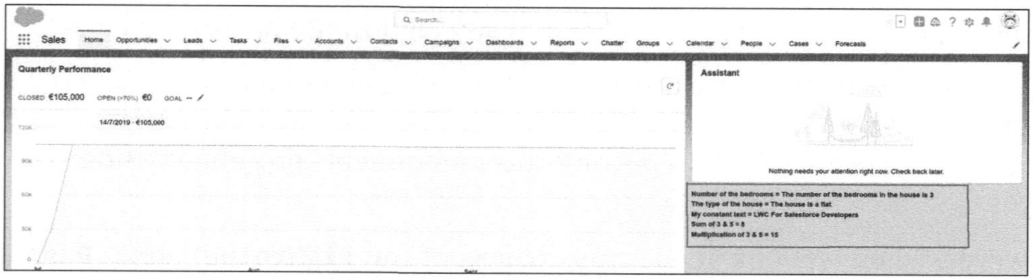

Figure 2.27: *The text is bold now*

Note: LWC is using standard CSS, there are only minor things specific to the Salesforce Platform. For details, please see the documentation.

Component SVG Icon

To include an SVG image as a custom icon for the component, we can put it in the LWC bundle by naming it as the component.

Let's add an example SVG resource to our firstLWC LWC, by naming it **`firstLWC.svg`** to use it as the custom component icon:

```
JS firstLWC.js   JS utils.js   <> firstLWC.html   firstLWC.js-meta.xml   # firstLWC.css   firstLWC.svg ×   JS firstLWC.test.js
force-app > main > default > lwc > firstLWC > firstLWC.svg
<svg version="1.1" baseProfile="full" width="300" height="200" xmlns="http://www.w3.org/2000/svg">
    <rect width="100%" height="100%" fill="red"></rect>
    <circle cx="150" cy="100" r="80" fill="green"></circle>
    <text x="150" y="125" font-size="60" text-anchor="middle" fill="white">SVG</text>
</svg>
```

***Figure 2.28**: SVG file to be used as a component custom icon*

Note: SVG files can also be directly uploaded into **`Static Resources`** and then can be imported via JavaScript files (or they can also be added directly into the HTML template files). That means, this is possible to use light SVG images in the LWCs.

Here is how the icon for our component is seen on the Salesforce Platform:

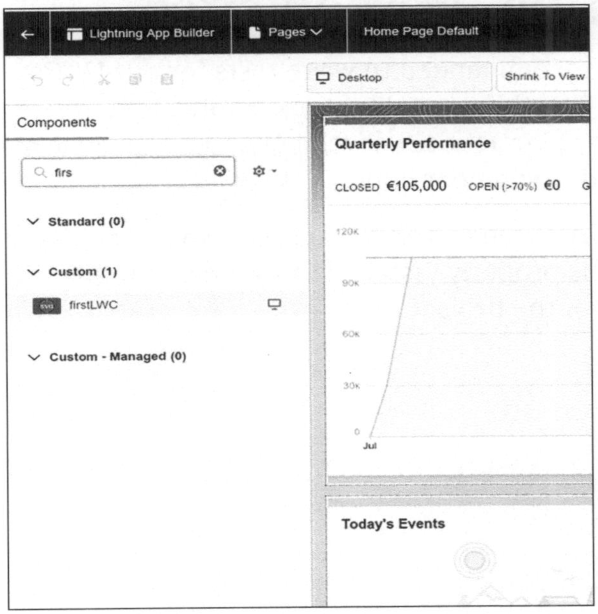

***Figure 2.29**: We now have a custom icon for our LWC*

Component Namespaces

In the Salesforce Platform, every component is part of a namespace. The default namespace is **c** (that stands for custom). So whenever we write an LWC of our own (which is not belonging to a managed package), it should be called with **c-** not depending on wherever (managed or unmanaged package, org with or without namespace etc.) it is used, example: `<c-my-component></c-my-component>`

If in the org, **Lightning Locker** is enabled instead of the new **Lightning Web Security**, we can use only other custom LWCs (with **c** namespace) or the LWCs from the standard **lightning** namespace, for example `<lightning-card> ... </lightning-card>`, `<lightning-accordion> … </lightning-accordion>` etc. Nevertheless, this is possible to use LWCs from other namespaces if **Lightning Web Security** is enabled, for example: `<othernamespace-component-1> … </othernamespace-component-1>`.

Tip: A custom LWC and a custom Aura component in the namespace can't have the same name, not dependent on whether **Lightning Locker** or **Lightning Web Security** is enabled.

Note: We're going to discuss **Lightning Locker** and **Lightning Web Security** in the next chapters, while we're working on the security concepts for LWCs.

LWC Testing Prerequisites

It is possible and recommended to write tests for our LWCs as we're writing for our Apex classes. The thing is unlike Apex testing, LWC testing is not mandatory (yet) but as a good QA practice, a developer should have the habit of writing tests related to all the development done.

LWC tests can be run using an NPM package: **sfdx-lwc-jest.** In order to be sure that this package is properly installed for our current project, we need to check the **package.json** of the project:

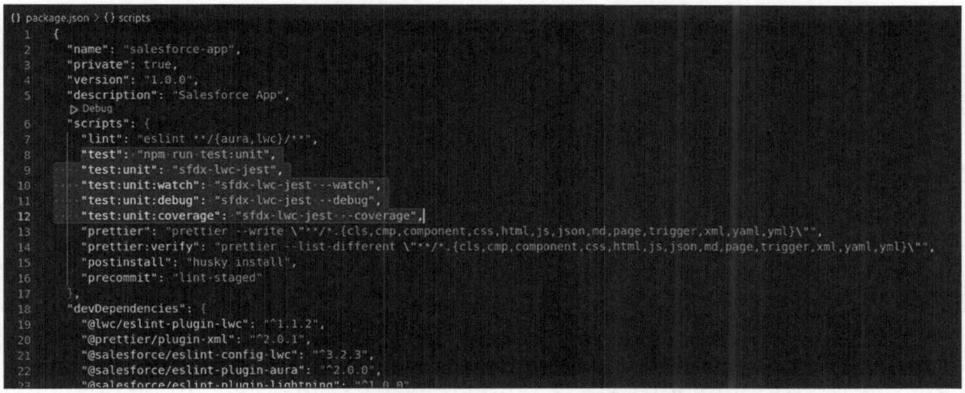

Figure 2.30: SFDX *project package.json file*

If we see the following lines, then we can be sure that our testing configuration is ready:

```
“test”: “npm run test:unit”,
“test:unit”: “sfdx-lwc-jest”,
“test:unit:watch”: “sfdx-lwc-jest --watch”,
“test:unit:debug”: “sfdx-lwc-jest --debug”,
“test:unit:coverage”: “sfdx-lwc-jest --coverage”,
```

If we see that **sfdx-lwc-jest** is not installed, we can install it by running this command:

```
sfdx force:lightning:lwc:test:setup
```

We should run this command while we're in the directory of our SFDX project.

If we encounter any error while running this command, we should check whether we have **node** and **npm** installed in our system. We can check these by running the following version commands:

```
node -v
npm -v
```

When we create our LWC, we notice that a **`__test__`** folder is created automatically for us (Refer to *Figure* 2.31). This folder is where we write and keep our LWC tests. If we notice that the folder somehow is not existing in the LWC bundle, we can create it by running the following command (while we're in the SFDX project directory):

```
sfdx force:lightning:lwc:test:create -f force-app/main/default/lwc/my-
Component
```

For now, we're stopping here. We're going to write some tests in the next chapter after we learn to code LWCs in detail.

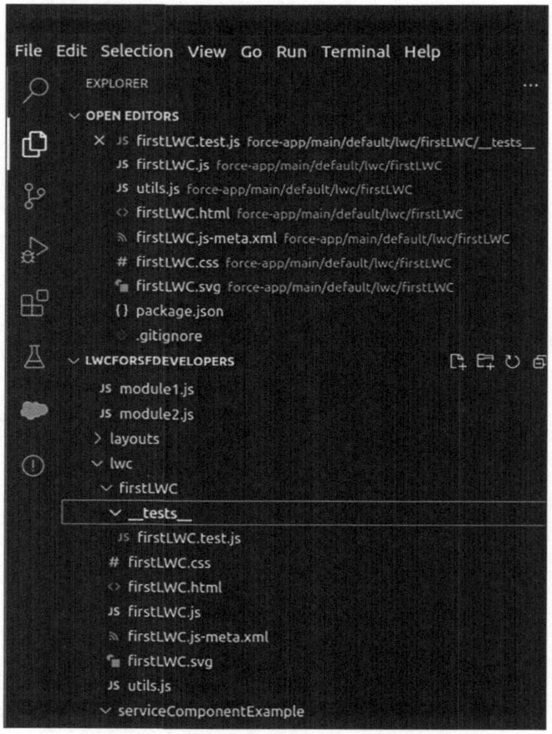

Figure 2.31: *LWC __tests__ folder*

LWC Local Development

Before concluding this chapter, we want to look at how to see the live changes while working with LWC, without needing to publish the component to a Salesforce org.

The developers coming from a web applications development background would know very well that while working with JS, HTML and CSS, one needs to publish the page to the web server consecutively, and refresh the browser page to see the latest version. This publishing process can be a real cumbersome and time-consuming, especially when the developer is working with the page styling.

To improve the developer experience, Salesforce is currently proposing a local development option while working with LWC: it is in the **beta** version though. With this capability, the developer doesn't need to publish LWC to a Salesforce org consecutively to see its latest version.

In order to install and configure it, we need to have a Salesforce org with DevHub enabled and we need a scratch org. And we should be working with LWCs under an SFDX project, not independently.

After we provide those prerequisites, we can install the **`LWC Local Development Server`** by using the following command:

```
sfdx plugins:install @salesforce/lwc-dev-server
```

Once we have the local development server ready to use, we can open, start and stop using the following commands from the VS Code command palette:

```
SFDX: Open Local Development Home
SFDX: Start LWC Local Development Server
SFDX: Stop LWC Local Development Server
```

The **`Open`** command starts the local development server and opens **`localhost:3333`** in the web browser.

The **`Start`** command is for starting the server and the **`Stop`** is for stopping it.

While the local development server is running, you can right-click any line under the LWC folder in VS Code and click on the **`SFDX: Preview Component Locally`** command. After that, SFDX will show you options whether you need to preview components on a Desktop or in iOS Simulator or an Android Emulator.

For further details, you can see the documentation.

Conclusion

In this chapter, we first prepared our development environment to start coding LWC. Once this was done, we looked into JavaScript modules as those are the main features which made the LWC framework modular design possible.

After we felt confident with JavaScript modules, we created our very first LWC and examined all the different files existing under its folder structure. We dove into the details of each file's purpose and configuration. We also saw how namespacing is working for LWCs.

We continued then by preparing our development environment to be able to start writing tests for our LWCs. Finally, we had the chance to look at how to work locally with LWCs without needing to publish them consecutively to a Salesforce org.

Later in the book, we'll learn the various aspects of LWC development along with how to work multiple HTML templates and how to write unit tests.

References

- Illuminated Cloud - https://www.illuminatedcloud.com/
- Code Builder - https://appexchange.salesforce.com/listingDetail?listingId=a0N3u00000Qsdi5EAB&tab=d
- Salesforce AppExchange - https://appexchange.salesforce.com/
- SFDX Developer Guide - https://developer.salesforce.com/docs/atlas.en-us.sfdx_dev.meta/sfdx_dev
- SFDX Command Reference - https://developer.salesforce.com/docs/atlas.en-us.sfdx_cli_reference.meta/sfdx_cli_reference
- Salesforce CLI - https://developer.salesforce.com/tools/sfdxcli
- SFDX - https://developer.salesforce.com/developer-centers/developer-experience
- Visual Studio Code download and install - https://code.visualstudio.com/download
- Salesforce Developer Edition org sign-up page - https://developer.salesforce.com/signup
- HTML Standard - https://html.spec.whatwg.org/multipage/custom-elements.html

- LWC Configuration File documentation - https://developer.salesforce.com/docs/component-library/documentation/en/lwc/lwc.reference_configuration_tags
- LWC CSS File documentation - https://developer.salesforce.com/docs/component-library/documentation/en/lwc/lwc.create_components_css_intro
- LWC Local Development Server documentation - https://developer.salesforce.com/tools/vscode/en/localdev/lwclocaldev

Chapter 3
LWC in Detail

Introduction

All the preparations are done and now we're ready to sail! In this chapter, we're going to learn various aspects of the LWC Framework including properties, data binding, rendering, decorators, composing components and their data flow, slots, lifecycle hooks, working with multiple HTML templates, how to access static resources and other various Salesforce resources. We'll also have the chance to see what is Shadow DOM and its difference from the standard DOM.

We'll continue by looking at how to define navigation in LWCs which will also provide the basis for how to work with files via LWCs. Afterwards, we are going to discuss some very useful standard modules of the LWC Framework such as Alert Modals, Confirm Modals, Prompt Modals and Toast Notifications. Finally, we conclude the chapter by making a start for how to work with the Salesforce backend, namely Apex classes and methods. Although to mention now, more details of working with Apex will be presented in the next chapter while we're learning to master the Lightning Data Service.

Structure

In this chapter, we will discuss the following topics:

- LWC basics
- Navigation in LWC
- Display notifications
- Importing APEX methods

LWC basics

Let's discuss the basics of LWC.

Shadow DOM

Before diving into the code, let's initially have some more theoretical background by discussing a little about Shadow DOM. The first thing we should mention is that Shadow DOM is not something specific to LWC but instead, it is one of the three Web Components standards along with HTML templates and custom elements. It is for encapsulating a specific DOM subtree (an encapsulated component) in the main web page's DOM, which gives the component to act like a standalone entity for CSS styles and JS DOM manipulations.

To understand practically, let's see an example:

parentComponent.html:

```
<template>
      <h1>Some Parent Title</h1>
      <div><p>Some parent content</p></div><br/><br/>
      <c-child-component></c-child-component>
</template>
```

parentComponent.css:

```
p { color: blue; }
```

parentComponent.js:

```
import { LightningElement } from 'lwc';
export default class ParentComponent extends LightningElement {
      renderedCallback() {
            let h1Content = this.template.querySelector('h1');
            h1Content.innerHTML = "Updated title!";
      }
}
```

The code for the **childComponent** LWC:

childComponent.html:

```
<template>
      <h1>Some Child Title</h1>
```

```
    <div><p>Some child content</p></div>
</template>
```

childComponent.css:

```
p { color: red; }
```

childComponent.js:

```
import { LightningElement } from 'lwc';
export default class ChildComponent extends LightningElement {}
```

After we deploy those two components and put the parent component in one of our Salesforce DE org's home pages, here is the result:

Figure 3.1: *Result of our simple example for "parent and child components"*

As we see, despite the child component being contained by the parent component, the parent component's CSS is not leaking into the child component: consequently, as their own CSS files point out child component's **p** tag is red, while the parent component's **p** tag is blue. We have this result because each component has its own encapsulation via the Shadow DOM.

As the Shadow DOM is implemented in the components, it is not possible to use the **window** or **document** global properties, instead of those we should use **this.template** while making the node selection in the HTML template of the component. In the previous code example, we see a simple usage for node selection in the **parentComponent**: Here, despite the HTML template file is defined as follows:

```
<h1>Some Parent Title</h1>
```

In the resulting screen, the title of the **parentComponent** becomes **updated title!** because we're doing a dynamic HTML update in the **parentComponent** JS controller by using **this.template** :

```
let h1Content = this.template.querySelector('h1');
h1Content.innerHTML = "Updated title!";
```

And one thing to note here is that `this.template.querySelector('h1')` of the `parentComponent` controller is not selecting the `h1` element of the `childComponent` but solely its own `h1` element because the `childComponent` is also encapsulated as its own.

Briefly, we can conclude that Shadow DOM enables local scoping for HTML and CSS. And this is one of the important aspects of component-based design in regard to maintenance and security.

Note: We can learn more details about DOM Standard by visiting DOM specs page: https://dom.spec.whatwg.org/

Tip: While working with LWCs, in order to stop Salesforce hold the cache, we should open **`Setup → Session Settings`** page and uncheck the **`Enable secure and persistent browser caching to improve performance`** checkbox. This is especially important when we work with small CSS changes in the components.

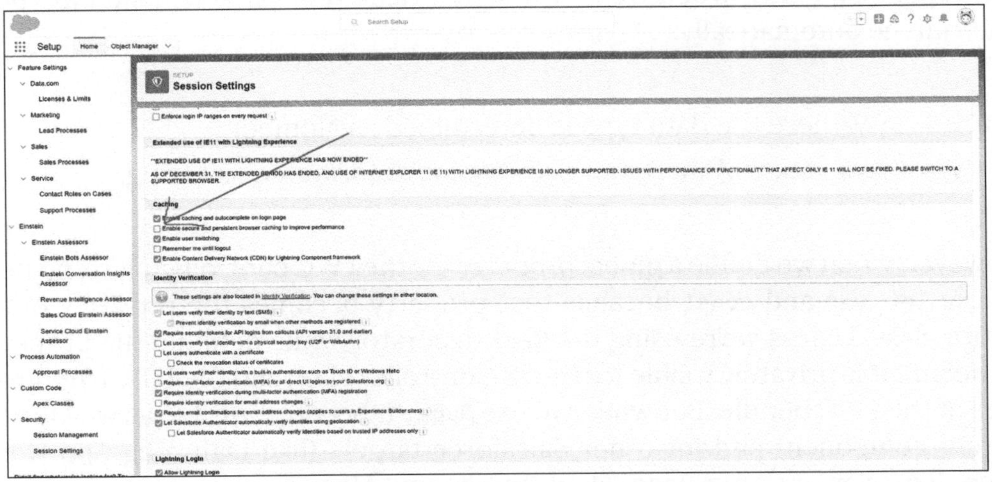

Figure 3.2: *Setup → Session Settings page*

Properties, data binding, setter, and getter methods

Until now, we already defined a couple of properties in our examples, so the topic of properties and data binding might already be captured.

As a LWC's controller is mainly a JavaScript class, we're able to define properties inside it, using JavaScript standard language rules. In the **parentComponent** we worked on in the previous section, we did already have a property:

```
let h1Content = this.template.querySelector('h1');
```

This **h1Content** property is in the **renderedCallback()** method, so as a JavaScript language rule we need to define it by using one of those keywords: **let, var** and **const** (Here we used **let**). As we already know, **let** and **var** are differing mainly regarding the scope where the property is valid. And when we need a property value that won't change, we use the **const** keyword. One practical aspect of JavaScript, despite the properties (variables) having data types, we don't need to state them explicitly: when we first assign a value to a variable, its data type is determined automatically:

```
let x = 3; // here the data type is determined as Number
var y = "Some text" // here the data type is determined as String
```

However, when we define a global property for the LWC controller class, no need to use **let**, **var** and **const** because that property becomes the property of the entire class. Unless we're using the **@api** decorator while defining the property, by default it is privately visible for the JS Controller class and the HTML template files of the LWC bundle. But when we use **@api,** it becomes visible as well for the parent component and for other Salesforce targets (like Lightning App Home Page, Experience Cloud page, Flow, and so on.) Here is an example of how to define properties inside the JS Controller class:

```
import { LightningElement } from 'lwc';
export default class someComponent extends LightningElement {
      myProperty; // property without a default value
```

```
    mySecondProperty = "myValue"; // property with a default value
}
```

Data binding

Data binding is nothing but it is the usage of the JavaScript controller class properties in the HTML template file, and vice-versa. In the previous code, we've already defined a class property called **mySecondProperty** with a default value of **myValue**: so, we can use it in the HTML template file like:

```
<template>
    <p>My second property is {mySecondProperty}</p>
    <lightning-formatted-text value={mySecondProperty} ></
lightning-formatted-text>
</template>
```

As we see, the properties can be used directly in the HTML (in the example, `{mySecondProperty}` is in the `<p>...</p>` tag) or can be used as the values for the tag attributes (in the example, it is used to initialize the `value` attribute of the `lightning-formatted-text` tag).

For the other direction, it is also possible to update the JavaScript controller property by using the actions (= technically they are called **events)** that happened in the frontend HTML template. As an example, let's look at this updated HTML template file:

```
<template>
  <lightning-input label="My Second Property" value={mySecondProperty}
onchange={updateSecondProperty}></lightning-input>
</template>
```

Now we defined a standard input field in the HTML. And as we can see, the default value is defined by using the existing `mySecondProperty` property. However, we have now an event listener, called **onchange**, which tracks whether or not the user updates the value of the input field. Thus, if the input field is updated by using the `updateSecondProperty` method (which would be defined in the JavaScript controller - please see the next section for event handler methods) it would be updating the value of the `mySecondProperty`.

Setter and getter methods

In JavaScript, so eventually in LWCs, if we need to execute some additional logic while setting or getting a property, we can define **`getter`** and **`setter`** methods similar to the Salesforce Apex language. Let's see within an example, here the **`someComponent`** LWC:

someComponent.js Controller:

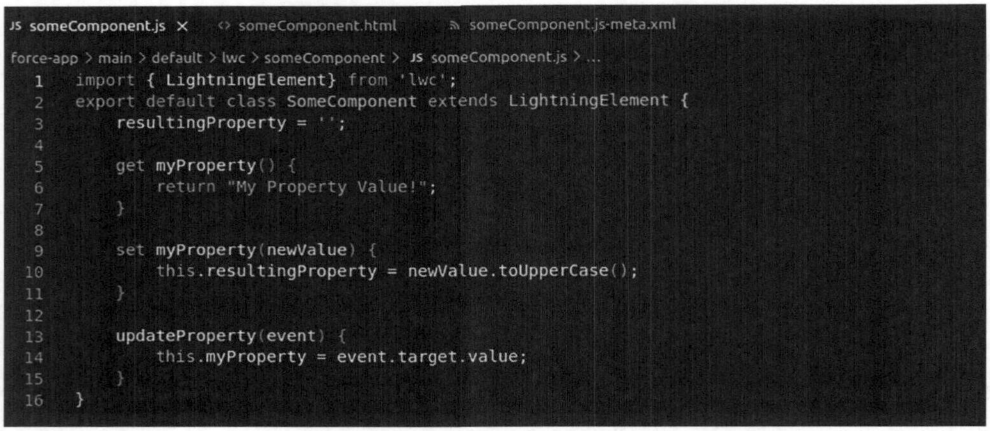

Figure 3.3: *LWC JavaScript Controller*

someComponent.html Template:

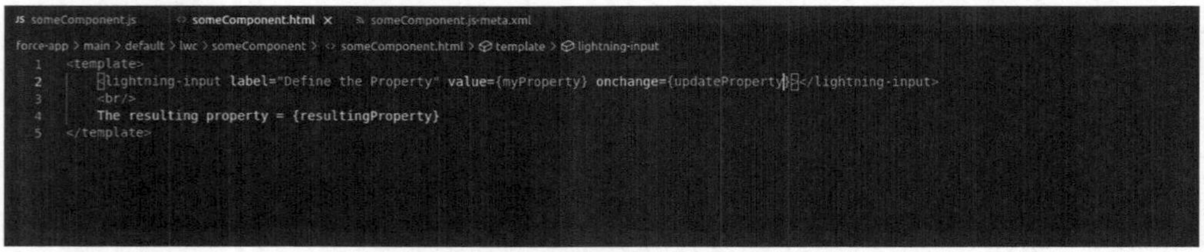

Figure 3.4: *LWC HTML Template*

After we deploy the component and run it, initially it is looking as:

Figure 3.5: *When we initially refresh the page*

When we change the initial default `My Property Value!` to something like `xyz`, it is seen that our `resultingProperty` is automatically updated as expected:

Figure 3.6: *We update the property in the input field which in turn updates the resulting property automatically*

Now let's examine how it is working. In the JavaScript controller **`someComponent.js`**, we have one regular property `resultingProperty` (without getter and setter methods) and one other property **`myProperty`** which is being got and set with the help of getter and setter methods.

```
resultingProperty = ‘’;

get myProperty() {
       return “My Property Value!”;
}
set myProperty(newValue) {
       this.resultingProperty = newValue.toUpperCase();
}
```

The `getter` method of the **`myProperty`** property is simply returning a static value:

My Property Value! that's why initially in the **lightning-input** field we see this default **My Property Value!** value.

Figure 3.7: *<lightning-input label="Define the Property"* `value={myProperty}` *onchange={updateProperty}></lightning-input>*

And the **setter** method of the **myProperty** is simply uppercasing its new value and doing the assignment to the **resultingProperty** property. As we know, **setter** methods are called automatically when there is an explicit assignment. Here, we do this explicit assignment for **myProperty** in the **event handler** method **updateProperty(),** so the **setter** method is automatically called here:

```
updateProperty(event) {
  this.myProperty = event.target.value; // explicit assignment for
"myProperty"
}
```

Event handler methods are automatically called when their triggering event happens. They get an **event** parameter in order to (mainly) have access to the source component of the event. Here for this **updateProperty()** event handler method, the triggering event is **change** and it is defined in the **<lightning-input>** component:

```
<lightning-input label="Define the Property" value={myProperty}
onchange={updateProperty}></lightning-input>
```

So basically when there is a change in the **<lightning-input>** field, the event is triggered and the new value is automatically shared with the **updateProperty()** method by using the **event** parameter:

```
updateProperty(event) {
  this.myProperty = event.target.value;
}
```

Here **event** is the change action, **event.target** is the **<lightning-input>** component and **event.target.value** is **<lightning-input>** field's new value obtained after the change action happens on the field. And when we do the assignment to **this.myProperty**, its setter method is automatically called which in turn automatically uppercase the new value and assigns it to the **this.resultingProperty.**

Thus, when we change the value of the input field, let's say to xyz, we obtain XYZ for the **resultingProperty** (please refer to *Figure* 3.6)

Briefly, when we need that some additional logic occurs while we're getting and/or setting the value of a property we should define the **getter** and/or **setter** methods. (By the way, we don't need to define always both of them at the same time, we can just define only **getter** or only **setter**, according to our needs.)

Tip: If a property with getter and setter will be a public property, then the **@api** decorator should be put only to one of those methods, not both. The best practice here is to annotate the getter with the **@api** decorator.

Conditional rendering, rendering lists, and iterators

In an LWC, it is possible to render dynamically HTML according to the values of the JavaScript controller properties. Now, we're going to look at how it can be achieved.

Conditional rendering

Let's look at this HTML template:

renderingComponent.html Template:

```
<template>
      <template lwc:if={isBlue}>
            <p style="color: blue;">Blue text!</p>
      </template>
      <template lwc:elseif={isRed}>
            <p style="color: red;">Red text!</p>
      </template>
      <template lwc:else>
            <p>Default text</p>
      </template>
```

```
</template>
```

Here we use three **directives**: **`lwc:if`**, **`lwc:elseif`** and **`lwc:else`**. The logic which is used here is exactly the same as building and **`if … else if … else`** block in a programming language like JavaScript, Apex, etc. We first check whether or not the first property is true with **`lwc:if.`** If it is false, then the second property is checked by using **`lwc:elseif`**. If this one is also false, then we're falling back to the default, with **`lwc:else`**.

Tip: **Directives** are special HTML attributes. The Lightning Web Components programming model has some custom directives that let us manipulate the DOM. For the details you can visit the documentation: HTML Template Directives

https://developer.salesforce.com/docs/component-library/documentation/en/lwc/lwc.reference_directives

---

So, if our JavaScript controller is defined like the following:

renderingComponent.js Controller:

```
import { LightningElement } from 'lwc';

export default class RenderingComponent extends LightningElement {

    isBlue = true;

    isRed = false;

}
```

We see the result as expected, in blue text:

***Figure 3.8:** isBlue property is true so we see blue text as expected*

Note We can wonder what would happen if both **`isBlue`** and **`isRed`** properties were **`true`** at the same time: here, **`isBlue`** is controlled in the initial block **`lwc:if.`** So as long as it continues to be true, the other blocks **`lwc:elseif`**, **`lwc:else`** will not be rendered even if they are also true.

It is possible to define as many conditions as needed by using additional **`lwc:elseif`** blocks:

renderingComponent.html Template:

```
<template>
      <template lwc:if={isBlue}>
            <p style="color: blue;">Blue text!</p>
      </template>
      <template lwc:elseif={isRed}>
            <p style="color: red;">Red text!</p>
      </template>
      <template lwc:elseif={isGreen}>
            <p style="color: green;">Green text!</p>
      </template>
      <template lwc:else>
            <p>Default text</p>
      </template>
</template>
```

In an HTML template, the first **`<template>… </template>`** element is called the **root template**. However, in our example you see that we utilized the condition directives on other **`<template>...</template>`** elements under the root template: those are called **nested templates**. This difference is important because the condition directives (**`lwc:if`, `lwc:elseif`**, **`lwc:else`**) *cannot be used in the root template.*

Note: Actually, the root template can only have **`lwc:preserve-comments`** and **`lwc:render-mode='light'`** directives. For more details, please visit the **`HTML Template Directives`** documentation page.

Besides the nested templates, the conditions directives can also be used directly on the HTML elements like **`<p>`**. Here is the updated example for our **`renderingComponent`** LWC:

```
<template>
      <template lwc:if={isBlue}>
            <p style="color: blue;">Blue text!</p>
      </template>
      <template lwc:elseif={isRed}>
```

```
            <p style="color: red;">Red text!</p>
        </template>
        <template lwc:elseif={isGreen}>
            <p style="color: green;">Green text!</p>
            <p lwc:if={isOrange} style="color: orange;">This is an orange 
text!</p>
        </template>
        <template lwc:else>
            <p>Default text</p>
        </template>
</template>
```

Rendering lists

When we discussed the data binding and the properties, careful readers might notice that all the examples were for single-valued properties. So, one may wonder how can we use also the **list properties** in HTML templates. Now, let's see this example:

JavaScript Controller:

```
import { LightningElement } from 'lwc';
export default class RenderingComponent extends LightningElement {
    contacts = [
        {
            Id: 1,
            Name: 'Jack Jones',
            Title: 'Product Manager',
        },
        {
            Id: 2,
            Name: 'Michelle Taylor',
            Title: 'Sales Manager',
        },
        {
            Id: 3,
```

```
            Name: 'Tim Wine',
            Title: 'Chief Marketing Officer',
        },
    ];
}
```

HTML Template:

```
<template>
    <ul class="slds-var-m-around_medium">
        <template for:each={contacts} for:item="con">
            <li key={con.Id}>{con.Name}, {con.Title}</li>
        </template>
    </ul>
</template>
```

In the JavaScript controller, we have a list property **contacts** which includes details for different contacts. In order to render all the contacts in the HTML template, we are using those directives on the nested template: **for:each** & **for:item**. Here, the former takes the **contacts** list property of the JavaScript controller as the value. For the latter, we can give any value we want: it is used as a parameter in the HTML only for capturing the values for different items in the list. We use **con** as its value in our example.

In the Lightning Web Components programming model, it is important that each element has a unique identifier in the HTML template. This **id** can be directly captured from the database (like the actual **Id** of the records) or it can be calculated dynamically (or be determined statically as in our example) in the JavaScript controller for each list's element.

After we're sure that we have a unique identifier for each list's element, we should use it in the HTML template by using the **key** directive. In our example, the **<li>...</li>** HTML elements are using this **key** directive to capture the unique identifier for each contact.

Note: The **key** directive is important because the framework is using this value to be able to identify uniquely different elements of the list property, when it is used with nested templates. Thus, when a value of an element is updated, the framework can instantly re-render the HTML template with the new value of that specific element.

Besides the nested templates, it is also possible to use those listing directives on the HTML elements:

```
<table key={tableKey} for:each={contacts} for:item="con">
  <tbody>
        <tr style="border:1px solid black;"><td>{con.Name},
{con.Title}</td></tr>
  </tbody>
</table>
```

However, this time **key** directive is needed once on the parent **<table> … </ table>** element instead of each **<tr> … </tr>** child element. When we don't use nested templates, there is no need to put a **key** directive on the child elements but should be put only on the parent element.

Iterators

When we need to apply special behavior to the first and/or last item in a list, instead of **for:each** and **for:item** directives, we can use the **iterator** directive. Let's see it in the following example, which uses the same **contacts** list as the list property:

```
<ul class="slds-var-m-around_medium">
      <template iterator:myit={contacts}>
            <li key={myit.value.Id} lwc:if={myit.first}
style="font-weight: bold;">{myit.value.Name}, {myit.value.Title}</li>
            <li key={myit.value.Id} lwc:elseif={myit.last}
style="font-style:italic">{myit.value.Name}, {myit.value.Title}</li>
            <li key={myit.value.Id} lwc:else>{myit.value.Name}, {myit.
value.Title}</li>
      </template>
</ul>
```

In the **iterator** directive, firstly we determine the parameter name that is used for each element of the list: It is **`myit`** in this example. So **`myit.value`** signifies the current element. (This is important: we are not using **`myit.Name`** but we are using **`myit.value.Name`** when we need to print out the name of the current contact element.)

`myit.first` is **`true`** if this we're on the first element and respectively **`myit.last`** is **`true`** if we're on the last element. By using the condition directives, we make the first element **`bold`** and the last element **`italic`**. We are using the default text format for all other contacts.

Here how it is looked when we deploy the component:

Figure 3.9: *First contact is bold; the last contact is italic. Other contacts are in the default format*

Decorators

Decorator is a design pattern in JavaScript which are used for wrapping a piece of code (like a function, class, and so on, without modifying its existing behaviors) with a **decorator** function (in order to extend its existing functionality or to further configure it). W3C ECMA International Technical Committee 39 (TC39) is currently working on standardizing them, and it is already in **Stage 3** (during the writing of this book).

Consider the following JavaScript code:

```
function readonlydecorator (target, key, descriptor) {
      descriptor.writable = false;
      return descriptor;
}

class SampleClass {
      @readonlydecorator property1;
      property2;
}
```

As decorators are not live yet in standard ECMAScript, this previous example code won't work in a browser. However, it can give you an idea about how useful the decorators are. Here, we define a **`decorator`** function (called **`readonlydecorator`**) which takes a prototype of a class property and makes that property **`readonly`** by updating its descriptor. In the example, **`property1`** becomes **`read-only`** but no changes happen for **`property2`**, because the decorator is used only for **`property1.`**

In the Lightning Web Components programming model, there are 3 decorators:

- **`@api`**: To make a property **`public`**, which means exposing it to parent components, lightning app pages, flow builders, experience builders, etc. By using it, it is also possible to make the methods **`public`**, which in turn builds the API for a component: thus, the parent component would be able to call those public methods.
- **`@track:`** After Spring 20 release, LWC's properties become reactive by default which means when a value of a property (with a primitive data type such as Boolean, Date, Datetime, Integer, String, Decimal etc.) is updated after an action happened on the page (or directly on the component), then the component is re-rendered automatically. However, for objects and arrays, unless you re-define them entirely, this is not the case. So, in order to enforce the re-rendering (when a property of an object or an element of an array is updated), this decorator should be used.
- **`@wire`:** It is used to define a **`wire adaptor`** to consume the reactive wire service.

In this chapter, we're going to look at **`@api`** and **`@track`** decorators. The **`@wire`** decorator will be examined in detail in the next chapter.

Tip: A property can only have one decorator.

@api decorator

As mentioned, the **`@api`** decorator is used to expose the properties and methods of an LWC. In order to see it in action, let's start by defining a simple component:

decoratorsComponent.js Controller:

```
import { LightningElement, api } from 'lwc';
export default class DecoratorsComponent extends LightningElement {
    @api myProperty = 'Default child text';
}
```

decoratorsComponent.html Template:

```
<template>
    {myProperty}
</template>
```

`decoratorsComponent` is a simple component having only one **`public`** property, called **`myProperty`**, which has a default value. When rendered, it is just printing out the property.

When we put it under a parent component, the parent component can assign a new default value to **`myProperty:`**

decoratorsParentComponent.js Controller:

```
import { LightningElement } from 'lwc';

export default class DecoratorsParentComponent extends LightningElement
{}
```

decoratorsParentComponent.html Template:

```
<template>
    <c-decorators-component my-property="This default parent text
overwrites the existing default value of the child component"></
c-decorators-component>
</template>
```

One thing to notice is that despite the name of the property being **`myProperty`** (written in camelCase) in the child component, we call it **`my-property`** (written in kebab-casing) while defining the attribute for the child component tag in the parent component's template.

So, when we deploy the child component standalone, we see its default value:

Figure 3.10: *decoratorsComponent child component standalone*

But if we deploy the parent component, it is seen (as expected) that the parent component overwrites the default value of the child component:

Figure 3.11: *decoratorsParentComponent parent component*

When a public property is defined in a component, its value should be updated always by its parent component, as a best practice. During the writing of this book, this practice is not enforced by Salesforce but the LWC rules existing in the linting utility (ESLint) would mark this kind of development as an error that should be fixed. So, this code (please refer to *Figure* 3.12) will work but will be marked as an error in VS Code.

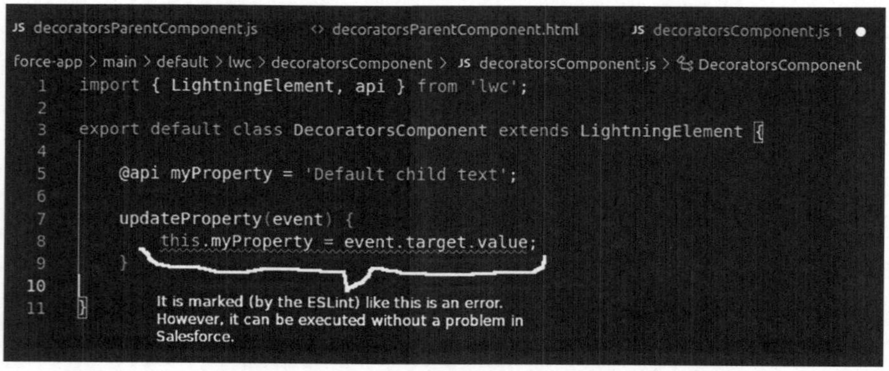

Figure 3.12: *Public properties shouldn't be updated in the component*

Therefore, as a best practice, the parent components should be responsible for updating the public properties of their child components. For an example of how to do it, please refer to *Figure* 3.13.

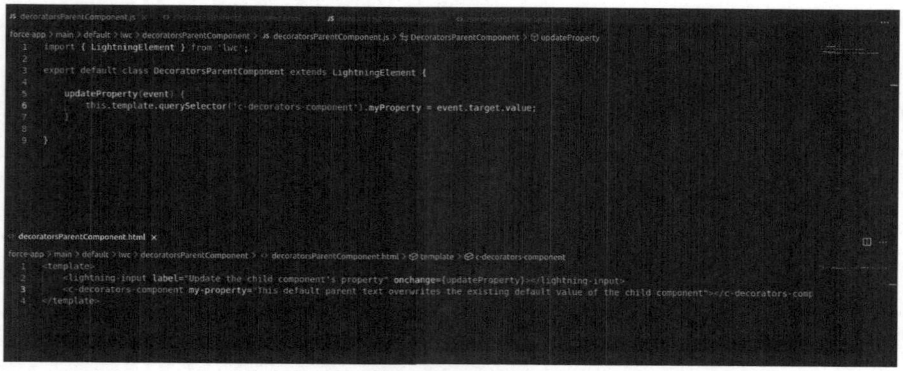

Figure 3.13: *Public properties of the child component are updated by the parent component*

In *Figure* 3.13, we see that the parent component has a **`lightning-input`** element (in its HTML template) which listens for the **`onchange`** event: when a change action happens on this **`lightning-input`** element, then the **`updateProperty`** method of the parent component will be called which will update the child's component public property **`myProperty`**. Here is the line which does the magic:

```
this.template.querySelector('c-decorators-component').myProperty
 = event.target.value;
```

As we see, instead of using the **`Document.getElementsByTagName`** selector, we're using **`this.template.querySelector`** (because we're in a shadow DOM) to select the child component from the parent component's HTML template.

Here is the resulting parent component's output:

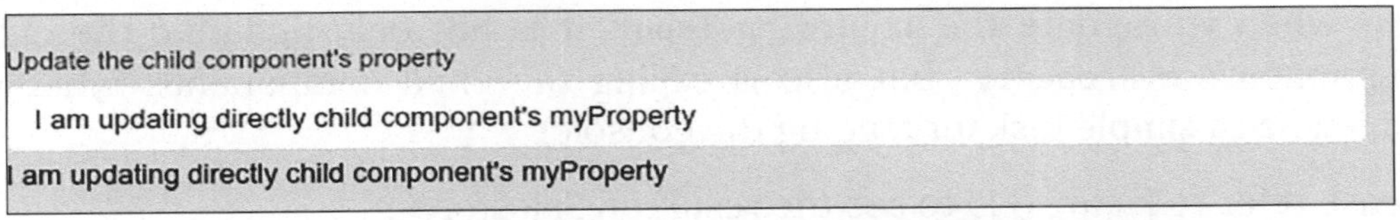

Figure 3.14: *When we enter a new value into the lightning-input, it is dynamically updating the child component's myProperty value*

So, we learned how the **`@api`** decorator works for properties. However, as mentioned before, the **`@api`** decorator can also be used to expose a child component's method. If we continue with our example, here is how to define a public method in a child component:

Child Component JS Controller (decoratorsComponent.js):

```
import { LightningElement, api } from 'lwc';
export default class DecoratorsComponent extends LightningElement {
    @api myProperty = 'Default child text';
    @api myMethod() {
        console.log('I am called from the parent component.');
    }
}
```

As **`myMethod`** is exposed via the **`@api`** decorator, now it is possible to call it from the parent component:

Parent Component JS Controller (decoratorsParentComponent.js):

```
import { LightningElement } from 'lwc';
export default class DecoratorsParentComponent extends LightningElement {
    updateProperty(event) {
        this.template.querySelector('c-decorators-component').myProperty
= event.target.value;
        this.template.querySelector('c-decorators-component').
myMethod();
    }
}
```

We simply update our current **updateProperty** method. Thus, we can see that now when we update the **lightning-input**, it is not only updating the child component's **myProperty** but also is calling the child component's **myMethod** (which has a simple task for logging the console).

Please refer to *Figure* 3.15 to see the result on Salesforce:

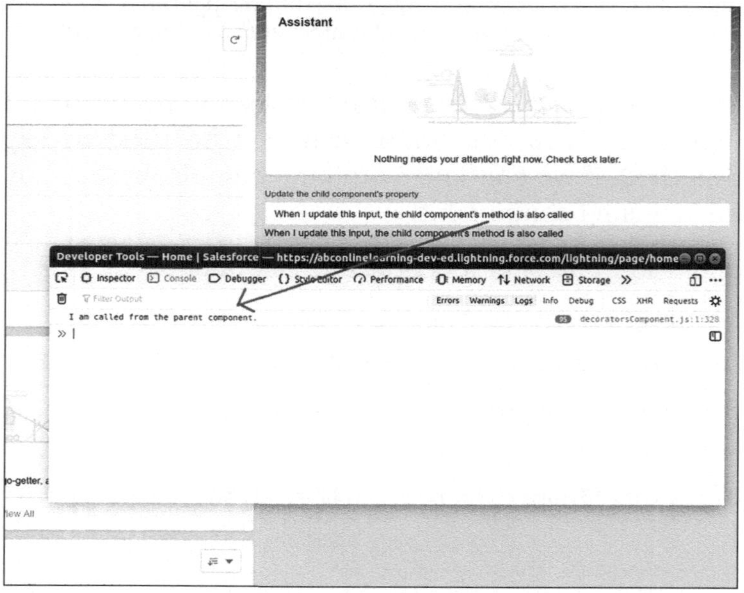

Figure 3.15: *Parent component calls the child component's "myMethod"*

Before concluding this @api decorator, we want to mention one final feature: **@api** decorator is not only used for this one-way communication between the parent components and the child components but it can be also used to expose the component's properties to other Salesforce non-code tools like Flows, Lightning App Builder, and so on. To see how it is functioning, let's update the configuration of the child component like the following:

Child Component Configuration File (decoratorsComponent.js-meta.xml):

```
<LightningComponentBundle xmlns=”http://soap.sforce.com/2006/04/
metadata”>
    <apiVersion>56.0</apiVersion>
    <isExposed>true</isExposed>
    <targets>
        <target>lightning__HomePage</target>
    </targets>
    <targetConfigs>
        <targetConfig targets=”lightning__HomePage”>
            <property name=”myProperty” type=”String”/>
        </targetConfig
    </targetConfigs>
</LightningComponentBundle>
```

We basically define a **`targetConfig`** for exposing the **`@api myProperty`** property to the **`Lightning App Builder`** for a **`Lightning Home Page`**: now it is possible to update the default value of this component while adding it into a **`Lightning Home Page`**. Please refer to *Figure* 3.16 for seeing how to configure it.

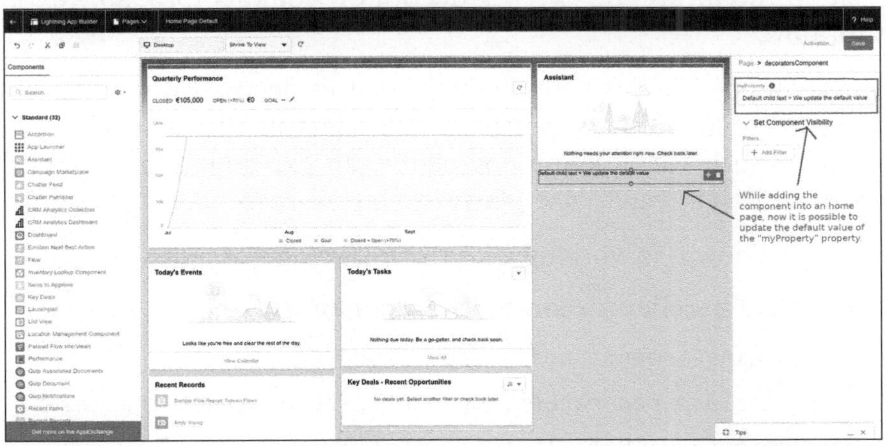

***Figure 3.16:** Now it is possible to update the component's exposed "myProperty" property's default value in the Lightning App Builder while editing a home page*

Figure 3.17 for the resulting page after the configuration is done:

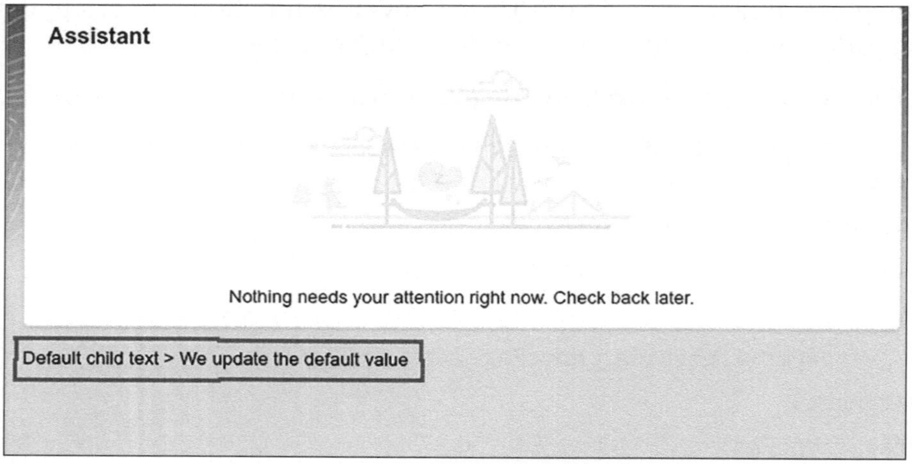

Figure 3.17: *The resulting page as expected*

@track decorator

In the previous section, we saw that the **`@api`** decorator is a very useful decorator which makes it very prevalent. Once, the same was also valid for the **`@track`** decorator: when the developers want a property to be reactive, they needed to use **`@track.`** But after Spring 20 release, the Salesforce Company made all primitive type properties (like Integer, String, Date, Datetime, Boolean etc.) reactive by default. So nowadays, we don't need to use at all the **`@track`** decorator for simple-valued properties of a LWC. As a pragmatic developer, we can even sense that, in the future, this **`@track`** decorator would be probably extinct, but not yet for now.

So, in one sentence, we need currently to use this decorator only and only if we want to make reactive the properties of an object or the elements of an array (that means even if we redefine completely an existing object or an existing array, again we don't need to use **`@track`** to have a re-rendering action).

Let's concretize how it is working with the following example:

Component JS Controller (decoratorsComponent.js):

```
import { LightningElement, api } from 'lwc';
export default class DecoratorsComponent extends LightningElement {
    @api myProperty = 'Default child text';
    myObject = {
```

```
        property1 : 'Some value',
        property2 : 5
    };
    myArray = [1,2,3];

    changeObject() {
        this.myObject = {
            property1 : 'Some new value',
            property2 : 8
        };
    }

    changeArray() {
        this.myArray = [4,5,6];
    }

    changeObjectProp1() {
        this.myObject.property1 = 'We updated only property1!';
    }

    changeArrayEl1() {
        this.myArray[0] = 1000;
    }

    @api myMethod() {
        console.log('I am called from the parent component.');
    }
}
```

Component HTML Template (decoratorsComponent.html):

```
<template>
    {myProperty}
    <br/><br/>
    <h1>My Object:</h1>
```

```
    <p>
        Property1 = {myObject.property1}<br/>
        Property2 = {myObject.property2}
    </p>
    <br/>
    <h1>My Array:</h1>
    <ul>
        <template for:each={myArray} for:item="el">
            <li key={el}>Element value = {el}</li>
        </template>
    </ul>
    <lightning-button label="Change Object" onclick={changeObject}></
lightning-button>
   <lightning-button label="Change Object's Property1" onclick=
{changeObjectProp1}></lightning-button>
    <lightning-button label="Change Array" onclick={changeArray}></
lightning-button>
    <lightning-button label="Change Array's First Element" on-
click={changeArrayEl1}></lightning-button>
</template>
```

As we can see, we basically defined one object (called **myObject**), one array (called **myArray**) with default values and those four buttons:

- **Change Object** button to redefine the **myObject** completely
- **Change Array** button to redefine the **myArray** completely
- **Change Object's Property1** button to update only **myObject→ property1**
- **Change Array's First Element** button to update only the first element of the **myArray.**

When we deploy the component, here is how it looks:

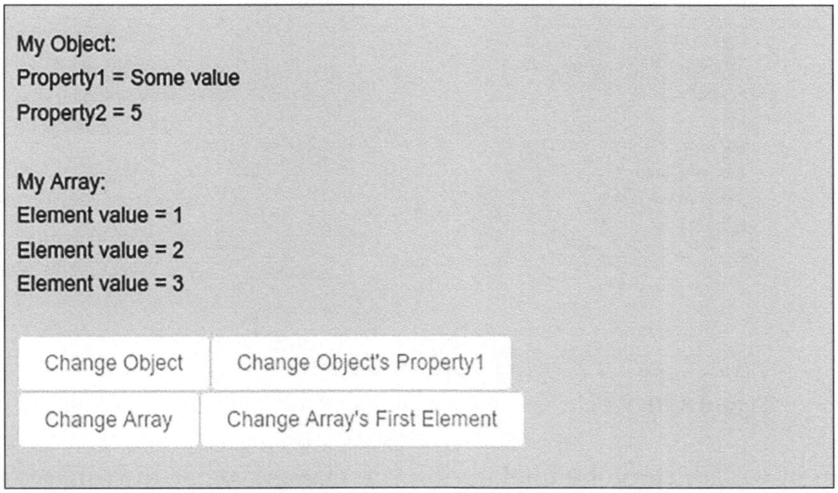

Figure 3.18: *Initial look of the component*

Until now, we didn't use the **`@track`** decorator, so let's observe what will happen when we click on the buttons (Please refer to *figures* 3.19-3.22).

As expected, when we click on the **`Change Object`** button, the component is re-rendered with the new object's property values (please refer to *Figure* 3.19).

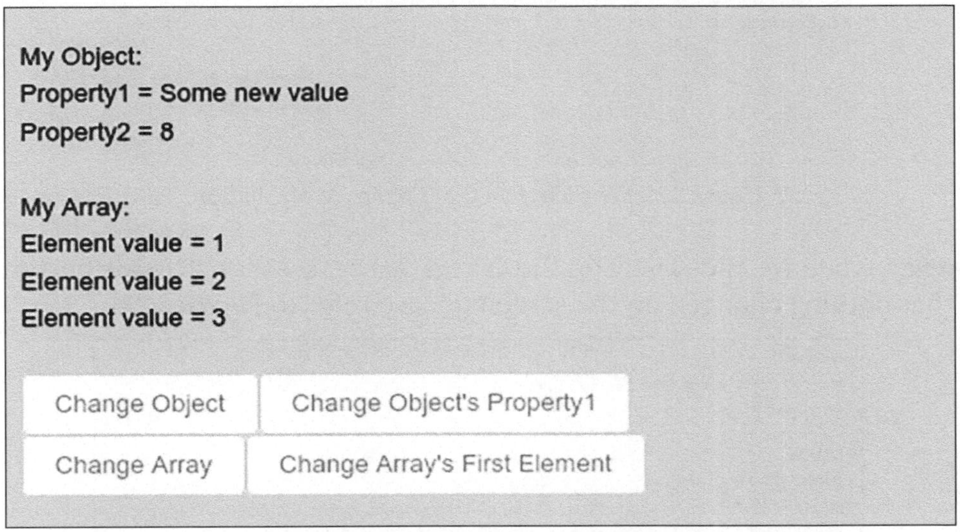

Figure 3.19: *We clicked on the "Change Object" button*

But when we try to update only the **`property1`** of the `myObject` but clicking on the **`Change Object's Property1`** button, nothing changed on the screen: no re-rendering at all. (Please refer to *Figure* 3.20).

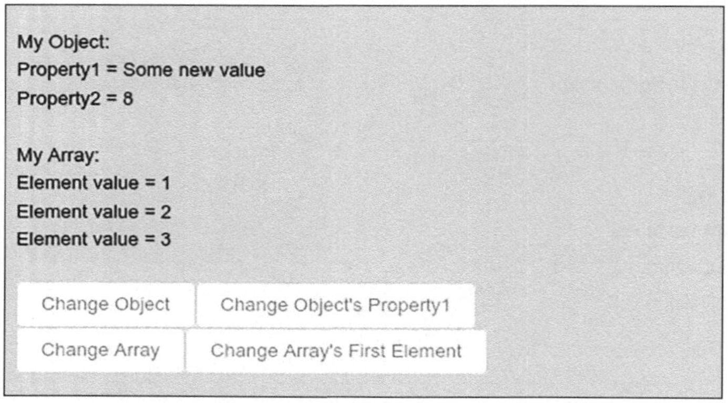

Figure 3.20: *We clicked on the "Change Object's Property1" button*

Again, when we continue by clicking on the **`Change Array`** button, we instantly notice that the component is re-rendered with the newly defined array (please refer to *Figure* 3.21).

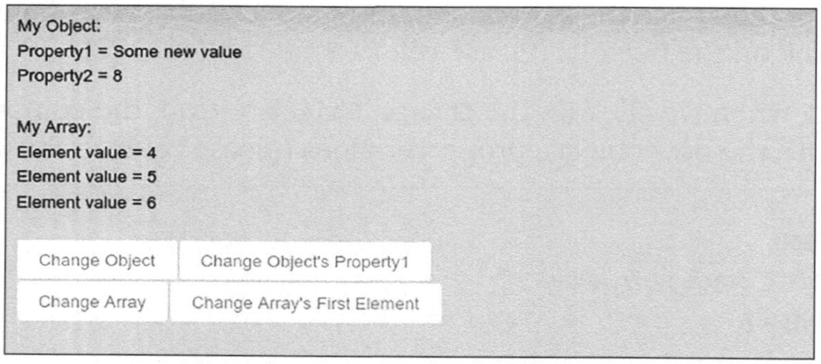

Figure 3.21: *We clicked on the "Change Array" button*

However, when we click lastly on the **`Change Array's First Element`** button, we see that nothing changed on the screen (please refer to *Figure* 3.22).

Figure 3.22: *We clicked on the "Change Array's First Element" button*

So, we see that we don't need to use the **@track** decorator for redefining objects and arrays. Nevertheless, we need it for updating individual properties and elements. Let's achieve this by making the following changes in the code:

Component JS Controller (decoratorsComponent.js):

```
import { LightningElement, api, track } from 'lwc';
export default class DecoratorsComponent extends LightningElement {
    @api myProperty = 'Default child text';
    @track myObject = {
        property1 : 'Some value',
        property2 : 5
    };
    @track myArray = [1,2,3];

    changeObject() {
        this.myObject = {
            property1 : 'Some new value',
            property2 : 8
        };
    }

    changeArray() {
        this.myArray = [4,5,6];
    }

    changeObjectProp1() {
        this.myObject.property1 = 'We updated only property1!';
    }

    changeArrayEl1() {
        this.myArray[0] = 1000;
    }

    @api myMethod() {
```

```
        console.log('I am called from the parent component.');
    }
}
```

Now, we added the **@track** decorator while defining initially the object and the array in the JS Controller file. However, we don't need to do any changes in the **Component HTML Template (decoratorsComponent.html)** file.

Note: Before using the decorators in the code, we need to import them initially in the component:

```
import { LightningElement, api, track } from 'lwc';
```

Now when we click on the **Change Object's Property1** button, we see that the component is re-rendered by having the updated value for the **myObject → property1** (please refer to *Figure* 3.23):

***Figure* 3.23:** *We clicked again on the "Change Object's Property1"* **button**

This time, when we click on the **Change Object's Property1** button we see that solely the **Property1** value is updated as expected.

And finally, when we click on the **Change Array's First Element** button, this time we see that only the first element of the array is updated (please refer to *Figure* 3.24):

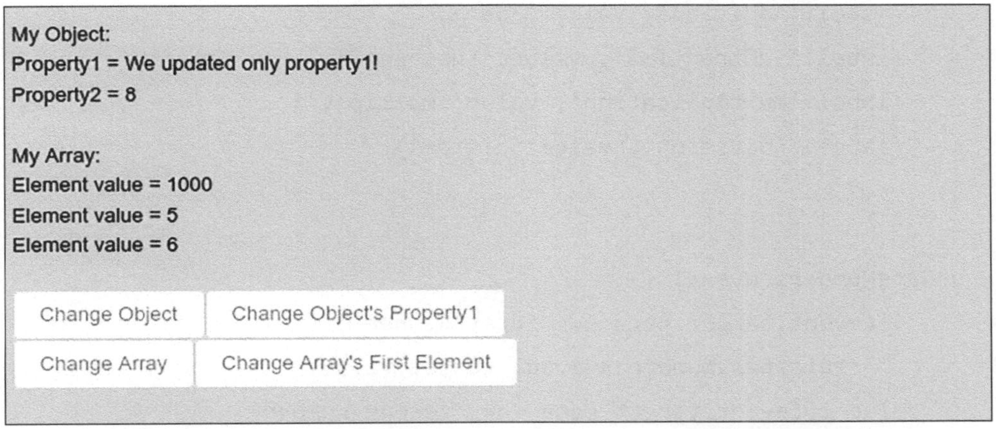

Figure 3.24: *Finally, we clicked on the "Change Array's First Element" button*

Thus, this was all for **`decorators`** for this chapter. As mentioned previously, there is a third decorator called **`@wire`** but we're going to examine it in the next chapter when we work on **`Lightning Data Service.`**

Composition and slots

This section will explain about Composition and slots.

Composition

Basically, by **`composition`**, we mean building parent-child component hierarchies in order to build complex parent components by using simpler building-block child components. We already did an example for a simple **parent-child** component pair while we were discussing the **`@api`** decorator. Now, let's examine in more detail this topic with the help of the following example (refer to *Figure 3.25* to see the output of the following components' code):

Parent Component Controller (compositionOwnerComponent.js)

```
import { LightningElement } from ‘lwc’;
export default class CompositionOwnerComponent extends LightningElement {
    firstNumber;
    secondNumber;
    result;
    options = [
        {label:’Please Select’, value:’0’},
```

```
        {label:'Addition', value:'add'},
        {label:'Subtraction', value:'subtract'},
        {label:'Multiplication', value:'multiply'},
        {label: 'Division', value:'divide'}
    ];

    updateNumbers(event) {
        if(event.target.name === 'first-number')
            this.firstNumber = event.target.value;
        else if(event.target.name === 'second-number')
            this.secondNumber = event.target.value;
    }
    handleChange(event) {
        const calculationType = event.target.value;
    if(this.firstNumber !== undefined && this.firstNumber !== null && this.
firstNumber !== '' && this.secondNumber !== undefined && this.secondNumber
!== null && this.secondNumber !== '') {
            this.template.querySelector('c-composition-composed-co
mponent').title = event.target.options.find(opt => opt.value === event.
detail.value).label + ' Result = ';
            this.result = this.template.querySelector('c-composi-
tion-composed-component').doTheCalculation(calculationType,this.
firstNumber,this.secondNumber);
        }
        else {
            this.template.querySelector('c-composition-composed-co
mponent').title = 'Please enter both numbers, then select the calcula-
tion type!';
            event.target.value = '0';
            this.result = '';
        }
    }
}
```

Parent Component HTML Template (compositionOwnerComponent.html):

```
<template>
    <lightning-input name=”first-number” label=”Enter first number”
value={firstNumber} onchange={updateNumbers}></lightning-input>
    <lightning-input name=”second-number” label=”Enter second number”
value={secondNumber} onchange={updateNumbers}></lightning-input>
    <lightning-combobox
        name=”calculation-type”
        label=”Please select the calculation type: “
        value=”0”
        options = {options}
        onchange={handleChange}
    ></lightning-combobox>
    <br/>
    <c-composition-composed-component title=’’>{result}</
c-composition-composed-component>
</template>
```

Child Component Controller (compositionComposedComponent.js):

```
import { LightningElement, api } from ‘lwc’;
export default class CompositionComposedComponent extends
LightningElement {

    @api title;

    @api doTheCalculation(type, a, b) {
        switch(type) {
            case ‘add’: return parseInt(a,10)+parseInt(b,10);
            case ‘subtract’: return parseInt(a,10)-parseInt(b,10);
            case ‘multiply’: return parseInt(a,10)*parseInt(b,10);
            case ‘divide’: return parseInt(a,10)/parseInt(b,10);
            default: return null;
        }
    }
```

```
}
```

Child Component HTML Template (compositionComposedComponent.html):

```
<template>
    <h1>{title} <slot></slot></h1>
</template>
```

We defined two components **`c-composition-owner-component`** and **`c-composition-composed-component`**. The latter is the child of the former. The child component has a public property title and has a public method **`doTheCalculation().`** As mentioned before, as a data flow best practice the parent components should always define and update the public properties of the child components. So here the value of the child component's title property is determined via the parent component's **`lightning-combobox→ handleChange`** method which is triggered when a change action happened on the **`lightning-combobox`**. Here is the line which is responsible for this assignment:

```
this.template.querySelector('c-composition-composed-component').title =
event.target.options.find(opt => opt.value === event.detail.value).label+
' Result = ';
```

By using the **`querySelector()`** method we query and find the child component in the parent component's HTML template and we do the assignment of the selected option's label of the lightning-combobox to the title property of the child component:

`this.template.querySelector('c-composition-composed-component').title` : We find the child component by using **`this.template.querySelector`** and reach its title property.

`event.target.options.find(opt => opt.value === event.detail.value).label` : This is a pure JavaScript code for obtaining the label of the selected option in the lightning-combobox.

So, it was how we update the child's component public **title** property from the parent's component.

Moreover, we can also initially define a default value while putting the child component into the parent component's HTML template:

```
<c-composition-composed-component title=''>{result}</c-composition-co
mposed-component>
```

In this example, we define an empty default value for the "title" property of the child component.

Note: Public properties, like the title in our example, should be primitive instead of object or array: if we need to pass an object or an array to the child components, as a best practice we need to slice this complex data structure in a higher-level component and pass the primitive values to the descendants.

Invoking a public method of a child component is very similar to what we do previously for using its public properties. Here is the line responsible (in our example) for invoking the child component's public method:

```
this.result = this.template.querySelector('c-composition-composed-co
mponent').doTheCalculation(calculationType,this.firstNumber,this.se
condNumber);
```

Again we use the **`querySelector()`** method to find the child component and directly use its **`doTheCalculation()`** public method. This method takes three parameters: the `calculationType` which holds the info about whether the user wants **addition**, **subtraction**, **multiplication** or **division** and the other two parameters are the numbers which will be used in the calculation. When this method is executed, it is returning a result which is being held in the local **`result`** parameter of the parent component. Then by using it, we're printing the result on the screen using the **`unnamed slot`** of the child component. (More on "slots" will come in the next section).

One additional thing to note is: in the LWC programming, the developers should avoid using any **`id`** attribute in the components. Instead of an **`id`** attribute, we can basically use **`name`** attribute. **`id`** attributes are not recommended because the Salesforce Platform, while processing the LWC, updates the **`id`** attributes according to the framework's needs. So, briefly, their values are being updated to some global custom values by the Salesforce Platform.

The **`updateNumbers()`** method of the parent component (which is triggered when a change action happened in one of the input fields) uses the **`name`** attribute to detect whether the change happens on the **`firstNumber`** or on the **`secondNumber`:**

```
updateNumbers(event) {
        if(event.target.name === 'first-number')
            this.firstNumber = event.target.value;
        else if(event.target.name === 'second-number')
            this.secondNumber = event.target.value;
}
```

Figure 3.25: *Screenshot of the component's run for a simple division calculation*

Briefly, we can do a resume like the following:

1. **Inheritance** is allowed in the LWC Framework, however, as a best practice the developers should compose components as explained earlier. If it is needed to share logic between the components, it can be easily done via modules. (More on modules can be found in the second chapter - *Creating Your First LWC.*)
2. Public attributes of the child components should always be defined and updated by the parent component.
    a. If the child component needs an update on one of its public properties, then it can fire an event that bubbles up; thus, the parent component can capture the signal and do the update for the child component. (More on **`events`** will come in the next chapters.)
3. Public methods of the child components can be easily invoked by the parent component as shown previously.

Before concluding this section, let's talk shortly about the **`container`** components:

```
<!-- owner.html -->
<template>
    <c-container-example>
        <c-item item-name="Item1"></c-item>
        <c-item item-name="Item2"></c-item>
    </c-container-example>
<template>
```

As we can see in this example, it is possible to define another type of parent component, which is called the container component. Here is how all relate to each other:

- Owner component
  - It is the component which owns the main **`template`**.
  - It can set public properties on composed components.
  - It can invoke the public methods of the composed components.
  - It listens any events fired by the composed components.
- Container component(s)
  - There can be many levels of hierarchy for container components:

    ```
    <template>
          <c-container-1>
                <c-container-2>
                      <c-item item-name="Item1"></c-item>
                </c-container-2>
          </c-container-1>
    </template>
    ```
  - It can read the public properties of the contained components but cannot update them.
  - It can call public methods of the contained components.
  - It can listen for some but not necessarily all the events bubbled by the contained components.
- Composed component(s)
  - Their public properties should be set by the parent (owner) component.
  - They can also use internally their public methods.
  - They can fire events to trigger actions on the parent component.

Slots

Slot is a web component standard which is used to push "mark-up" (not data) from parent to child components. There are two types of slots:

- Unnamed Slots
- Named Slots

Note: By mark-up, we mean a bunch of HTML tags and texts. However, when we say data, we mean **primitive** or **non – primitive** data that can be used, updated or read throughout the application via the components' properties.

In the example of the previous Composition section, we've already used a sample for the **`unnamed slot`**:

Parent Component HTML Template (compositionOwnerComponent.html):

```
<template>
   // … we omitted irrelevant code to provide a better focusing on "slot" usage …
 <c-composition-composed-component title=''>{result}</c-composition-composed-component>
</template>
```

Child Component HTML Template (compositionComposedComponent.html):

```
<template>
    <h1>{title} <slot></slot></h1>
</template>
```

By using the **`<slot></slot>`** tags in the child component's HTML template, we provide a placeholder which can be filled directly by the parent component. In this example, we see that the parent component puts **`{result}`** in the content of the **`<c-composition-composed-component>`** child component which in turn is put directly inside of the child component's **`<slot>...</slot>`** tag. So, this way, when the **`result`** property of the parent component is updated, it is possible to see the changes directly in the child component's html template.

Briefly, by using the **`slots`**, the parent components can update the markup of the child components.

When we need to use only one slot in a component, the **`unnamed slot`** will do the work, as shown in the previous example. However, if there is a need to change the markup of the child component partially then we need to use **`named slots`**. Let's see the following example for seeing them in action:

Parent Component HTML Template:

```
<template>
        <c-slot-child-component>
                <div slot="slot1">This is the 'slot1' content</div>
                <div slot="slot2">This is the 'slot2' content</div>
        </c-slot-child-component>
</template>
```

Child Component HTML Template:

```
<template>
        <slot name="slot1">Default content for slot1</slot>
        <slot name="slot2">Default content for slot2</slot>
</template>
```

Basically, here **`<div slot="slot1">...</div>`** of the parent component will replace the Default content for **`slot1 text`** and the **`<div slot="slot2">...</div>`** mark-up will replace the **`Default content for slot2`** text respectively, in the child component HTML template.

For slots, there is a specific **`onslotchange`** event that can be used to handle the lifecycle of the content that is passed in:

Child Component HTML Template:

```
<template>
        <slot name="slot1" onslotchange={handleSlotChange}>Default
content for slot1</slot>
        <slot name="slot2" onslotchange={handleSlotChange}>Default
content for slot2</slot>
</template>
```

Child Component JS Controller:

```
import { LightningElement } from 'lwc';
export default class SlotChildComponent extends LightningElement {
    handleSlotChange(event) {
        const slot = event.target;
        console.log("slot change event is triggered! "+slot.name);
        if(slot.name == "slot1") console.log("Slot 1 is updated!");
        if(slot.name == "slot2") console.log("Slot 2 is updated!");
    }
}
```

Slots can be used to add dynamically any HTML markup we need: so it is also possible to use them to dynamically add/remove child components in a parent component (please refer to *figures* 3.26 and 3.27):

slotOwnerComponent.js:

```
import { LightningElement } from 'lwc';
export default class SlotOwnerComponent extends LightningElement {
    addOneMoreChildComponent = false;

    handleAdd(){
        this.addOneMoreChildComponent = true;
    }
}
```

slotOwnerComponent.html:

```
<template>
    <c-slot-parent-component>
        <c-slot-child-component>
            <div slot="slot1">This is the 'slot1' content</div>
            <div slot="slot2">This is the 'slot2' content</div>
        </c-slot-child-component>
        <template lwc:if={addOneMoreChildComponent}>
```

```
            <c-slot-child-component></c-slot-child-component>
        </template>
    </c-slot-parent-component>
<lightning-button label="Add One More Child Component" onclick=
{handleAdd}></lightning-button>
</template>
```

slotParentComponent.js:

```
import { LightningElement } from 'lwc';
export default class SlotParentComponent extends LightningElement {}
```

slotParentComponent.html:

```
<template>
    <slot></slot>
</template>
```

slotChildComponent.js:

```
import { LightningElement } from 'lwc';
export default class SlotChildComponent extends LightningElement {
    handleSlotChange(event) {
        const slot = event.target;
        console.log("slot change event is triggered! "+slot.name);
        if(slot.name == "slot1") console.log("Slot 1 is updated!");
        if(slot.name == "slot2") console.log("Slot 2 is updated!");
    }
}
```

slotChildComponent.html:

```
<template>
    <slot name="slot1" onslotchange={handleSlotChange}>Default content
for slot1<br/></slot>
        <slot name="slot2" onslotchange={handleSlotChange}>Default
content for slot2<br/></slot>
```

```
</template>
```

In this example, the **`slotOwnerComponent`** component is updating the **`<slot></slot>`** of the **`slotParentComponent`** by adding one more **`slotChildComponent`** when the button is clicked.

Before we click on the button:

Figure 3.26: *Initially, the "parent component" has only one "child component"*

After we click it:

Figure 3.27: *When we click on the button, a second "child component" with default texts is added*

Lifecycle hooks

When a component is initialized or inserted into the DOM or rendered etc. there are a handful of functions that get invoked automatically: they are called **Lifecycle Hooks.**

- **`constructor()`** is invoked when the component instance is created.
- **`connectedCallback()`** is invoked when the component is inserted into the DOM.
- **`disconnectedCallback()`** is invoked when the component is removed from the DOM.
- **`renderedCallback()`** is invoked when the component is completely rendered.
- **`errorCallback()`** is invoked when there is an error in any of the lifecycle hooks or when there is an error in event handling.

In the official documentation of Lightning Web Components, the flow of the component lifecycle is explained by very good diagrams (please refer to *Figures* 3.28 and 3.29):

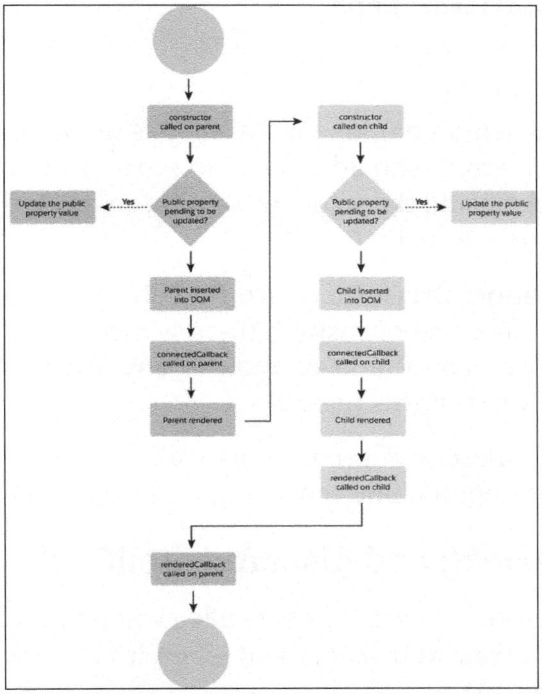

Figure 3.28: *The Flow of the Component Lifecycle from creation through render*

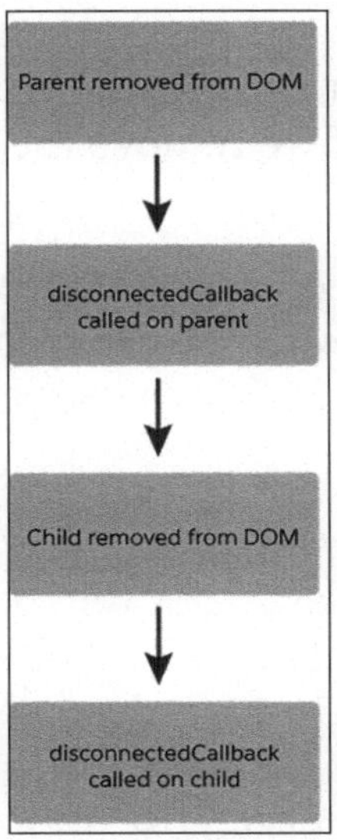

Figure 3.29: *The Flow of the Component when it is removed from the DOM*

So basically, except the **`renderedCallback()`** hook, every other hook is called first on the parent component and then later on the child component but for **`renderedCallback()`** the parent is waiting for the completion of the execution of the child's **`renderedCallback()`** hook.

Constructor()

This method fires when a component instance is created. The first statement of a **`constructor()`** method should always be **`super()`** in order to establish the correct prototype chain and the value for **this**. So **`super()`** is required as the first statement in order to use **`this`**.

In the instance creation phase, there are no public **`properties`**, **`attributes`** or **`children`**. So we cannot use or inspect them while we're in the **`constructor()`** method. And also, we cannot add or remove any attributes as those are not reachable yet while we're at this phase.

This is the phase where we programmatically create the instance of the component: this does not include rendering or being inserted into the DOM.

connectedCallback() and disconnectedCallback()

As mentioned previously, those hooks are called when the component is inserted into the **`DOM (=connectedCallback())`** and when it is removed from the **`DOM (= disconnectedCallback()).`**

As the component is inserted into the DOM, we can use **`connectedCallback()`** to coordinate behavior with the environment, fetch data, set up initial configurations and/or listen for events, etc. We should be aware that this hook can be called more than once if we remove the component from one place and put it in another place.

Most of the time, we would need to use **`disconnectedCallback()`** to reset the work which is previously done by the **`connectedCallback(),`** briefly whenever we have specific actions to be done when the component is removed from the DOM.

renderedCallback()

Whenever the HTML template of the component is rendered, this **`renderedCallback()`** hook is invoked. As we know, there is a default reactivity for the primitive properties in LWC which means whenever a value of a primitive property is changed then the template re-renders automatically. So briefly we can easily understand that for almost every action that happens, for every event which is triggered on the component, this hook will eventually be invoked. That's why, as a best practice, we should use this hook only we need to do global actions related to the whole component: for managing other partial renders on the component, we should use independent event handlers.

One thing to note, as this hook is called whenever there is an update on the component's state, we should be careful not to make additional state updates in it: if we do, then it can cause an infinite loop due to the subsequent recursive executions of this hook.

Tip: Normally a component would be re-rendered many times in a session so if we need to invoke **`renderedCallbak()`** only once, we may need to use a Boolean property like **`hasRendered`**.

Note: When a template is re-rendered, the LWC engine attempts to reuse the existing elements, so in the following cases it will skip re-rendering of the element:

- If the **`key`** attribute of an iteration element stays the same, then the engine will assume that it doesn't change so it will not re-render it.
- Elements received as **`slot`** content, if the diffing algorithm didn't notice a difference.

---

errorCallback()

As mentioned previously, whenever there is an error in one of the other hooks or in an event handling, then this hook is invoked. By using it, we can detect whether or not an error happens in the component and consequently, we can manage beautifully the situation for the user either by printing the error on the screen or by passing the component into another view.

This hook should have 2 arguments:

- **`error`** which is the JavaScript native **`error`** object
- **`stack`** which is a string for obtaining the details of the error

Example:

```
import { LightningElement } from 'lwc';
export default class Boundary extends LightningElement {
    error;
    stack;
```

```
    errorCallback(error, stack) {
        this.error = error;
    }
}
```

Working with multiple HTML templates

We understood how the different lifecycle hooks function. Apart from those specific hook functions, we have also a very useful method which gives us the ability to render different HTML templates according to custom conditions or custom actions on the component: the **`render()`** method. Let's see it in an example (please refer to *Figure* 3.30):

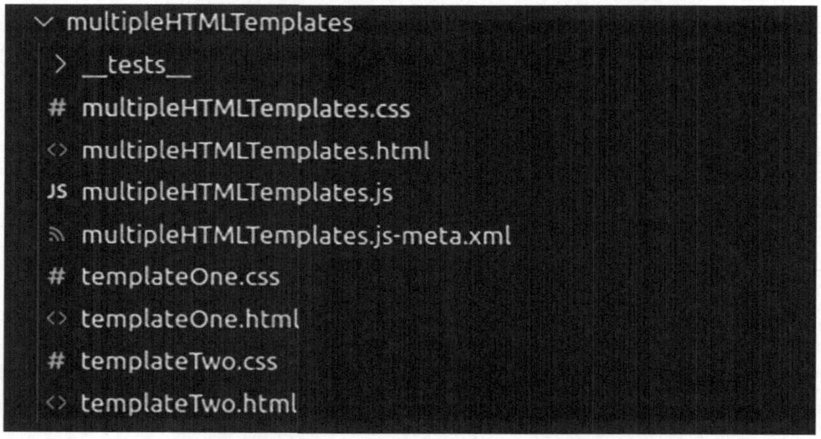

Figure 3.30: *A LWC with multiple HTML templates*

We see that the component **`multipleHTMLTemplates`** has three different HTML templates:

- `multipleHTMLTemplates.html`
- `templateOne.html`
- `templateTwo.html`

In addition, we need to note that every HTML template has a companion CSS file having the same name, which means every template is using its own CSS descriptions:

- `multipleHTMLTemplates.css`
- `templateOne.css`
- `templateTwo.css`

If we don't define any custom condition or any custom action, the component will eventually use its default template **multipleHTMLTemplates.html** and will ignore the other two templates. However, by using the **render()** method, we can decide which template to use:

multipleHTMLTemplates.js:

```
import { LightningElement } from 'lwc';
import templateOne from './templateOne.html';
import templateTwo from './templateTwo.html';
import defaultTemplate from './multipleHTMLTemplates.html';
export default class MultipleHTMLTemplates extends LightningElement {
    templateCounter = 1;

    render() {
        if(this.templateCounter % 3 === 1) return templateOne;
        else if(this.templateCounter % 3 === 2) return templateTwo;
        return defaultTemplate;
    }
    increaseCounter(){
        this.templateCounter++;
    }
}
```

In the JavaScript controller, we define the **render()** method to select the template according to the remainder of the division of the **templateCounter** by **3**. When the remainder is **1** the component renders the **templateOn**, if it is **2** the component renders the **templateTwo** and finally if it is **0** the component renders the **default template**. By clicking on the button, we increase the **templateCounter** by one, so with each click we have a new template rendered (please refer to *Figures* 3.31,- 3.33):

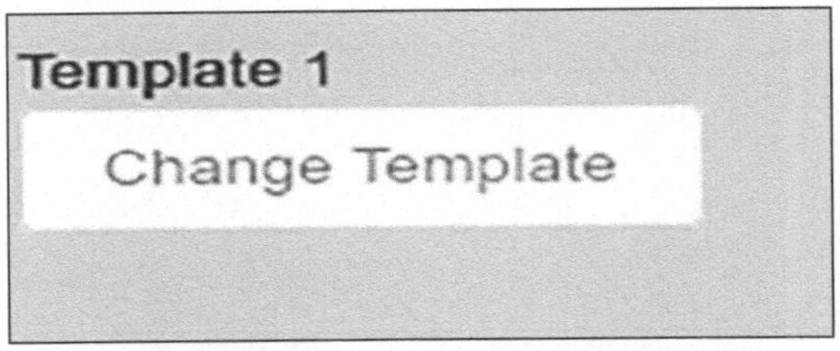

Figure 3.31: *Initially, the "templateOne" is rendered*

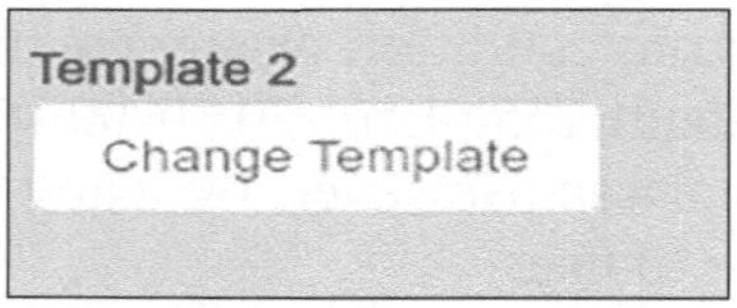

Figure 3.32: *We clicked once on the button, "templateTwo" is rendered*

Figure 3.33: *We clicked a second time on the button, "default template" is rendered*

Static resources and third-party JS libraries

For modern security exigencies, it is not a good idea to use static resources (like images, documents, third-party JavaScript libraries, etc.) by calling them directly from third-party external URLs, servers, websites, platforms, etc. JavaScript is a very strong language that can listen and trigger any event (visible or hidden to the user) while the user is working on the browser screen: so, when we use directly an image or a JavaScript file from another web server (even if this server is run by a very trustworthy, reliable company like Google, Facebook, etc.), we basically give them the power to execute any code in our web application. Naturally, by default, Salesforce is not allowing to use any third-party resource from external platforms.

What we need to do is to upload those resources directly into our Salesforce org, and then we would be able to use them in our LWCs.

This can be done by using the **`New`** button in **`Setup → Static Resources`**:

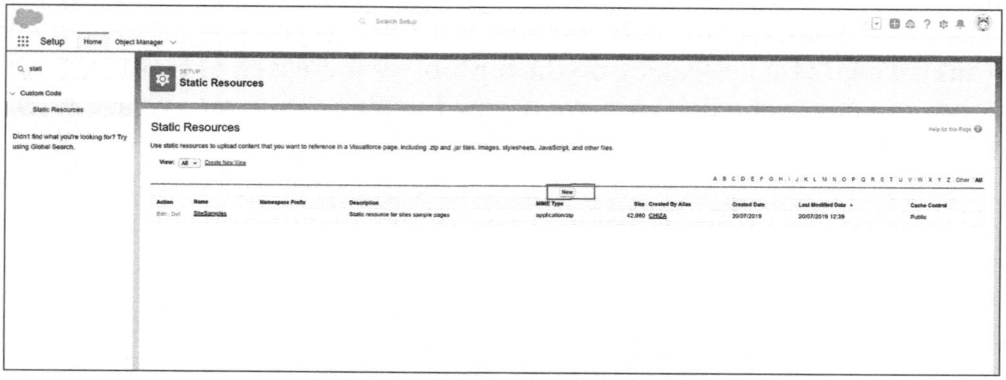

Figure 3.34: *"Static Resources" screen in Salesforce org Setup*

For example, we uploaded 2 resources, please refer to *Figure* 3.35:

- JS file: ExternalJS. Please find its content as follows:

```
window.externalJS = (function() {
  return {
     doTheSum: function(a, b) {
            return a + b;
     }
  };
}());
```

- Image file: `ImageResource`

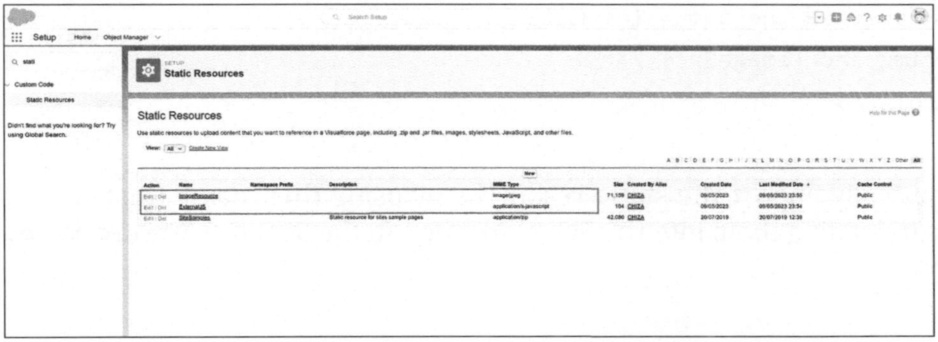

***Figure* 3.35**: *Two Third-Party Resources are uploaded into the Salesforce org*

After we have these resources uploaded into the Salesforce org, we can directly use them by importing them into our LWC:

staticResourcesComponent.js:

```
import { LightningElement } from ‘lwc’;
import { loadScript } from ‘lightning/platformResourceLoader’;
import JSLib from ‘@salesforce/resourceUrl/ExternalJS’;
import ImageRes from ‘@salesforce/resourceUrl/ImageResource’;

export default class StaticResourcesComponent extends LightningElement {
    imageSrc = ImageRes;
    a = 5;
    b = 3;
    result;
```

```
    renderedCallback() {
        loadScript(this, JSLib).then(() => {
            this.result = externalJS.doTheSum(this.a, this.b);
        });
    }
}
```

staticResourcesComponent.html:

```
<template>
    Result of the sum = {result}
    <img src={imageSrc} />
</template>
```

We basically import the static resources by using their name (that we've given while uploading them into the Salesforce org, in the **Setup → Static Resources** menu):

```
import JSLib from '@salesforce/resourceUrl/ExternalJS';
import ImageRes from '@salesforce/resourceUrl/ImageResource';
```

ExternalJS is the name for the uploaded JS file static resource and ImageResource is the name for the uploaded image file static resource (please refer again to *Figure* 3.35). While importing them, we can give any name we want: here we choose to use **JSLib** and **ImageRes** as their names in the JS controller.

For using the image, we define a property **imageSrc** in the JS controller and by using it we become able to define the source URL of the image tag in the html template:

```
<img src={imageSrc} />
```

However, for being able to load the JS file into our LWC, we need to use a standard method of the LWC Framework's core library, which is called **loadScript**. So, in the beginning, we import that method:

```
import { loadScript } from 'lightning/platformResourceLoader';
```

Then, by using this **loadScript** method, we use the **doTheSum** function of the **externalJS** object of our **ExternalJS** JavaScript file static resource:

```
loadScript(this, JSLib).then(() => {
    this.result = externalJS.doTheSum(this.a, this.b);
});
```

Here is the resulting LWC on the Salesforce org:

***Figure 3.36**: By using the "doTheSum" method of the third-party JS file we're able to calculate the "result" and we're able to see the image on the screen which is called directly from the Salesforce org static resources*

Generally, the storage of Salesforce orgs is not sufficient for uploading every resource on them and in addition, it is not also cheap to increase the storage limits of Salesforce orgs. After all, the Salesforce Company is not an **Infrastructure-as-a-Service (IaaS)** provider like Amazon Web Services, Google Cloud, etc. It is a **Software-as-a-Service (SaaS)** provider, as we know.

So, most companies need to keep their files (not on Salesforce but) on IaaS providers. That means, while working on real-world scenarios, our LWCs should be able to load resources from third-party servers.

In order to achieve this, we need to define those third-party servers' URLs as **CSP (Content Security Policy) Trusted Sites** on Salesforce Setup by using the **New Trusted Site** button:

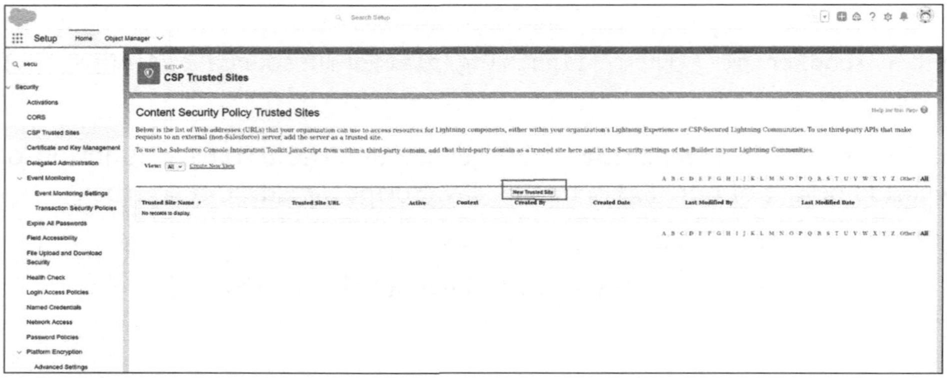

Figure 3.37: *"Content Security Policy Trusted Sites" screen in Salesforce org Setup*

In addition, we need to add the same site's URL under the `Remote Site Settings` in Salesforce Setup, by using the `New Remote Site` button:

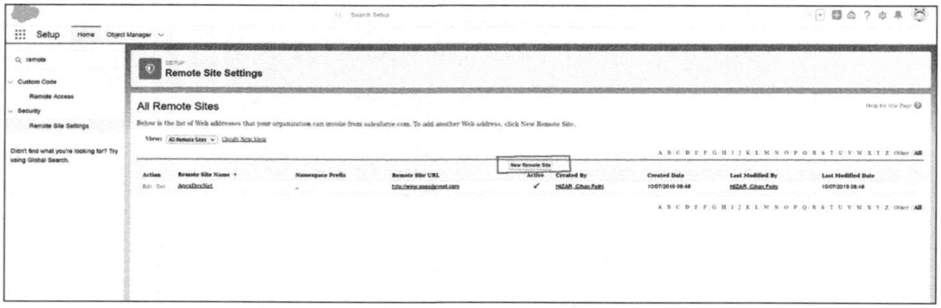

Figure 3.38: *"Remote Site Settings" screen in Salesforce org Setup*

One important note to mention: The third-party JavaScript files and libraries should **always** be uploaded into Salesforce static resources: We can **never** call a third-party JavaScript API from a third-party site. They should all reside in Salesforce org. However, for image files, pdf documents etc. we can work with third-party cloud providers as described.

Navigation in LWC

In LWCs, in order to let the user navigate to internal pages (like record pages, custom tabs, lightning apps etc. - namely, any page that exists in the Salesforce org) or to external websites we use the **lightning/navigation** navigation service. Let's see an example to capture how it functions:

navigationServiceExample.js:

```
import { LightningElement } from 'lwc';
```

```
import { NavigationMixin } from 'lightning/navigation';
export default class NavigationServiceExample extends
NavigationMixin(LightningElement) {
    url;
    connectedCallback() {
        this.accountListViewPageReference = {
            type:   'standard__objectPage',
            attributes: {
                objectApiName: 'Account',
                actionName: 'list'
            },
            state: {
                filterName: 'Recent'
            }
        };

        this[NavigationMixin.GenerateUrl](this.accountListViewPage
Reference)
        .then(listPageUrl => this.url = listPageUrl);
    }
    handleClick() {
        this[NavigationMixin.Navigate](this.accountListViewPage
Reference);
    }
}
```

navigationServiceExample.html:

```
<template>
   Recent Accounts Page URL = {url}<br/><br/>
  <lightning-button label="Open Recently Viewed Accounts" onclick=
{handleClick}></lightning-button>
</template>
```

In order to use the LWC navigation service, first we need to import it and then extend it:

```
import { NavigationMixin } from 'lightning/navigation';
export default class NavigationServiceExample extends NavigationMix-
in(LightningElement)
```

Thus, we are able to add two APIs to our component's class:

```
[NavigationMixin.GenerateUrl](pageReference)
[NavigationMixin.Navigate](pageReference, [replace])
```

`[NavigationMixin.GenerateURL]` is used to create the URL of the page we want to navigate. This can be useful if we want to define our own **`anchor <a>`** tag having a value for its **`href`** attribute by this generated URL. And **`[NavigationMixin.Navigate]`** is used to open the page: it is the actual **navigation** action.

Both APIs are using a **`pageReference`** type object, that we create like the following:

```
this.accountListViewPageReference = {
            type:   'standard__objectPage',
            attributes: {
                objectApiName: 'Account',
                actionName: 'list'
            },
            state: {
                filterName: 'Recent'
            }
        };
```

Here, we can give any name we want while defining the object. In this example, we give **`accountListViewPageReference`** as its name. This object has two mandatory properties (type and attributes) and one optional property (state). Here, we want to open an Account object list view page, so that's why we give **`standard__objectPage`** as the value of the **`typ`** property and we define the **`attributes`** property accordingly. The optional **`state`** property is used to declare that we want to see the **`recent accounts list`**.

Note: In order to learn different type, attributes and state values of the PageReference object, for different page types, we can consult the official documentation:

https://developer.salesforce.com/docs/component-library/documentation/en/lwc/reference_page_reference_type

---

Tip: `[NavigationMixin.Navigate]` API has a second optional variable **`replace`** which is used to override the browser's current history: when it is **`true`**, the current page is overridden by the navigated page: that means, when the user clicks on the **`back`** button of the browser, (s)he will not be able to return to the original page which starts the navigation.

By default its value is **`false`**, and for most cases this is what we need.

So, if we deploy this `navigationServiceExample` component, here how it looks on Salesforce org:

Figure 3.39: *"navigationServiceExample" Component on Salesforce org*

When we click on the **`Open Recently Viewed Accounts`**, the **`recent list`** view for the **`Account`** object is opened, as expected:

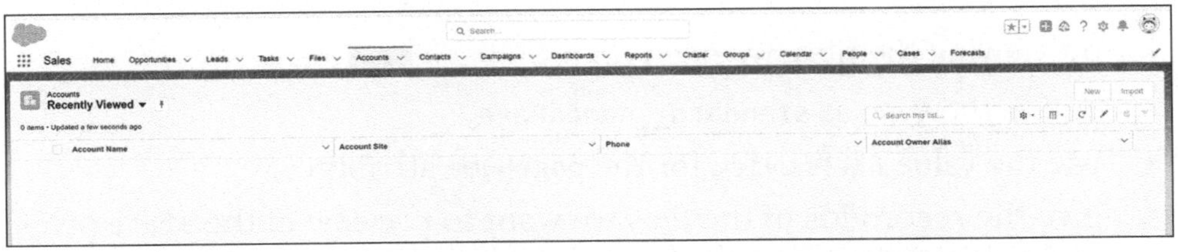

Figure 3.40: *After we click on the "Open Recently Viewed Accounts" button*

Note: The **lightning/navigation** service is supported only in Lightning Experience, Experience Builder sites and the Salesforce mobile app. It cannot be used if we put our LWC into a Visualforce page or we run it through Lightning Out.

Navigate to files

Navigating to files is no different from what we saw until now for the navigation service. We're using the same **NavigationMixin** module with a **pageReference** object specific to preview the files. Here is a quick example:

```
import { LightningElement } from 'lwc';
import { NavigationMixin } from 'lightning/navigation';
export default class OpenFileSample extends NavigationMixin
(LightningElement) {
    navigateToFiles() {
      this[NavigationMixin.Navigate]({
        type: 'standard__namedPage',
        attributes: {
            pageName: 'filePreview'
        },
        state : {
            recordIds: '069xx0000000A4BAAA,069xx0000000A3CAAQ',
            selectedRecordId:'069xx0000000A4BAAA'
        }
      })
    }
}
```

So, for previewing the files, we need to:

- define the **type** as **standard__namedPage,**
- use the value **filePreview** for the **pageName** attribute,
- give the record Ids of the files we want to preview in the **state** property of the **pageReference** object.

And that's it.

selectedRecordId is an optional **state** property, which is used to determine which file would be downloaded first. If it is not used, the first **id** in the **recordIds** list is used by default for download.

However, if we don't want to **preview** the files but instead of, we want to give the user the ability to directly download the files then we can use the **lightning/fileDownload** module. Here is an example:

```
import { LightningElement } from 'lwc';
import { generateUrl } from 'lightning/fileDownload';
export default class Download extends LightningElement {
    recordId;
    url;
    handleClick() {
        this.url = generateUrl(this.recordId);
    }
}
```

Briefly, by using the **generateUrl** method of the **lightning/fileDownload** module, we can directly obtain the download URL of the file.

Display notifications

Creating feedback for the user is one of the important aspects of web development. After all, standard users don't know how to debug a web application, so all they have are only those Alert, Prompt, Confirm modals and Toast notifications. Luckily for us, while working with the LWC Framework, we don't need to rediscover America because Salesforce already provides those functionalities via its standard modules.

There are 4 types of notifications in the LWC Framework:

- **Alert Modals:** For showing a read-only feedback message to the user.
- **Confirm Modals:** For getting the confirmation of the user to proceed further.
- **Prompt Modals:** For receiving input from the user before proceeding further.
- **Toast Notifications:** These are more user-friendly alert modals which provide instant feedback to the user.

In order to see all of them in action, here is the LWC we created:

displayNotifications.js

```
import { LightningElement } from 'lwc';
import LightningAlert from 'lightning/alert';
import LightningConfirm from 'lightning/confirm';
import LightningPrompt from 'lightning/prompt';
import { ShowToastEvent } from 'lightning/platformShowToastEvent';

export default class DisplayNotifications extends LightningElement {
    async handleAlertClick() {
        await LightningAlert.open({
            message: 'This is the error message in the alert box.',
            theme: 'error',
            label: 'A Simple Alert Example'
        });
    }

    async handleConfirmClick() {
        const result = await LightningConfirm.open({
            message: 'It is where we write the confirmation message',
            variant: 'headerless'
        });
    }

    handlePromptClick() {
        LightningPrompt.open({
            message: 'Your answer please:',
            label: 'A Simple Prompt Example',
            defaultValue: ''
        }).then((result) => {
            // put the actions to be done here after the user responds
        });
    }
```

```
    showNotification() {
        const evt = new ShowToastEvent({
            title: 'A Simple Toast Notification Example',
            message: 'It is successful!',
            variant: 'success'
        });
        this.dispatchEvent(evt);
    }
}
```

diplayNotifications.html:

```
<template>
    <lightning-button onclick={handleAlertClick} label="Open Alert
Modal"></lightning-button><br/>
    <lightning-button onclick={handleConfirmClick} label="Open Confirm
Modal"></lightning-button><br/>
    <lightning-button onclick={handlePromptClick} label="Open Prompt
Modal"></lightning-button><br/>
    <lightning-button label="Show Notification" onclick=
{showNotification}></lightning-button>
</template>
```

So, in order to use those standard modules, we need to first import them, as usual:

```
import LightningAlert from 'lightning/alert';
import LightningConfirm from 'lightning/confirm';
import LightningPrompt from 'lightning/prompt';
import { ShowToastEvent } from 'lightning/platformShowToastEvent';
```

And then in the event handler methods, we use their methods to create various modals and the toast notification:

```
LightningAlert.open({ … })
```

```
LightningConfirm.open({ … })
LightningPrompt.open({ … })
const evt = new ShowToastEvent({ … }); this.dispatchEvent(evt);
```

For **Alert Modal,** apart from the error theme, there are default, shade, inverse, alt-inverse, success, info, warning and offline themes. Each theme has its own color.

For **Confirm Modal**, we can also define a theme. We have the same themes as the Alert Modal. For the variant property, we can also give the valueheader", which is the default value for the variant property.

For **Prompt Modal**, we can also define a theme and we have the same themes as Alert Modal and the Confirm Modal. By using the variant property, here also we can define whether or not we want a header or not on the modal.

The Toast Notification is functioning like an LWC custom event. (We'll discuss the LWC events in the following chapters.) Here, apart from the success value, the variant property can get info, warning and error values. **Info** is the default value for this variant property.

In Toast Notification, we can also define a mode:

- **`dismissible`**: Remains visible until the user clicks the close button or 3 seconds has elapsed, whichever comes first.
- **`pester`**: Remains visible for 3 seconds.
- **`sticky`**: Remains visible until the user clicks the close button.

When we deploy this **`displayNotifications`**, it is running like the following (refer to *Figures* 3.41–3.45):

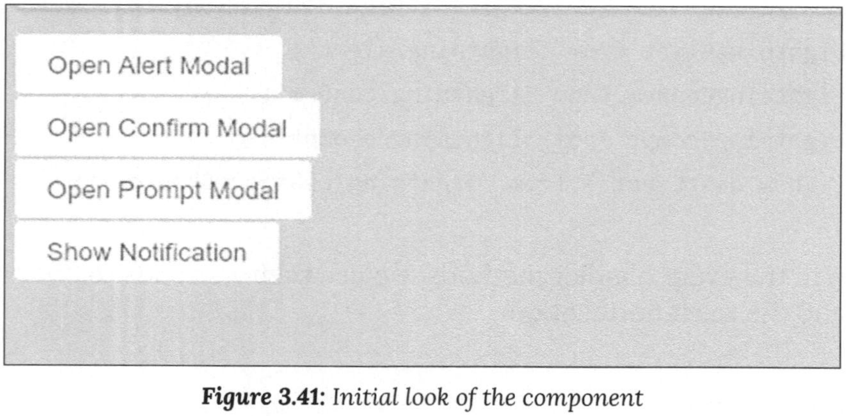

Figure 3.41: *Initial look of the component*

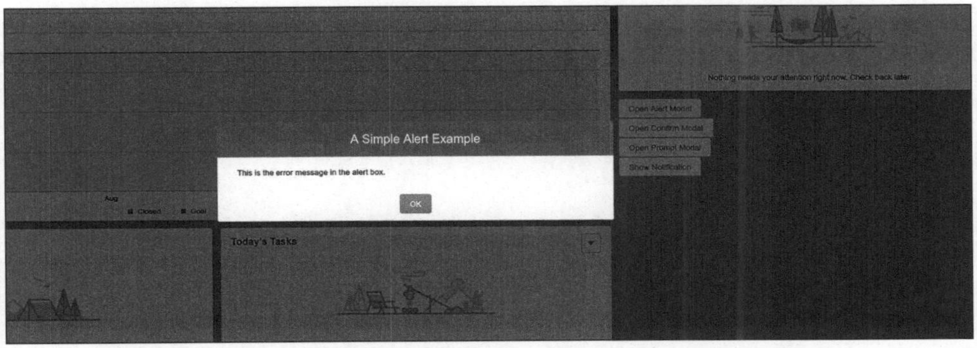

Figure 3.42: *When we click on the "Open Alert Modal" button*

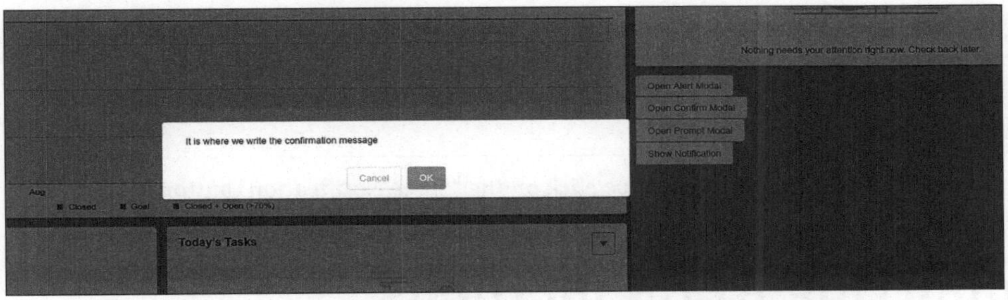

Figure 3.43: *When we click on the "Open ConfirmModal" button*

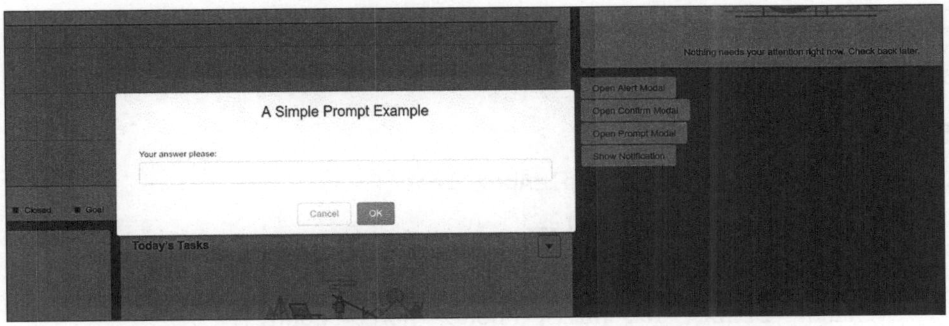

Figure 3.44: *When we click on the "Open Prompt Modal" button*

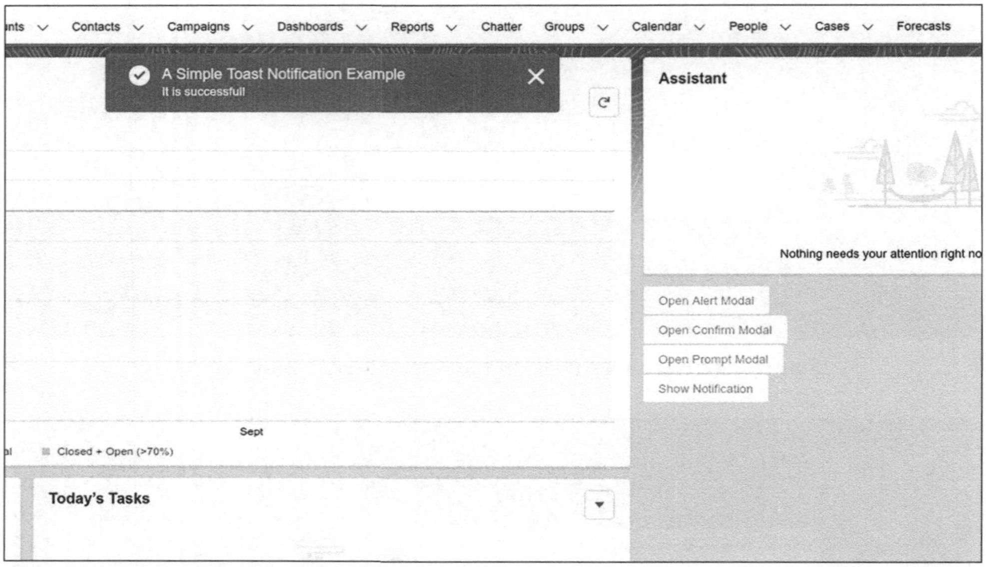

Figure 3.45: *When we click on the "Show Notification" button*

Importing APEX methods

For concluding this chapter, let's see lastly how to obtain backend data in our LWCs.

Let's start by writing a very simple Apex class to query for all the accounts:

simpleApexClass.cls:

```
public with sharing class simpleApexClass {
    @AuraEnabled(cacheable=false)
    public static List<Account> getAllAccounts() {
        return [SELECT Id, Name, Phone FROM Account];
    }
}
```

As we see, this simple Apex class has only one method **`getAllAccounts`** which returns all the accounts of the Salesforce org. This Apex class can function as an LWC backend controller because of the existing **`@AuraEnabled`** annotation in one of its methods. Briefly, if we want that a method of an Apex class can be imported by an LWC, we need to annotate it with **`@AuraEnabled.`**

Here we put **cacheable=false** which means we don't want to cache the result of the query in the client side: so, whenever the user refreshes the page, or (s)he reconnects to the LWC which uses this Apex method, Salesforce will re-query for all the accounts. (Although, in a real-life scenario in a production environment, for having a good performance on the pages, most of the time we need to prefer to use **cacheable=true**.)

Now, let's see the LWC which imports and uses this Apex class:

lwcForApex.js:

```
import { LightningElement } from 'lwc';
import getAccounts from '@salesforce/apex/simpleApexClass.
getAllAccounts';
export default class LwcForApex extends LightningElement {
    accounts;
    connectedCallback() {
        getAccounts().then(result => {
            this.accounts = result;
        })
        .catch(error => {console.log(error)});
    }
}
```

lwcForApex.html:

```
<template>
    <h1><b>List of Accounts:</b></h1>
    <template for:each={accounts} for:item="acc">
        <p key={acc.Id}>{acc.Name}, {acc.Phone}</p>
    </template>
</template>
```

As usual, everything starts by importing the needed method at the beginning of the LWC:

```
import getAccounts from '@salesforce/apex/simpleApexClass.
getAllAccounts';
```

Then we use this method in order to obtain the data from the backend and assign it to a property of the LWC:

```
getAccounts().then(result => {
   this.accounts = result;
})
```

When we deploy both the Apex class and the LWC to the Salesforce org, here is how it looks:

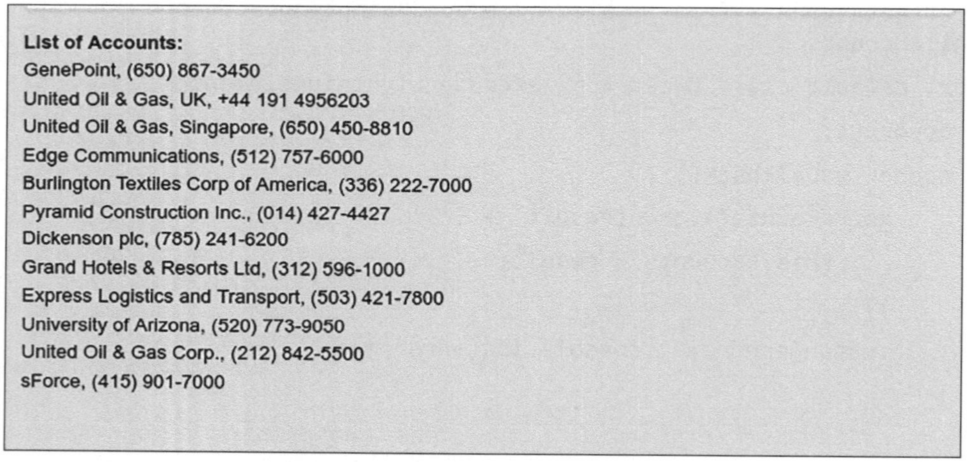

Figure 3.46: *LWC is showing the backend data*

This was a very simple example that we added here to be able to give a more complete picture of the basics for working with LWCs. In the following chapter, we're going to see various methods and services to connect from LWCs to Salesforce backend.

Conclusion

This was one of the important chapters of this book. Now we have a very good understanding of how to work with LWCs as we developed the know-how for various topics like Shadow DOM, properties, data binding, setter and getter methods, conditional rendering, rendering lists and iterators, decorators, composition, slots, lifecycle hooks, working with multiple HTML templates, how to work with static resources and third-party JavaScript libraries, navigation and notifications in LWC, using backend data via importing Apex class methods.

In the next chapter, we'll focus on using the Salesforce data.

References

- DOM Standard - https://dom.spec.whatwg.org/
- HTML Template Directives - https://developer.salesforce.com/docs/component-library/documentation/en/lwc/lwc.reference_directives
- TC39 - Decorators Proposal - https://github.com/tc39/proposal-decorators
- ESLint Linting Tool for VS Code - https://marketplace.visualstudio.com/items?itemName=dbaeumer.vscode-eslint
- The Flow of the Component Lifecycle - https://developer.salesforce.com/docs/component-library/documentation/en/lwc/lwc.create_lifecycle_hooks
- LWC Navigation Service PageReference Types - https://developer.salesforce.com/docs/component-library/documentation/en/lwc/reference_page_reference_type

CHAPTER 4
Using Salesforce Data

Introduction

As one may quickly notice, Salesforce is basically a huge database. The objects are the tables, the fields are the columns, and the records are the rows. A list view in Salesforce is nothing but a representation of an object (similar to a data table) with its records (similar to rows) and fields (similar to columns). A record page of an object is simply a representation of a data record with all of its properties (another fancy name for fields) in a user-friendly page layout.

So, in this chapter, we're focusing on how to work with Salesforce data via LWCs. Interacting with data is mainly handled via high-level technical features – already developed for us by Salesforce – which are aggregated under the brand name Lightning Data Service. Therefore, we'll start by understanding what it is and what it covers. While working on it, we'll also have the chance to meet (and learn how to use) the `@wire` decorator. Finally, we'll conclude the chapter by showing how to use Apex classes and methods by importing them into our LWCs.

Structure

In this chapter, we will discuss the following topics:

- Lightning Data Service introduction
- Lightning Data Service base components
- Lightning Data Service Wire adapters and functions
- Working with Apex

Lightning Data Service introduction

Lightning Data Service (LDS) provides us the ability to capture data from the Salesforce backend without needing to use any Apex implementation. It respects (by default) CRUD (Create-Read-Update-Delete) access, field-level security (FLS) settings, and sharing settings. Thus, only the records and fields that the user has permission are loaded and shown on the pages.

LDS also takes care of caching the data. When a page consists of multiple components displaying the same record, they all share the same cached version of the record. This approach results in significant performance improvements because the data is loaded once and shared among all components, regardless of how many are using it. LDS maintains a client-side cache of the loaded data, which results in much faster access than re-requesting it from the server. However, it re-requests the data from the server when the request occurs after the cache lifetime has passed.

LDS can also detect changes in the data. So, when a change occurs in any supported data or metadata, all components (which are using a relevant LDS adapter) will receive updated values, even if the cache lifetime has not passed.

Note: LDS is built on top of the User Interface API, so it supports all custom objects and all the standard objects that the User Interface API supports.

So, how do we use LDS? We can easily benefit from it by using the following functionalities in our LWCs:

- Base components (**`lightning-record-form`**, **`lightning-record-view-form`**, and **`lightning-record-edit-form`**)
- Wire adapters (such as `getRecord`) and functions (such as **`createRecord()`**, **`updateRecord()`**, and **`deleteRecord()`**)

When we don't require a complex solution (which involves obtaining data related to different objects and fields under specific conditions), LDS is the way to move forward. However, if it is not sufficient for our case, then we need to use Apex classes and methods. We will also explain how it is achieved throughout this chapter.

LDS base components

As mentioned earlier, there are three base components that benefit from the LDS features:

- lightning-record-form
- lightning-record-view-form
- lightning-record-edit-form

As their names imply, they are used for creating, reading, or updating the records throughout LDS, without needing any Apex class implementation.

`lightning-record-form` can be used to view and create/edit records, but it does not allow building a custom layout. In contrast, the other two base components allow building custom layouts for the fields, but they are limited to one function only: **`lightning-record-view-form`** is for view records, and **`lightning-record-edit-form`** is for creating/updating records.

lightning-record-form

Let's directly start with an example:

ligthningRecordForm.html:

```
<template>
    <lightning-record-form
        record-id={recordId}
        object-api-name={objectApiName}
        layout-type="Compact"
        mode="view"
        columns="2"
    >
    </lightning-record-form>
</template>
```

lightningRecordForm.js:

```
import { LightningElement, api } from 'lwc';

export default class LightningRecordForm extends LightningElement {
    @api recordId;
    @api objectApiName;
}
```

As a first impression, we can quickly notice that while using this base component, most of the configuration is done in the front-end (**HTML** file). Therefore, in addition to not needing an Apex class for getting the record data, while using this base component, we don't even need to have a complex JS controller.

Tip: **`recordId`** and **`objectApiName`** are two specifics properties, which are provided by Salesforce. As their names imply, they are dynamically filled by Salesforce with the respective **`record ID`** and **`object API name`** values of the record page we're on.

So, let's say, if we're on an **`Account`** record page, the **`objectApiName`** would get the value **`Account`** (which is the API name of the standard **`Account`** object), and **`recordId`** would get the record ID of the account record.

`lightning-record-form` can have two different **`layout-type`**: **`Compact`** or **`Full`**. When we use **`Compact`**, Salesforce gets the fields that exist in the compact layout of the object. Similarly, if the value is **`Full`**, then all the fields from the object's page layout are used. These layouts are determined by the Administrator users on the object setup page.

The **`mode`** attribute of the component can have three different values: **`view`**, **`readonly`**, and **`edit`** (please refer to Figures 4.2–4.4, respectively). The **`columns`** attribute is used for stating the number of columns we want to have in the layout of the component. (In this example, we are using 2 columns.)

Initially, our component appears as follows when we put it on an account record page:

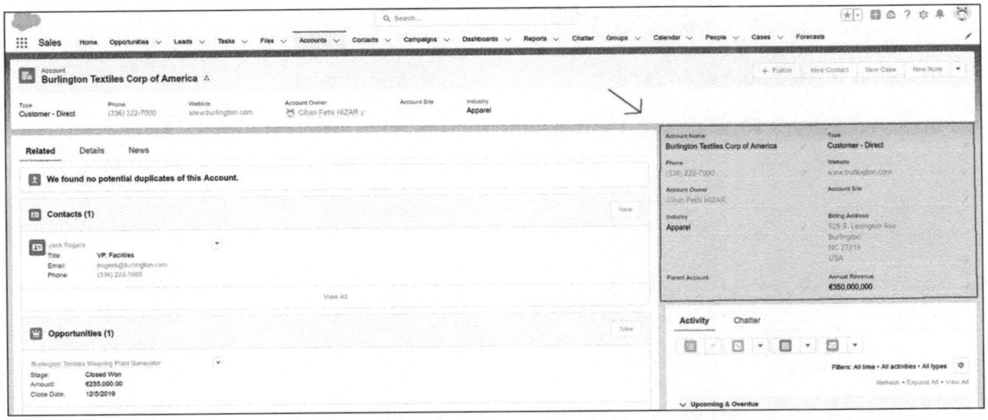

Figure 4.1: *lightning-base-component directly captures the "recordId" from the record page where it resides, and thus it can show the details of the respective record*

As it is in the view mode, the fields' values are initially in **`read-only`**, but it is possible to switch to the edit mode by clicking any of the **`pencil`** icons:

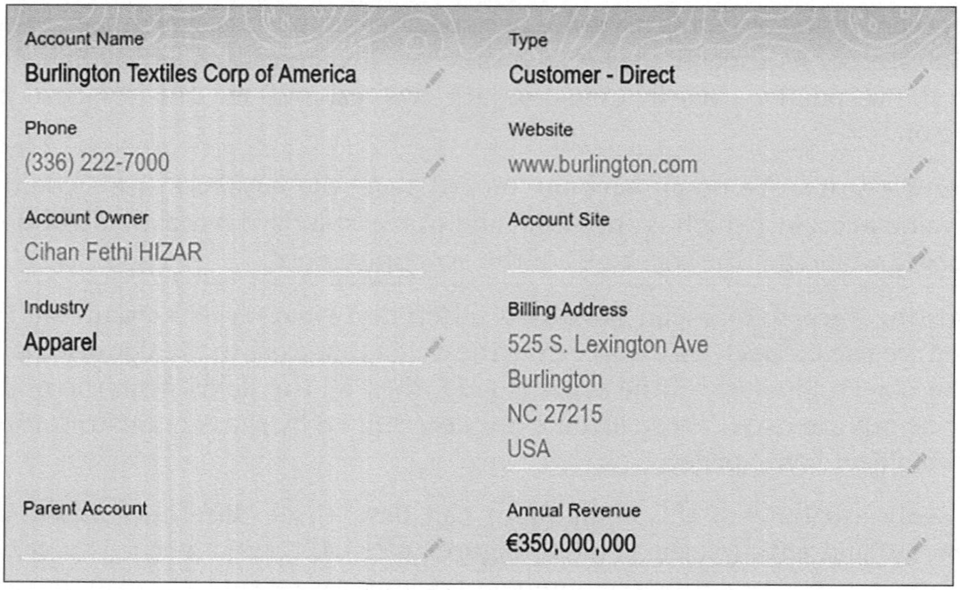

***Figure 4.2:** lightning-base-component in "view" mode*

However, if we use the **`readonly`** mode, then there won't be any **`pencil`** icon, which means it is not possible to edit the fields at all:

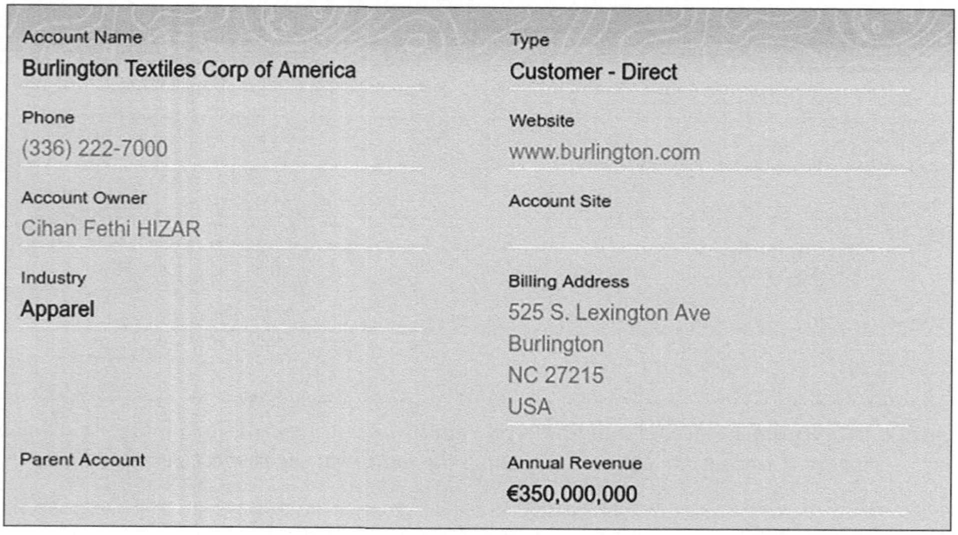

***Figure 4.3:** lightning-base-component in "readonly" mode*

Finally, if we click the **`pencil`** icon while we're in the view mode or deploy the component directly in the edit mode, it will look something like this:

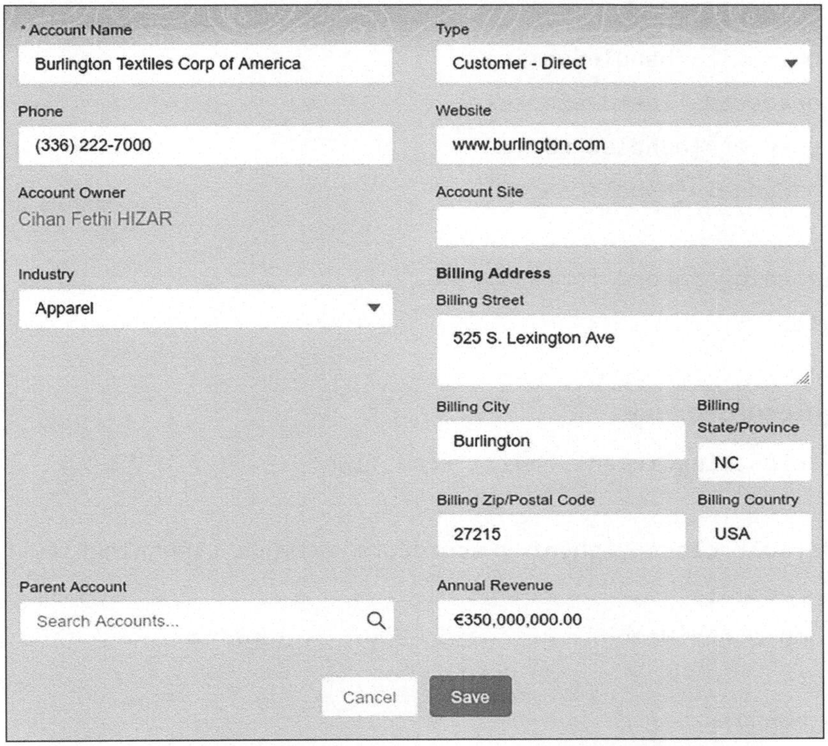

Figure 4.4: *lightning-base-component in "edit" mode*

While in **`edit`** mode, we can change any value of the existing fields using the **`Save`** button. On the other hand, clicking **`Cancel`** will restore all the fields' values to their initial values, as expected.

These **`Save`** and **`Cancel`** buttons are automatically added by Salesforce when in **`edit`** mode. However, we have the option to define custom actions when a **`Save`** or a **`Cancel`** click occurs. Here, let's explore an improved version of our initial example:

ligthningRecordForm.html:

```
<template>
    <lightning-record-form
        record-id={recordId}
        object-api-name={objectApiName}
```

```
        layout-type="Compact"
        mode="edit"
        columns="2"
        onsubmit={handleSubmit}
        onsuccess={handleSuccess}
        onerror={handleError}
        oncancel={handleCancel}
    >
    </lightning-record-form>
</template>
```

lightningRecordForm.js:

```
import { LightningElement, api } from 'lwc';

export default class LightningRecordForm extends LightningElement {
    @api recordId;
    @api objectApiName;

    handleSubmit() {
        console.log("The record is submitted.");
    }

    handleSuccess() {
        console.log("The record is successfully saved.");
    }

    handleError() {
        console.log("An error is occurred while saving the record!");
    }

    handleCancel() {
        console.log("Cancelled: No changes are done!");
    }
```

```
}
```

As seen in this improved example code, we've added four new attributes to our **lightning-record-form** base component:

- **onsubmit**: It is called when the user clicks the **Save** button. By using it, we can override the standard submit action.
- **onsuccess**: When the record is successfully submitted, a **Success** event is triggered, and we can use it to define our custom follow-up actions.
- **onerror**: When Salesforce encounters an error while submitting the record, an **error** event is triggered. So, we can use it for beautifully handling this error feedback.
- **oncancel**: It is called when the user clicks on the **Cancel** button. Similar to **onsubmit**, it can be used to override the standard cancel action.

It is also possible to create records by using this **lightning-record-form** base component. The only thing we need to do is to remove the **record-id** attribute from the component while in edit mode:

ligthningRecordForm.html:

```
<template>
    <lightning-record-form
        object-api-name={objectApiName}
        layout-type="Compact"
        mode="edit"
        columns="2"
    >
    </lightning-record-form>
</template>
```

When we do this, the record layout is loaded in **Full** layout by default (even if we determine **Compact**), with all fields empty, allowing the user to fill them and create a new record by clicking the **Save** button:

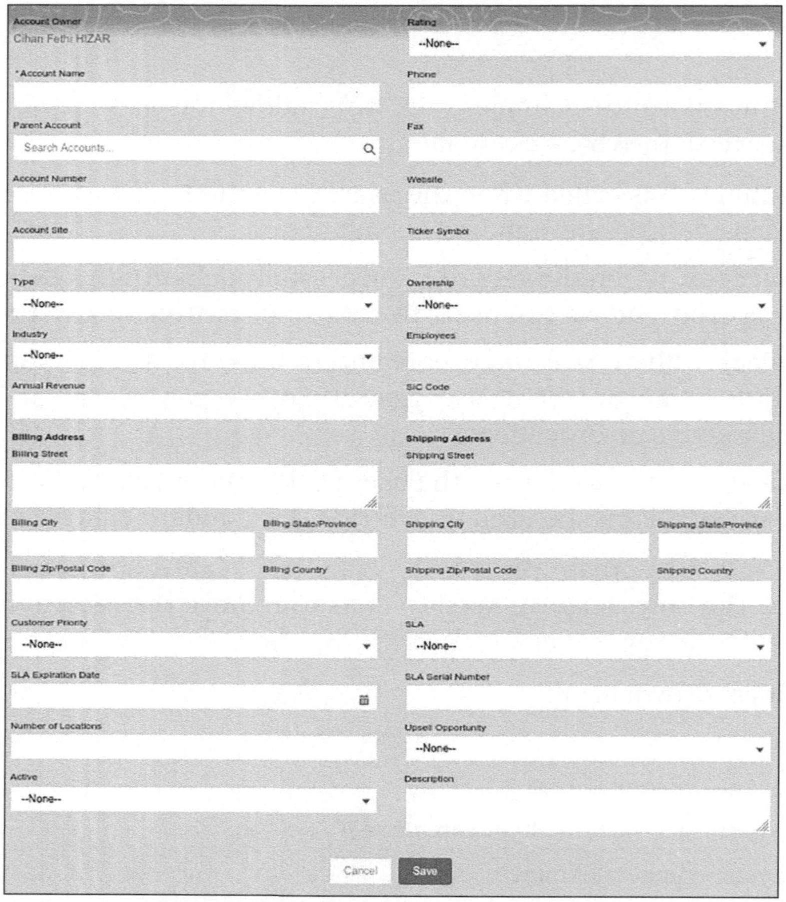

Figure 4.5: *lightning-base-component in "edit" mode for creating a new record*

Lots of fields, just for creating a new record! Surely, nobody will like such a layout. Fortunately, instead of using the **`layout-type`** attribute, we can determine the fields we need by using the **`fields`** attribute:

ligthningRecordForm.html:

```
<template>
    <lightning-record-form
        object-api-name={objectApiName}
        fields={fields}
        mode=”edit”
        columns=”2”
        onsubmit={handleSubmit}
```

```
        onsuccess={handleSuccess}
        onerror={handleError}
        oncancel={handleCancel}
    >
    </lightning-record-form>
</template>
```

lightningRecordForm.js:

```
import { LightningElement, api } from 'lwc';

import ACCOUNT_NAME_FIELD from "@salesforce/schema/Account.Name";
import ACCOUNT_PHONE_FIELD from "@salesforce/schema/Account.Phone";
import ACCOUNT_WEBSITE_FIELD from "@salesforce/schema/Account.Website";

export default class LightningRecordForm extends LightningElement {
    @api recordId;
    @api objectApiName;

    fields = [ACCOUNT_NAME_FIELD, ACCOUNT_PHONE_FIELD, ACCOUNT_WEBSITE_
FIELD];
}
```

To use the **fields** attribute, we need to define the fields (that we want) in the JS controller. It is an array, but its elements (for example, **Account.Name, Account.Phone, Account.Website**) should be imported first.

This way, we now only see the fields we need for creating a new account:

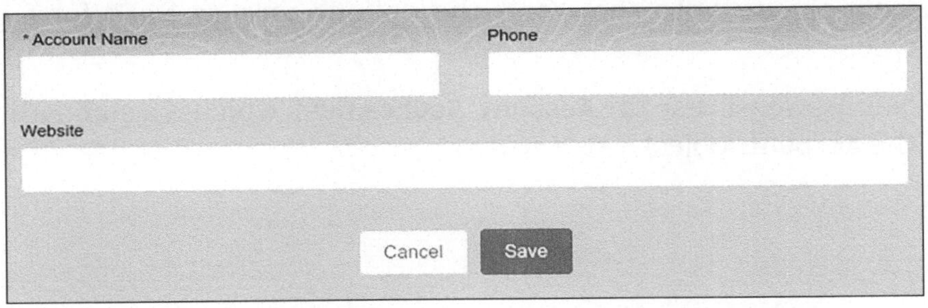

Figure 4.6: *lightning-base-component having the fields we chose*

Note: The **fields** attribute can also be used in **view** and **readonly** modes, and it is not specific for **edit** mode. Moreover, if we decide to use the fields attribute, then we won't need to use **layout-type** attribute anymore, and vice-versa is also true.

Tip: If we don't want to import the fields one by one in the JS controller, there is a simpler way to define the fields:

lightningRecordForm.js:

```
import { LightningElement, api } from 'lwc';
export default class LightningRecordForm extends LightningElement {
   @api recordId;
   @api objectApiName;

   fields = ['Name', 'Phone', 'Website'];
  }
```

As demonstrated earlier, it is also possible to determine the fields just by using the field API names in a string array. However, it's important to note that, in this version, we can only add the fields that are not **lookup** or **master-detail**; namely, we cannot use the relational fields in this version. In addition, it will not be possible to determine whether or not a field exists until runtime.

Briefly, we would suggest to always use the longer version, which involves importing the fields first.

Before concluding this section on **lightning-record-form**, let's touch on how to work with different record types for an object. In real-time scenarios, record types would confront us most of the time when different option value sets for a picklist field would be configured by using different record types. So, while working with the **lightning-record-form** base component, simply putting the picklist field into the **fields** array would not be a sufficient solution if the requirement forces us to show only the options that are valid for a specific record type.

As an example, we will use the **Account Source** field, which is a standard picklist field of the **Account** object.

Let's assume that our **`Account`** object has two record types: **`Direct Account`** and **`Indirect Account`**:

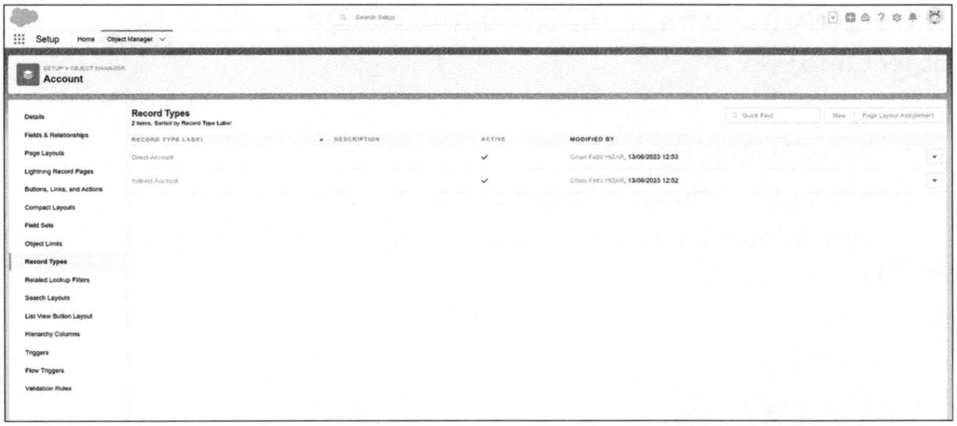

Figure 4.7: *Account object has two record types*

If the **`Account Source`** field has different sets of option values for each record type and if the request on which we're working requires that we should list only the values of the **`Direct Account`** record type, then we should capture and use the **`record type id`** as follows:

lightningRecordForm.js:

```
import { LightningElement, api, wire } from 'lwc';

import { getObjectInfo } from 'lightning/uiObjectInfoApi';
import ACCOUNT_OBJECT from '@salesforce/schema/Account';
import ACCOUNT_NAME_FIELD from "@salesforce/schema/Account.Name";
import ACCOUNT_PHONE_FIELD from "@salesforce/schema/Account.Phone";
import ACCOUNT_WEBSITE_FIELD from "@salesforce/schema/Account.Website";
import ACCOUNT_ACCOUNTSOURCE_FIELD from "@salesforce/schema/Account.
AccountSource";

export default class LightningRecordForm extends LightningElement {
    @api recordId;
    @api objectApiName;

    fields = [ACCOUNT_NAME_FIELD, ACCOUNT_PHONE_FIELD, ACCOUNT_WEBSITE_
```

```
FIELD, ACCOUNT_ACCOUNTSOURCE_FIELD];

    @wire(getObjectInfo, { objectApiName: ACCOUNT_OBJECT })
    objectInfo;

    get recordTypeId() {
        const rtis = this.objectInfo.data.recordTypeInfos;
        return Object.keys(rtis).find(rti => rtis[rti].name === "Direct
Account");
    }
}
```

ligthningRecordForm.html:

```
<template>
    <lightning-record-form
        object-api-name={objectApiName}
        record-type-id={recordTypeId}
        fields={fields}
        mode="edit"
        columns="2"
        onsubmit={handleSubmit}
        onsuccess={handleSuccess}
        onerror={handleError}
        oncancel={handleCancel}
    >
    </lightning-record-form>
</template>
```

We will discuss the details of the **`@wire`** in the next section of this chapter, however, for now, it's important to know that **`@wire`** is used to bring the object metadata of the **`Account`** object by using the **`getObjectInfo`** wire adapter. Then, in the same syntax, it also assigns this metadata to the **`objectInfo`** property of the LWC class. Thus, it is possible to capture the **`record type id`** value by using the **`record type name`** (which is **`Direct Account`** in this example) in the getter function.

Note: We could also capture the **`record type id`** by simply using an Apex method instead of the **`wire adapter`**. However, whenever possible, we should always prefer the wire adapters over Apex methods for improved performance and stability in the code.

Finally, the only thing left to do is to use the **`recordTypeId`** in our **`lightning-record-form`** base component, and the rest is dealt by Salesforce. Thus, we'll see that the **`Account Source`** field will now show only the option values selected for the **`Direct Account`** record type.

lightning-record-view-form

As mentioned earlier, **`lightning-record-view-form`** is the base component that can be used for viewing the records. However, unlike the **`lightning-record-form`**, by using **`lightning-record-view-form`**, we can only view the records in readonly mode.

Let's examine it in an example:

lightningRecordViewForm.js:

```
import { LightningElement, api } from 'lwc';

export default class LightningRecordViewForm extends LightningElement {
    @api recordId;
    @api objectApiName;
}
```

lightningRecordViewForm.html:

```
<template>
    <lightning-record-view-form
        record-id={recordId}
        object-api-name={objectApiName}
    >
        <lightning-output-field field-name="Name"></lightning-output-field>
```

```
        <lightning-output-field field-name="Phone"></lightning-output-field>
        <lightning-output-field field-name="Website"></
lightning-output-field>
    </lightning-record-view-form>
</template>
```

As noticed instantly, while using the **`lightning-record-view-form`** base component, instead of importing the fields in the JS controller, we need to display them directly in the HTML template file using **`lightning-output-field`** tags, where the **`field-name`** attributes should take the API name of the object's fields as the values. This provides us with the flexibility to change the style by wrapping those tags with custom-styled div or by directly inline-styling them.

Briefly, whenever we need a custom design, we may use **`lightning-record-view-form`** instead of **`lightning-record-form`**.

Apart from this difference, it's worth noting that the **`lightning-record-view-form`** component has two main attributes (**`record-id`** and **`object-api-name`**), which is way less than the **`lightning-record-form`**, where we do all the configuration directly using different attributes such as **`mode`**, **`fields`**, **`layout-type`**, and more, as we may remember.

Consequently, when we deploy this component into an account record page, it'll appear as follows:

***Figure 4.8:** "lightning-record-view-form" component in use*

lightning-record-edit-form

The **`lightning-record-edit-form`** base component is used for editing the record or creating new records. We may use this component instead of the **`lightning-record-form`** base component when a custom design is needed because, here, the fields are put directly in the HTML using **`lightning-input-field`** tags, which gives us the ability to implement a custom design.

Let's see an example:

lightningRecordEditForm.js:

```
import { LightningElement, api } from 'lwc';

export default class LightningRecordEditForm extends LightningElement {
    @api recordId;
    @api objectApiName;
}
```

lightningRecordEditForm.html:

```
<template>
    <lightning-record-edit-form
        record-id={recordId}
        object-api-name={objectApiName}
    >

        <lightning-input-field field-name="Name"></lightning-input-field>
        <lightning-input-field field-name="Phone"></lightning-input-field>
        <lightning-input-field field-name="Website"></lightning-in-
put-field>
        <lightning-input-field field-name="AccountSource"></
lightning-input-field>

         <lightning-button type="reset" label="Cancel"></
lightning-button>
        <lightning-button type="submit" label="Save"></lightning-button>
    </lightning-record-edit-form>
</template>
```

Everything is quite similar to the **`lightning-record-view-form`**, but this time, we're using **`lightning-input-field`** tags instead of **`lightning-output-field`** tags. The **`lightning-input-field`** tag is a specific tag of Salesforce, which can have a matching format according to the type of the data (for example, **`select box`** for **`picklist`** fields, **`text box`** for **`text`** fields, and more).

While working with **`lightning-record-edit-form`**, we need to manually define the **Save** button and **Cancel** button, unlike **`lightning-record-form`** where these buttons automatically appear in the case of **`edit`** mode. So, we have two buttons of types **`submit`** and **`reset`** inside the **`lightning-record-edit-form`**.

When we deploy this component into an account record page, we obtain the following result:

***Figure 4.9:** "lightning-record-edit-form" component in use*

If we want to create a record instead of editing one, all we need to do is remove **`record-id={recordId}`** from the component. Then, all the fields in the form will start to appear empty, and when the user fills the form and clicks the **Save** button, a new account record will be saved. If we want the fields to be pre-populated by some default values, we can use the **`value`** attribute in **`lightning-input-field`**:

```
<lightning-input-field field-name="Name" value="Default Name"></
lightning-input-field>
```

Note: It is also possible to use **<lightning-input>** tags instead of **<lightning-input-field>** tags, but this should be considered only if we want to implement our custom validation rules on the client side.

Tip

```
<lightning-button type="reset" label="Cancel"></lightning-button>
```

will not properly reset all the field types in the **`lightning-record-edit-form`**. So, to have a proper reset functionality across different field types, we need to override the standard reset action by using an event listener like **`onclick={resetCustom}`**:

```
<lightning-button type="reset" label="Cancel" onclick=
{resetCustom}></lightning-button>
```

lightning-record-edit-form also supports **error**, **submit**, and **success** events like **lightning-record-form**:

```
<lightning-record-edit-form
        record-id={recordId}
        object-api-name={objectApiName}
        onerror={handleError}
        onsubmit={handleSubmit}
        onsuccess={handleSuccess}
        onload={handleLoad}
>
```

onerror, **onsubmit**, **onsuccess**, and **onload** event listeners function similarly to **lightning-record-form**. However, we haven't discussed the **onload** listener; it listens to the **form initial loading** event, responsible for the initial loading of the record data.

Similarly, if we want to override the **submit** button, we can define an event listener as follows:

```
<lightning-button type="submit" label="Save"
onclick={customSaveAction}></lightning-button>
```

Before closing this section, it's important to mention that while using **lightning-record-view-form** and **lightning-record-edit-form**, it is also possible to import the fields initially and then use them in **lightning-output-field or lightning-input-field** tags. Thus, if a field does not exist, we would have the chance to capture the error before runtime.

JS Controller:

```
import { LightningElement, api } from 'lwc';
import NAME_FIELD from '@salesforce/schema/Account.Name';
```

```
export default class AccountCreator extends LightningElement {
    @api recordId;
    @objectApiName;
    nameField = NAME_FIELD;
}
```

HTML Template:

```
<template>
<lightning-record-edit-form record-id={recordId} object-api-name=
{objectApiName}>
        <lightning-input-field field-name={nameField}><
/lightning-input-field>
        <lightning-button type="submit" label="Save"></lightning-button>
    </lightning-record-edit-form>
</template>
```

LDS Wire adapters and functions

If a data retrieval request cannot be handled using the LDS base components, then our next option is to use the Wire Service with wire adapters and functions. While LDS base components mostly allow us to work with only a single record of an object, the Wire Service enables us to work with multiple records of different objects. All of this is possible by using the **`@wire`** decorator.

The Wire Service

With the Wire Service, it is possible to connect to Salesforce record data without the need to use any Apex code and SOQL queries. As the name wire implies, we can consider this service as a cord that binds the backend records' data to a client property (or client function). However, as we will show, in the upcoming sections, it is even possible to use the Wire Service to directly bind a client property (or a client function) to an Apex class (which provides record data).

Basically, the syntax of the Wire Service is as follows:

```
@wire(adapterId, adapterConfig)
```

```
propertyOrFunction;
```

Here, the **adapterId** is the wire adapter we use to obtain data. There are standard wire adapters like **getRecord** and **getObjectInfo**, or we can use our own Apex method for an **adapterId**. Briefly, we can consider the **adapterId** as the data provider. It should always be imported at the beginning of the LWC JS Controller as:

```
import { adapterId } from 'adapterModule';
```

adapterConfig is basically an object that contains the parameters and configuration values our adapter needs to provide us with the data. Most of the time, we state the name of the objects and fields in **adapterConfig**, to obtain the data accordingly.

propertyOrFunction is the property (or the function) name that we provide in LWC. By using it, we're able to display the data (which is provided by the Wire Service) in the HTML template. It functions like all other properties/functions of LWC, but it retrieves the backend data as soon as the LWC is loaded. When its type is a property, it will have data and error properties. If its type is a function, then the results returned will be an object with data and error properties.

To concretize what we've discussed until now, let's look at the following two examples:

Example1: Decorate a property with @wire:

```
import { LightningElement, api, wire } from 'lwc';
import { getRecord } from 'lightning/uiRecordApi';
import ACCOUNT_NAME_FIELD from '@salesforce/schema/Account.Name';

export default class WireProperty extends LightningElement {
    @api recordId;

    @wire(getRecord, { recordId: '$recordId', fields: [ACCOUNT_NAME_
FIELD] })
    record;
}
```

Here, **getRecord** is the **adapterId**.

`{ recordId: '$recordId', fields: [ACCOUNT_NAME_FIELD] }` is the **`adapterConfig`**.

And **`record`** is the property name for our LWC. We can use the returning backend data with **`record.data`** property, and we can investigate whether any error occurred by using **`record.error`** property.

Example2: Decorate a function with @wire:

```
import { LightningElement, api, track, wire } from 'lwc';
import { getRecord } from 'lightning/uiRecordApi';

export default class WireFunction extends LightningElement {
    @api recordId;
    @track record;
    @track error;

    @wire(getRecord, { recordId: '$recordId', fields: ['Account.Name'] })
    wiredFunction({ error, data }) {
        if (data) {
            this.record = data;
            this.error = undefined;
        } else if (error) {
            this.error = error;
            this.record = undefined;
        }
    }

    get name() {
        return this.record.fields.Name.value;
    }
}
```

In this **Example2, `adapterId`** and **`adapterConfig`** are the same as in the previous **Example1.** However, this time, instead of a property, we decorate a function called **wiredFunction**. This function has one parameter, which is an object with two properties: **error** and **data**. This object holds the resulting data (or error) of the Wire Service. So, by using it, we can implement any control code needed in the body of the function. (In this example (Example2), we simply do some checks and assignments accordingly.)

Finally, **$recordId** is reactive in both examples. This means that when we update the **recordId** in the LWC, the Wire Service will instantly provide the updated data while the component is being re-rendered.

Tip: data and error properties are hard-coded standard property names of Salesforce, so we should always use them.

While working with the Wire Service, it is an important best practice to import the object and field references instead of directly hard-coding their API names while defining the **adapterConfig.** Thus, the admins won't be able to update the API names of those objects and/or fields.

In addition, this way it is possible to import the parent objects and fields through traversing (up to three) relationship fields of the main object (for example, **Opportunity.Account.Owner.Username**).

As mentioned earlier, when we work with references, if there is an error with the API names, we can capture it before runtime.

Here are some examples related to importing references:

```
import ACCOUNT_OBJECT from '@salesforce/schema/Account';
import ACCOUNT_NAME_FIELD from '@salesforce/schema/Account.Name';
import OPPORTUNITY_ACCOUNT_OWNERID_FIELD from '@salesforce/schema/Op-
portunity.Account.OwnerId';
```

As seen in the previous examples (Example1 and Example2), the Wire Service is reactive, which means it can work with reactive variables (that are prefixed with **$**). Thus, when the value of the reactive variable changes, the Wire Service provides updated data accordingly. The good thing is that if the data already exists in the client cache, the Wire Service will not bother itself to re-connect to the backend one more time, but instead, it will directly use the existing client cache data.

getRecord wire adapter

getRecord is one of the popular wire adapters used in projects. We already had some examples in the previous section. Now, let's examine a complete LWC that uses the **getRecord** wire adapter.

getRecordWireAdapter.js:

```
import { LightningElement, api, wire } from 'lwc';
import { getRecord, getFieldValue } from 'lightning/uiRecordApi';
import ACCOUNT_NAME_FIELD from "@salesforce/schema/Account.Name";
import ACCOUNT_PHONE_FIELD from "@salesforce/schema/Account.Phone";
import ACCOUNT_WEBSITE_FIELD from "@salesforce/schema/Account.Website";

const FIELDS = [ACCOUNT_NAME_FIELD, ACCOUNT_PHONE_FIELD, ACCOUNT_
WEBSITE_FIELD];

export default class GetRecordWireAdapter extends LightningElement {
    @api recordId;

    @wire(getRecord, {recordId : '$recordId', fields: FIELDS})
    accountRecord;

    get name() {
       return this.accountRecord.data ? this.accountRecord.data.fields.
Name.value : 'Data error1';
    }

    get phone() {
      return this.accountRecord.data ? this.accountRecord.data.fields.
Phone.value : 'Data error2';
    }

    get website() {
      return this.accountRecord.data ?
getFieldValue(this.accountRecord.data,ACCOUNT_WEBSITE_FIELD) : 'Data
error3';
```

```
    }
}
```

getRecordWireAdapter.html:

```
<template>
    <lightning-formatted-text value={name}></lightning-formatted-text
><br/>
    <lightning-formatted-phone value={phone}></lightning-formatted
-phone><br/>
    <lightning-formatted-url value={website}></lightning-formatted-url>
</template>
```

Here, after we import the **`getRecord`** wire adapter and the **`getFieldValue()`** function, we define our **`FIELDS`** array using the imported fields. Then, we decorate our **`accountRecord`** property with the **`getRecord`** wire adapter and its **`adapterConfig`** (which is formed of the **`recordId`** and the **`fields`**). The rest is just standard LWC functionality.

However, we can point out two ways of obtaining the field value: the former is by directly using the object properties (like **`this.accountRecord.data.fields.Name.value`**), and the latter is by using the **`getFieldValue()`** function of the Salesforce JavaScript API.

Note: Instead of importing the fields one by one, we could also define the **`FIELDS`** array as an array of strings:

```
FIELDS = ['Account.Name', 'Account.Phone', 'Account.Website'];
```

At first sight, it might seem like an easier syntax, but as explained previously, it comes with its risks. As a best practice, we should always initially import the fields and use those imported references in our code.

When we deploy this component into an account record page, here is the resulting look:

Figure 4.10: *getRecordWireAdapter LWC*

createRecord() function

`createRecord()` is a Salesforce JavaScript API function used for creating records. It allows more flexibility when dealing with use cases where using the **`lightning-record-form`** (or **`lightning-record-edit-form`**) base component is not sufficient.

Let's see how we can use it:

createRecordFunction.html:

```
<template>
  <lightning-input label="Name" type="text" data-name="name"></
lightning-input>
  <lightning-input label="Website" type="url" data-name="website"></
lightning-input><br/>
  <lightning-button variant="brand" label="Create Account"
onclick= {handleSave}></lightning-button>
</template>
```

createRecordFunction.js:

```
import { LightningElement } from 'lwc';
import { createRecord, getFieldValue } from 'lightning/uiRecordApi';
import ACCOUNT_OBJECT from '@salesforce/schema/Account';
import ACCOUNT_NAME_FIELD from '@salesforce/schema/Account.Name';
import ACCOUNT_WEBSITE_FIELD from '@salesforce/schema/Account.Website';

export default class CreateRecordFunction extends LightningElement {

 handleSave() {
  const fieldValues = {};
```

```
  fieldValues[ACCOUNT_NAME_FIELD.fieldApiName] =
this.template.querySelector('[data-name="name"]').value;
  fieldValues[ACCOUNT_WEBSITE_FIELD.fieldApiName] =
this.template.querySelector('[data-name="website"]').value;

  const recordData = {
        apiName : ACCOUNT_OBJECT.objectApiName,
        fields : fieldValues
    };

   createRecord(recordData)
   .then(newAccount => {
     console.log("Id = "+newAccount.id);
     console.log("Name = "+newAccount.fields.Name.value);
     console.log("Website = "+getFieldValue(newAccount,ACCOUNT_
WEBSITE_FIELD));
    })
    .catch(errorObj => {
        console.log("An error occurred: "+errorObj.body.error);
    });
  }
}
```

Initially, in the HTML template, we create a simple form consisting of two fields: **Name** and **Website**. We put the custom **handleSave** action into the click event listener of the button. So, all the magic happens in this **handleSave()** method of the JS controller.

To use the **createRecord()** function, we first need to import it. Meanwhile, we also import the **getFieldValue()** method to enhance our example. The **createRecord()** method needs an input of type **recordInput** object, which has two properties: the **apiName** of the Salesforce object that we're going to create a record, and the (meta)data for its fields with their values (which would be entered by the user in the form).

So, in our example, we create the **`recordData`** (which is a **`recordInput`** object). Then, using this object, we call the **`createRecord()`** function. After its execution is done, the **`createRecord()`** function returns a `Promise` object. If the creation of the record is successful, then the **`then()`** part is executed. If we encounter any error, we can **`catch()`** it.

Note: As we know, JavaScript is a single threaded language, which means only one operation can be executed at a time; so, the code is executed line by line. However, when the users are using our JavaScript application on their browser UI (such as when they click a button (or more generally when they do any action) to request data), we need to obtain the data from backend servers as we cannot make the users wait for the data to load synchronously. That's why we need to be able to make certain requests asynchronously to avoid blocking users on theirs browsers.

For writing clean, readable asynchronous calls in our JavaScript code, we use **Promise** objects. As its name implies, it promises that it will deliver the needed data sometime in the future. So, all we need to do is write callback functions for either a positive result (which means we obtain the data without problem) or a failure (which means we encounter an error and cannot obtain the data).

In Salesforce LWC, every imported Apex method returns a **Promise** object. That's why, we use an imported Apex method as follows:

```
import { createRecord } from 'lightning/uiRecordApi';

…

createRecord(recordData)
   .then(newAccount => {
       console.log("Id = "+newAccount.id);
       console.log("Name = "+newAccount.fields.Name.value);
       console.log("Website = "+getFieldValue(newAccount,ACCOUNT_
WEBSITE_FIELD));
       })
    .catch(errorObj => {
       console.log("An error occurred: "+errorObj.body.error);
```

```
});
```

We need to define a callback functionality to be used when we obtain the resulting data as expected (this callback is the **`then()`** block) and another callback functionality to be used when we encounter an error (and this one is the **`catch()`** block).

To learn more about JavaScript Promises, we can visit MDN Promise documentation: https://developer.mozilla.org/en-US/docs/Web/JavaScript/Reference/Global_Objects/Promise

---

Here, in our example, when the creation is successful, we log the record data into the console. We want to point out how different data types are being called:

- For obtaining the resulting **`record id`**, we can directly use **`newAccount.id`**.
- For all other fields' values, we can use the longer version, such as **`newAccount.fields.Name.value`**, or the shorter version by using the **`getFieldValue()`** function, such as **`getFieldValue(newAccount, ACCOUNT_WEBSITE_FIELD)`**.

As an additional note, we can re-look how we obtain the values of the two form fields:

```
fieldValues[ACCOUNT_NAME_FIELD.fieldApiName] = this.template.
querySelector('[data-name="name"]').value;
fieldValues[ACCOUNT_WEBSITE_FIELD.fieldApiName] =
this.template.querySelector('[data-name="website"]').value;
```

As we can see, we're using the **`querySelector`** method of the template to obtain the values entered (by the user) into each field.

Note: While working with the **`createRecord()`** function, we need to use explicit properties (**`objectApiName`** and **`fieldApiName`**) to obtain the API names of the object and its fields:

```
ACCOUNT_OBJECT.objectApiName
ACCOUNT_NAME_FIELD.fieldApiName
    ACCOUNT_WEBSITE_FIELD.fieldApiName
```

When we deploy and run this **`createRecordFunction`** LWC on Salesforce:

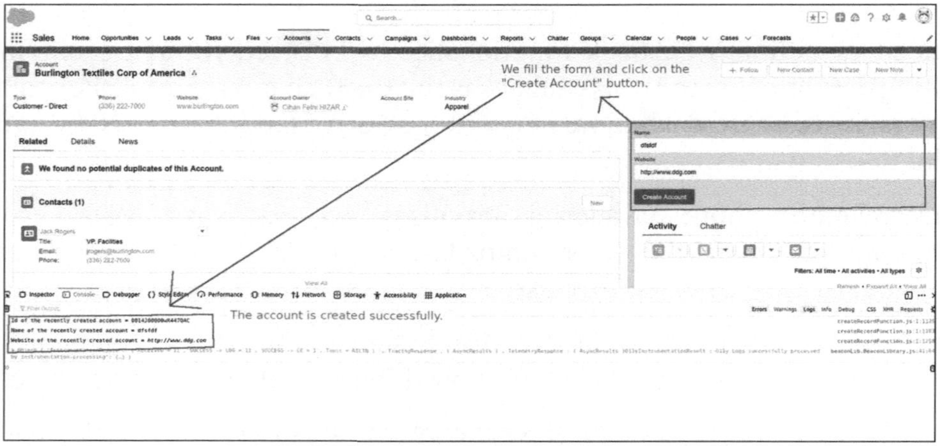

Figure 4.11: *createRecordFunction LWC*

updateRecord() function

There are small differences between **`updateRecord()`** function and **`createRecord()`** function. Let's discuss these distinctions in an example:

updateRecordFunction.html:

```
<template>
  <template if:true={currentAccount}>
   <lightning-input label=”Name” type=”text” data-name=”name”
value={currentAccount.Name}></lightning-input>
   <lightning-input label=”Website” type=”url” data-name=”website”
value={currentAccount.Website}></lightning-input>
    <lightning-button variant=”brand” label=”Update Account”
onclick={handleUpdate}></lightning-button>
  </template>
</template>
```

updateRecordFunction.js:

```
import { LightningElement, api, wire } from ‘lwc’;
import getCurrentAccount from
‘@salesforce/apex/updateRecordController.getCurrentAccount’;
import { updateRecord } from ‘lightning/uiRecordApi’;
```

```
import ACCOUNT_ID_FIELD from '@salesforce/schema/Account.Id';
import ACCOUNT_NAME_FIELD from '@salesforce/schema/Account.Name';
import ACCOUNT_WEBSITE_FIELD from '@salesforce/schema/Account.Website';

export default class UpdateRecordFunction extends LightningElement {

    @api recordId;
    currentAccount;
    @wire(getCurrentAccount, {accountId: '$recordId'})
    wiredFunction({error, data}) {
        if(data) {
            this.currentAccount = data;
        }
        else if(error) {
            console.log("Error occurred while decorating the
'wiredFunction'.");
            console.log(error);
        }
    }

    handleUpdate() {
      const fieldValues = {};
     fieldValues[ACCOUNT_ID_FIELD.fieldApiName] = this.currentAccount.Id;
       fieldValues[ACCOUNT_NAME_FIELD.fieldApiName] = this.template.
querySelector('[data-name="name"]').value;
       fieldValues[ACCOUNT_WEBSITE_FIELD.fieldApiName] = this.template.
querySelector('[data-name="website"]').value;

        const recordData = {
            fields : fieldValues
        };

        updateRecord(recordData)
          .then(updatedAccount => {
```

```
            console.log("Account is updated successfully!");
            console.log("New Account Name = "+updatedAccount.fields.Name.
value);
            console.log("New Account Website = "+updatedAccount.fields.
Website.value);
          })
          .catch(errorObj => {
             console.log("An error occurred: "+errorObj.body.error);
          });
    }
}
```

As it is an **update** function, we need a record to update. To capture a record, we decorate a function (called **wiredFunction()**) with an Apex class method: **getCurrentAccount()**.

updateRecordController.cls:

```
public with sharing class updateRecordController {

    @AuraEnabled(cacheable=true)
    public static Account getCurrentAccount(String accountId){
        try {
            return [SELECT Id, Name, Website FROM Account WHERE Id =
:accountId LIMIT 1];
        } catch (Exception e) {
            throw new AuraHandledException(e.getMessage());
        }
    }
}
```

This Apex method provides an account record by using an **accountId** as the input. Naturally, that input is provided by our LWC with the following line:

```
@wire(getCurrentAccount, {accountId: '$recordId'})
```

```
wiredFunction({error, data}) {… }
```

We'll discuss more on this topic – wiring Apex methods – in the next section. For now, we only need to understand that we capture the account record (to update it later) from the Apex method **`getCurrentAccount()`**.

`handleUpdate()` is almost the same as the previous **`handleSave()`** method, with only one difference. Here, in the **`currentAccount`** record, we also have the **`id`** of the record. Thus, Salesforce doesn't need to have an explicit **`objectApiName`** property to understand the type of the object; it can directly understand the object we're working on by using this **`id`** information.

So, while defining the **`recordInput`** object this time, we don't add an **`apiName`** property, adding only the **`fields`** property is sufficient:

```
const recordData = {
            fields : fieldValues
        };
```

When our **`recordInput` object** (which is called **`recordData`** in this example) is ready, we simply call the **`updateRecord()`** function. Its implementation is similar to our previous **`createRecord()`** example.

When we deploy and run this **`updateRecordFunction`** LWC and **`updateRecordController`** Apex class on Salesforce:

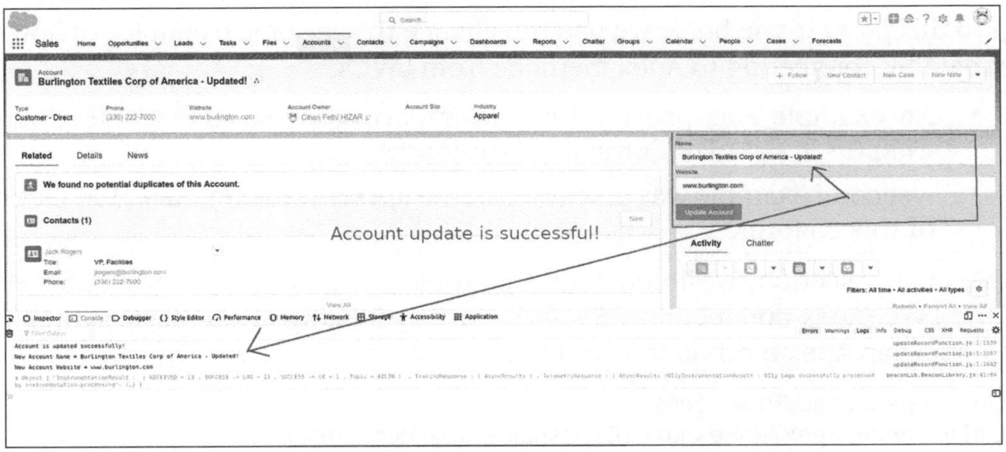

Figure 4.12: *updateRecordFunction LWC*

deleteRecord() function

The **`deleteRecord()`** function is much simpler than the **`createRecord()`** and **`updateRecord()`** functions. It only needs a **`recordId`** and then provides a **`Promise`** object, similar to the former ones.

We'll explain it via a pseudo-code (for further details, please visit the link in the *References* section of this chapter):

```
import { deleteRecord } from 'lightning/uiRecordApi';

….

deleteRecord(recordId)
.then(() => {
      // the deletion is complete, show confirmation message to the user
      // navigate the user to another page if necessary, by using
NavigationMixin
})
.catch(error => { … });
```

Working with APEX

Up to this point in the book, we had the chance to see some examples of how to get data by connecting to Apex methods from LWCs:

- An example was provided in the *Importing Apex methods* section of *Chapter 3, LWC For Salesforce Developers*.
- A second example was discussed in the **`updateRecord() function`** section of this chapter.

Now, in this section, we'll conclude this topic by working on various aspects of the LWC-Apex connections. So, let's start by looking at the basic syntax for importing an Apex method into an LWC:

```
import apexMethodName from
'@salesforce/apex/Namespace.Classname.apexMethodReference';
```

Here, "`apexMethodName`" is the name we assign for calling the Apex method in LWC. As a best practice, we should always use the same name of the Apex method (which would be "`apexMethodReference`").

To see a living example, let's revisit the code of the **`updateRecord() function`** section in *Chapter 4*:

```
import getCurrentAccount from '@salesforce/apex/updateRecordController.
getCurrentAccount';
```

To recall, in that example, we had defined an Apex class called "`updateRecordController`", in which there is a method named "`getCurrentAccount()`":

updateRecordController.cls:

```
public with sharing class updateRecordController {

    @AuraEnabled(cacheable=true)
    public static Account getCurrentAccount(String accountId){
        try {
            return [SELECT Id, Name, Website FROM Account WHERE Id =
:accountId LIMIT 1];
        } catch (Exception e) {
            throw new AuraHandledException(e.getMessage());
        }
    }
}
```

That's why we import it from **`@salesforce/apex/updateRecordController.getCurrentAccount`**. In this example, we don't have a **`namespace`**, the import is simply using the pattern **`classname.apexMethodReference`**.

Tip: When the LWC and the Apex class are in the same namespace (and in the same package), we don't need to specify the **`namespace`** while importing. However, if the class is in a managed package, we need to mention its **`namespace`.**

If we closely examine the definition of the Apex method, we notice that there is an annotation at the beginning of the method: **@AuraEnabled(cacheable=true).** This annotation states that the method is invokable from an LWC component. Besides, these Apex methods should always be **static** and either **global** or **public**. Hence, in our example, it is defined as **public static**:

```
@AuraEnabled(cacheable=true)
public static Account getCurrentAccount(String accountId) { … }
```

When **cacheable=true,** it means that unless the data is stale (namely, expired), LWC will continue to use the data existing in the client cache. On the contrary, when the **cacheable=false**, LWC will always connect to the backend to re-request the data, whether it is stale or not.

Note: When **cacheable=true**, we cannot use DML operations in the Apex method.

We understood how we define and import Apex methods for using them in LWCs. Once an Apex method is imported in an LWC, we have two options for how to call it:

- We can call it "imperatively"
- Or, we can wire it.

Call Apex methods imperatively

If we recall our example from the *Importing Apex methods* section of *Chapter 3*:

simpleApexClass.cls:

```
public with sharing class simpleApexClass {
    @AuraEnabled(cacheable=false)
    public static List<Account> getAllAccounts() {
        return [SELECT Id, Name, Phone FROM Account];
    }
}
```

lwcForApex.js:

```
import { LightningElement } from 'lwc';
import getAccounts from '@salesforce/apex/simpleApexClass.getAllAccounts';
export default class LwcForApex extends LightningElement {
```

```
    accounts;

    connectedCallback() {
        getAccounts().then(result => {
            this.accounts = result;
        })
        .catch(error => {console.log(error)});
    }
}
```

It is a simple example of how to call imperatively an Apex method. As we can see, after importing the method by giving the name **`getAccounts`**, we can use it directly in our LWC. In the imperative calls, the methods return a Promise object, which is why we use the **`then()… catch()`** structure for dealing with the data returned from the backend:

```
getAccounts().then(result => {
            this.accounts = result;
        })
        .catch(error => {console.log(error)});
```

In this example, we do the call inside the **`connectedCallback()`** lifecycle hook. However, we can do it in any LWC function we want. This means we can do the call at the exact moment we need, such as when a trigger we track is triggered. In summary, there's no need to directly load the data while initially running the LWC. Moreover, in imperative calls, we can work with cache **`(= @AuraEnabled(cacheable=true))`** or not **`(= @AuraEnabled(cacheable=false))`** according to our needs.

If we needed to pass a parameter to the Apex method, we could accomplish it as follows:

Apex Method:

```
public with sharing apexClass() {

    @AuraEnabled(cacheable=true)
```

```
    public static List<Account> getAccounts(String searchKey) { … }

}
```

LWC JS Controller:

```
import { LightningElement } from 'lwc';
import getAccounts from '@salesforce/apex/apexClass.getAccounts';
export default class LwcForApex extends LightningElement {
    accounts;
    mySearchKey = 'Burlington';

    connectedCallback() {
        getAccounts({searchKey: this.mySearchKey}).then(result => {
            this.accounts = result;
        })
        .catch(error => {console.log(error)});
    }
}
```

Wiring Apex methods

We've already seen that the basic syntax for Wire Service is as follows:

```
@wire(adapterId, adapterConfig)
propertyOrFunction;
```

Similarly, for wiring the Apex methods, the syntax is as follows:

```
@wire(apexMethodName, {apexMethodParams})
propertyOrFunction;
```

If we recall the example from the **updateRecord() function** section of *Chapter 4*:

updateRecordController.cls:

```
public with sharing class updateRecordController {
    @AuraEnabled(cacheable=true)
    public static Account getCurrentAccount(String accountId){ … }
}
```

updateRecordFunction.js:

```
import { LightningElement, api, wire } from 'lwc';
import getCurrentAccount from
'@salesforce/apex/updateRecordController.getCurrentAccount';
…

export default class UpdateRecordFunction extends LightningElement {
    @api recordId;
    currentAccount;
    @wire(getCurrentAccount, {accountId: '$recordId'})
    wiredFunction({error, data}) {
        if(data) {
            this.currentAccount = data;
        }
        else if(error) {
            console.log("Error occurred while decorating the 'wiredFunc-
tion'.");
            console.log(error);
        }
    }
…
}
```

It is a simple example for wiring an Apex method **(= getCurrentAccount()** of the **updateRecordController** class) to an LWC function **wiredFunction({error, data}).**

When wiring an Apex method to a function, we should always use an input object, which is **`{error, data}`.** Here, its **`error`** property is for capturing any error that might happen, and its "`data`" property is for showing the retrieved data when there are no errors.

In this example, we also pass a parameter **(= "`accountId`")** to the Apex method by using the **`recordId`** property of the LWC.

If we wanted to wire this Apex method to a property instead of a function, then the syntax would be as follows:

```
@wire(getCurrentAccount, {accountId: '$recordId'})
wiredProperty;
```

This way, the **`wiredProperty`** would have two properties: **`data`** and **`error`**. Thus, before doing any assignment, we would need to check whether **`wiredProperty.error`** is null or not. If there is no error, then we will do an assignment as follows:

```
this.currentAccount = wiredProperty.data;
```

Note: When wiring an Apex method, its annotation should always be

`@AuraEnabled(cacheable=true))`

because the Wire Service should always work with cache.

If there is no need to pass a parameter to the Apex method, then the syntax would be as follows:

```
@wire(getCurrentAccount)
wiredProperty;
```

or

```
@wire(getCurrentAccount)
wiredFunction({error, data}) { … };
```

More about client-side caching

When we set the Apex method **`cacheable=true`**, the default refresh time is automatically configured in Lightning Experience and the Salesforce mobile app by Salesforce. However, as we cannot assume this actual default cache duration (because it is constantly improved by Salesforce with new releases), sometimes we may need to refresh the cache before waiting for its automatic expiration.

There are two methods used for clearing the cache:

- **`refreshApex()`** from **`@salesforce/apex`**
- **`otifyRecordUpdateAvailable(recordIds)`** from **`lightning/uiRecordApi`**

`refreshApex()` is used when we wire the Apex method to a property or to a function. On the other hand, **`notifyRecordUpdateAvailable(recordIds)`** is used for refreshing the records when LWC calls the Apex method imperatively.

In addition, **`notifyRecordUpdateAvailable(recordIds)`** is also used for dropping the cache while working with non-Apex wire adapters like **`getRecord`**.

Note: For further details and examples on this topic, please visit the link in the *References* section of this chapter.

getSObjectValue() Function

Before we conclude this *Working with Apex* section, we also want to mention a useful function called **`getSObjetValue()`**.

As we can see, when working with Apex methods, we mainly obtain an SObject (or a list of SObjects) in the returned data. So, by using this **`getSObjectValue()`** function, an LWC can capture the field values of the returned records by using the imported field references. Thus, our code will ensure that it will continue to work even if the names of the object and/or fields change.

Let's see a simple example of how it is used:

LWC JS Controller:

```
import { LightningElement, wire } from 'lwc';
import { getSObjectValue } from '@salesforce/apex';
import getContact from '@salesforce/apex/myContactController.getContact';
```

```
import NAME_FIELD from '@salesforce/schema/Contact.Name';
import EMAIL_FIELD from '@salesforce/schema/Contact.Email';

export default class ApexStaticSchema extends LightningElement {
    @wire(getContact) contact;

    get name() {
        return this.contact.data ? getSObjectValue(this.contact.data,
NAME_FIELD) : '';
    }

    get email() {
        return this.contact.data ? getSObjectValue(this.contact.data,
EMAIL_FIELD) : '';
    }
}
```

Conclusion

The data is the most important aspect of a development project, and it is not different in the Salesforce ecosystem as well. In this chapter, we had the chance to learn various ways to communicate with the Salesforce backend to capture data via **high-level** features like LDS Base Components, the Wire Service, adapters, standard functions, and more. All of these are developed by Salesforce to ease our lives while developing customizations for Salesforce orgs. We also saw that for our specific needs, it is even possible to connect with custom Apex methods to capture custom data needed for our applications.

In the next chapter, we will focus more on how to control our LWCs' states when different user interactions and system changes happen continuously in real time. Namely, we'll learn how to work with events and Lightning Message Service.

References

- User Interface API - https://developer.salesforce.com/docs/atlas.en-us.uiapi.meta/uiapi/ui_api_get_started.htm

- lightning/ui*Api Wire Adapters and Functions - https://developer.salesforce.com/docs/component-library/documentation/en/lwc/lwc.reference_ui_api
- @salesforce Modules - https://developer.salesforce.com/docs/component-library/documentation/en/lwc/lwc.reference_salesforce_modules
- deleteRecord() function - https://developer.salesforce.com/docs/component-library/documentation/en/lwc/reference_delete_record
- Client-Side Caching - https://developer.salesforce.com/docs/component-library/documentation/en/lwc/lwc.apex_result_caching

CHAPTER 5

Events In LWC

Introduction

Most of the time, a page in a Salesforce Lightning application, a record page or a home page, and more, will consist of many LWCs. This is expected because, as we can recall from the *Problem-solving with small reusable components* section of *Chapter 1, Introduction*, our solutions will be implemented (almost all the time) by many LWC parent-child hierarchies along with independent components. So, building a structure that assures the communication (~data passing) between LWCs is one of the important aspects of LWC programming. This is where we start to benefit from the "events" to build this communication.

Hence, in this chapter, we will focus on how to work with events throughout LWCs. We'll first start with the basics and then improve our know-how by studying how to configure them in detail. We'll observe that we can split the events into two sub-topics: events for parent-child components' communications and events for independent components' data passing via publish-subscribe or via Lightning Message Service. We'll examine all of these in this chapter.

Structure

In this chapter, we will discuss the following topics:

- Event basics
- Event propagation
- Publish–Subscribe events (pubsub module)
- Lightning Message Service

Event basics

When someone discusses events in LWC, we may think of, by default, the communication between the parent and the child components. To dive into the subject, we will discuss the following titles:

- Dispatch and handle events
- About event targets
- Passing data in events

Dispatch and handle events

As we know, modern browsers already support standard DOM events such as **`click`**, **`mouseover`**, **`change`**, and more. As discussed in *Chapter 1, Introduction*, LWC is a framework that highly benefits from the latest ECMAScript developments. So, it is normal that we can already work with these standard DOM events.

As an example, let's revisit the following component (which we've first shared in *Chapter 3, LWC In Detail*):

someComponent.js:

```
import { LightningElement} from 'lwc';
export default class SomeComponent extends LightningElement {
    resultingProperty = '';

    get myProperty() {
        return "My Property Value!";
    }

    set myProperty(newValue) {
        this.resultingProperty = newValue.toUpperCase();
    }

    updateProperty(event) {
        this.myProperty = event.target.value;
    }
}
```

someComponent.html:

```
<template>
 <lightning-input label="Define the Property"
value={myProperty} onchange={updateProperty}></lightning-input>
    <br/>
    The resulting property = {resultingProperty}
</template>
```

In this example, we see that the component is listening for the standard DOM **`change`** event over the **`lightning-input`** standard LWC.

Note: We have shared a reference for all the available standard DOM events at the end of this chapter.

Standard DOM events are (most of the time) used for detecting users' actions on a page. However, to achieve solid communication (for being able to pass data) between parent and child components, we need to define our custom events.

In LWC, it is easily possible to define the custom events using the **`CustomEvent`** interface. To dispatch these events, all we need is to call the **`dispatchEvent()`** method of the **`EventTarget`** interface. Let's see this with a simple example:

Child controller - eventChildComponent.js:

```
import { LightningElement } from 'lwc';
export default class EventChildComponent extends LightningElement {
    sendCustomEvent() {
        this.dispatchEvent(new CustomEvent('mycustomevent'));
    }
}
```

Child template - eventChildComponent.html:

```
<template>
    <lightning-button label="Send Event" onclick={sendCustomEvent}></
lightning-button>
</template>
```

Parent controller - eventParentComponent.js:

```
import { LightningElement } from 'lwc';
export default class EventParentComponent extends LightningElement {
    handleCustomEvent() {
        console.log("Custom event is fired from the child component");
    }
}
```

Parent template - eventParentComponent.html:

```
<template>
    <c-event-child-component onmycustomevent={handleCustom
Event}></c-event-child-component>
</template>
```

We have two components: one parent and one child. The child component has a simple button that creates a custom event (using the **`CustomEvent`** interface) when the user clicks it, and then at the same time, it dispatches the event using the **`dispatchEvent()`** method of the **`EventTarget`** interface:

```
this.dispatchEvent(new CustomEvent('mycustomevent'));
```

Note: `CustomEvent` and **`EventTarget`** interfaces are automatically implemented in all LWCs, so no need to manually import and implement them.

The **`CustomEvent`** constructor has one mandatory variable: the name of the custom event. Here, in our example, we determined **`mycustomevent`** as the name of the event. While defining a name for a custom event, it's important to consider the following best practices:

- No uppercase letters
- No spaces
- (If we need to separate the words, we can) use underscores between words
    - Hence, here, in this example, we would also determine our custom event's name as **`my_custom_event`.**
- The custom event name shouldn't start with **`on`**.

- We listen for an event in a parent component using the **on** prefix as **oncustomeventname.** This is why if we use **on** at the beginning of the name of the custom event, the event listening markup would become **onon**customeventname, which can be confusing.

In our example, since the custom event is directly created and dispatched by the child component itself, we use the **this** keyword for the **EventTarget** object while dispatching the event in the child component:

```
this.dispatchEvent(new CustomEvent('mycustomevent'));
```

Note: It is also possible to dispatch events from other HTML tags of template. In such cases, we need to use the HTML component (which can be determined by using **this.template.querySelector()** method) instead of **this** keyword while calling the **dispatchEvent()** method. We'll discuss this topic in the next section.

In order to be able to capture the event, the parent component should listen for it via an event listener:

```
<c-event-child-component onmycustomevent={handleCustom
Event}></c-event-child-component>
```

Here, the event listener is declaratively attached in the parent component template by using the attribute **onmycustomevent** over the child component tag. Basically, as a general rule of thumb, the names of the event listeners are determined as **on + custom event** name, while we define them declaratively. Hence, here, it is used as **onmycustomevent**.

To achieve something in the parent component (when the event happens), we need to wire a method to the event listener. So, here, we wire the method **handleCustomEvent**. The only thing that remains to do is to define this method in the parent component controller:

```
handleCustomEvent() {
        console.log("Custom event is fired from the child component");
    }
```

Apart from attaching the event listener declaratively in the template, we could also attach it programmatically. To show this in action, let's update the parent component as follows:

Parent controller - eventParentComponent.js:

```
import { LightningElement } from 'lwc';
export default class EventParentComponent extends LightningElement {
    constructor() {
     super();
     this.template.addEventListener('mycustomevent2',this.handle
CustomEventProgrammatically);
    }

    handleCustomEventProgrammatically() {
        console.log("We caught the child component's event
programmatically");
    }

    handleCustomEvent() {
        console.log("Custom event is fired from the child component");
    }
}
```

In this updated example, our parent component starts to listen to a second event called **`mycustomerevent2`** using the **`addEventListener()`** standard DOM method. When we use this method, we don't need to put any declarative expression in the parent component template file, we leave it as it is initially.

As seen, moreover, we put the event listener directly in the **`constructor()`** method. Thus, as soon as the parent component is created, it starts to listen for the event. In the description of the event listener, we add the handler function we want to use (which is **`handleCustomEventProgrammatically`**), and we define this function in the JS controller.

Tip: As we know, **`<c-event-child-component>`** is directly owned by the parent component's template file (which means that this tag explicitly exists in the parent component's template file). However, if this child component tag was added dynamically via a named spot into the parent component's template file, then we would need to use **`this.addEventListener()`** instead of **`this.template.addEventListener()`** to define the event listener.

In order to see this new event handler in action, we naturally need to add this new **`mycustomevent2`** event in the child component controller:

Child controller - eventChildComponent.js:

```
import { LightningElement } from 'lwc';
export default class EventChildComponent extends LightningElement {
    sendCustomEvent() {
        this.dispatchEvent(new CustomEvent('mycustomevent'));
        this.dispatchEvent(new CustomEvent('mycustomevent2',
{bubbles:true}));
    }
}
```

One thing to notice is that this time we need to make **`bubbles = true`** while creating the custom event, because unless we do this, this new event won't be able to propagate outside of the child component (up to the parent component) due to **Shadow DOM** default restrictions. (The **`bubbles`** property is related to **event propagation**, and we'll explore it in more detail in later sections.)

Tip: The LWC framework manages and cleans the event listeners as part of the component lifecycle. However, if we add listeners to different objects such as **`window`**, **`document`**, **`div`**, and more, we're responsible for removing them ourselves.

The **`disconnectedCallback()`** lifecycle hook is the place where we should do these removals.

To see in action what we've done until now, we can deploy our parent and child components to a record page:

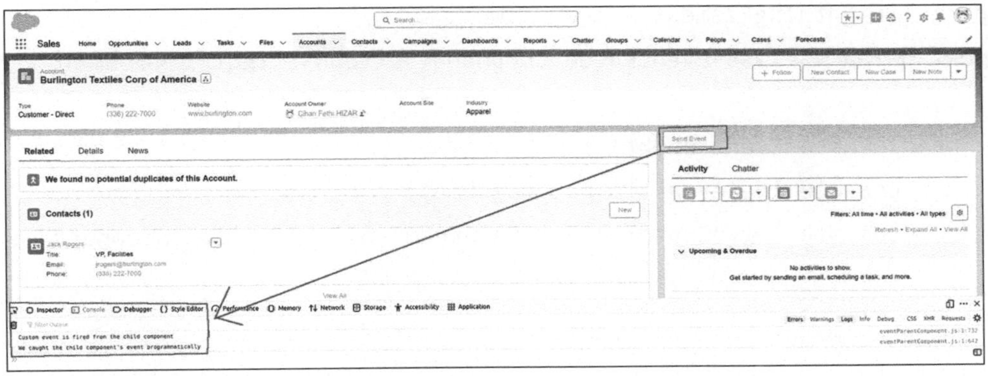

Figure 5.1: *When we click the button, we see that the events are fired successfully*

About event targets

By using the "`event.target`" property, it is possible to capture the source object of an event. Let's see how it works by updating our previous child component as follows:

```
import { LightningElement } from 'lwc';
export default class EventChildComponent extends LightningElement {
    sendCustomEvent(event) {
        console.log(event.target.tagName);
        this.dispatchEvent(new CustomEvent('mycustomevent'));
        this.dispatchEvent(new CustomEvent('mycustomevent2',
{bubbles:true}));
    }
}
```

When we run this code, we'll see **`LIGHTNING-BUTTON`** in the console. This is because the click event, which calls this **`sendCustomEvent()`** method, happens over the **`<lightning-button>`** standard component of the child component.

However, when we run the following controller for the parent component, we'll see **`C-EVENT-CHILD-CONTROLLER`** in the console. This is because, for the parent component, the source of the event is the **`c-event-child-controller`** child component:

```
import { LightningElement } from 'lwc';
export default class EventParentComponent extends LightningElement {
    ...
    handleCustomEvent(event) {
        console.log(event.target.tagName);
        console.log("Custom event is fired from the child component");
    }
}
```

Here is the screenshot for the updated components' resulting page in Salesforce org:

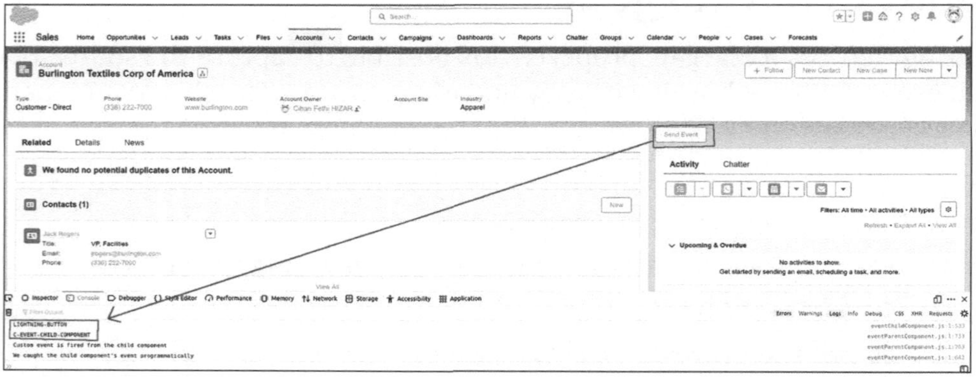

Figure 5.2: *The event.target objects are different for the parent and the child components*

When an event bubbles up (which means it travels from child up to parent component(s)), the target of the event (which is the source tag that dispatches the event) will be different in every shadow roots of the components in the hierarchy. This dynamic change of the **`event.target`** along the hierarchy is known as **event retargeting**.

Here, in our example, we used the **`tagName`** property of the **`event.target`** object to determine the tag name of the source component. Nonetheless, the **`event.target`** object has many other properties, with the **`value`** property being another popular example.

If we return to our initial example with the **`someComponent`** LWC, we would see this **`value`** property in action:

someComponent.js:

```
import { LightningElement} from 'lwc';
export default class SomeComponent extends LightningElement {
    ...

    updateProperty(event) {
        this.myProperty = event.target.value;
    }
}
```

someComponent.html:

```
<template>
 <lightning-input label="Define the Property" value={myProperty}
onchange={updateProperty}></lightning-input>
    ...
</template>
```

Briefly, for all the components that can have a value (such as **`input`** box, **`select`** box, and more), we can use the **`event.target.value`** to capture the **`value`** at the time of the event happening. Moreover, this **`value`** property is not read-only, which means that it is even possible to update the value of the input component in real time:

Template:

```
<lightning-input onchange={uppercaseInputValue}></lightning-input>
```

Controller:

```
uppercaseInputValue(event) {
        event.target.value = event.target.value.toUpperCase();
}
```

In this previous example, whenever a user enters a value into the **`lightning-input`** box, the entry will automatically be uppercased.

Before concluding this section, let's finally look at how to dispatch an event from a tag of a component's template. For this one, let's improve our child component as follows:

Child controller - eventChildComponent.js

```
import { LightningElement } from 'lwc';

export default class EventChildComponent extends LightningElement {

    constructor() {

        super();

        this.template.addEventListener('tag_dispatch', this.handle
TagDispatch);

    }

    handleTagDispatch() {

        console.log('We detected an event from lightning-formatted-text
tag!');

    }

    renderedCallback() {

        this.template.querySelector('lightning-formatted-text').
dispatchEvent(new CustomEvent('tag_dispatch', {bubbles:true}));

    }


    sendCustomEvent(event) {

        console.log(event.target.tagName);

        this.dispatchEvent(new CustomEvent('mycustomevent'));

        this.dispatchEvent(new CustomEvent('mycustomevent2',
{bubbles:true}));

    }


}
```

Child template - eventChildComponent.html

```
<template>

    <lightning-button label="Send Event" onclick={sendCustomEvent}></
lightning-button>

    <br/><br/>
```

```
    <lightning-formatted-text value="Initial value"></lightning-format-
ted-text>
</template>
```

In the **renderedCallback()** lifecycle hook, we dispatch an event (which is called **tag_dispatch)** whose source is **lightning-formatted-text** tag of the child component's template. By using the **constructor()** lifecycle hook, we add the event listener to the component. Once again, here, we also use **bubbles = true** in the definition of this custom event because the events of sub-tags can be caught only and only if the event is bubbling up.

When we deploy the updated child component, we see that as soon as the component is loaded into the page, the event is fired and handled as expected:

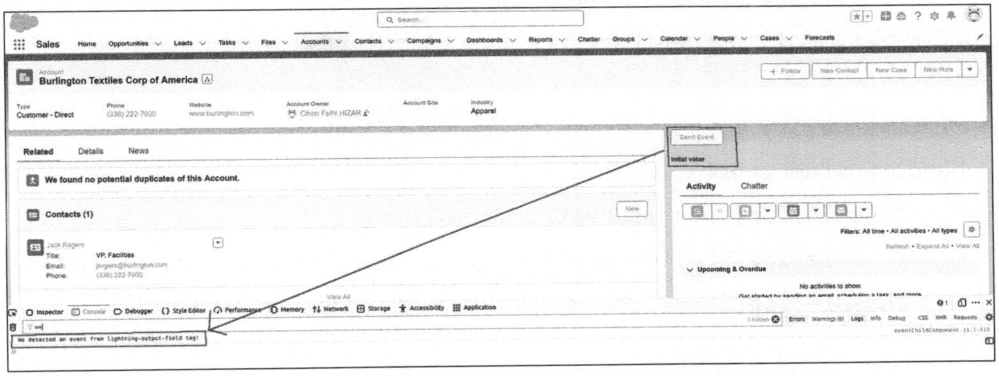

Figure 5.3: *We dispatch the event from a sub-component of the child component*

Passing data in events

Until now, in all of our examples, we have fired basic events that don't have any data. However, as one can easily expect, the events are mainly used for passing data between components.

Fortunately, it is extremely easy. Let's improve our parent and child components once again to see it in action:

Child controller – eventChildComponent.js

```
import { LightningElement } from 'lwc';
export default class EventChildComponent extends LightningElement {
    ...
```

```
    sendCustomEvent(event) {
       console.log(event.target.tagName);
       this.dispatchEvent(new CustomEvent('mycustomevent', {detail:
'Hey! I am the child component!'}));
       this.dispatchEvent(new CustomEvent('mycustomevent2',
{bubbles:true}));
    }

}
```

Parent controller - eventParentComponent.js:

```
import { LightningElement } from 'lwc';
export default class EventParentComponent extends LightningElement {
    ...

    handleCustomEvent() {
        console.log(event.target.tagName);
        console.log("Custom event is fired from the child component");
        console.log('Here the data captured: '+event.detail);
    }
}
```

Briefly, all we need to do is add an object with a **`detail`** property while creating the custom event in the child component:

Child controller:

this.dispatchEvent(new CustomEvent('mycustomevent', `{detail: 'Hey! I am the child component!'}));`

Then, in the event handler of the parent component, we can directly use the received data by using this **`detail`** property:

```
console.log('Here the data captured: '+event.detail);
```

As a best practice, we should always send primitive data with the **`detail`** property, even though it is also possible to send an object. If we need to send an object, before sending it via **`detail`** property, we should copy its data to another object and then add this new object to the **`detail`** property. Thus, this ensures that the event handler of the parent component would not modify the original object (permanently, without our will and knowledge!) but would work only with the data that it receives.

When we deploy the updated parent and child components, the result will look something like this:

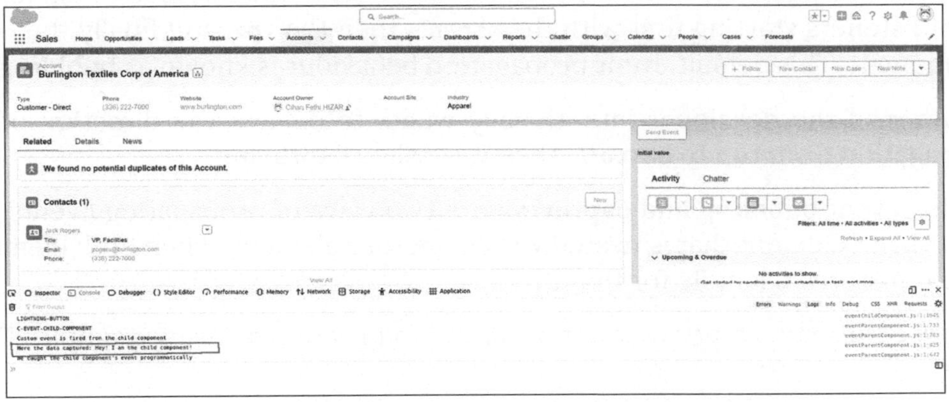

Figure 5.4: *When we click the "Send Event" button, the data is also shared with the parent component*

Event propagation

Before we jump into event propagation in LWC, let's first understand how it works in standard JavaScript.

Event propagation in JavaScript

HTML documents are formed of nested components. Even if the user sees only a piece of text on a web page, the text should actually be part of a **`<span>`** tag, which may be a part of **`<p>`** tag, which in turn may be a part of **`<div>`** tag, and so on...

```
<div>
   <p>
      <span>
```

```
        Some text
      </span>
   </p>
</div>
```

Just like the successive waves that happen after we throw a stone into a lake, when we trigger an event on a child component, JavaScript tries to find the event listeners from the **bottom to the top** throughout the entire hierarchy. Here, in our previous example, when we click the Some text, JavaScript will look for the event listeners starting first with the **`<span>`,** then the **`<p>`,** and finally the `<div>` component. This default event propagation behaviour is known as **bubbling**.

However, if the developer intentionally wants to change the direction of the propagation from **top to bottom**, then it is called **capturing**.

Briefly, event **bubbling** and **capturing** are two ways of propagating events that occur in an element that is nested within another element, when both elements have registered a handle for that event.

Let's see these two types of event propagation in action by using a simple HTML page:

js-propagation-examples.html:

```
<html>
<head></head>
<body>
      <div id="div1" onclick="javascript:alert('div');">
            <p onclick="javascript:alert('p');">
                  <span onclick="javascript:alert('span');">
                        Click me for "bubbling"!
                  </span>
            </p>
      </div>
      <div id="div2" name="capture">
            <p name="capture">
                  <span name="capture">
                        Click me for "capturing"!
```

```
                    </span>
              </p>
        </div>

<script type="text/javascript">
      var capturingComponents = document.querySelectorAll("[name =
'capture']");
      capturingComponents.forEach(ele => {
            ele.addEventListener(
                  "click",
                  event => console.log(event.currentTarget.tagName),
                  true
            );
      });
</script>
</body>
</html>
```

bubbling is the default behaviour in standard JavaScript. This is why, defining **`onclick`** event listeners on the **`<div id='div1'>`** component and its child components, **`<p>`** and **`<span>`**, is more than sufficient to experience the default **bubbling** behaviour. As expected, when we run this HTML page in a browser and click the **`Click me for "bubbling"!`** text, we will first see an **`alert box of "span"`**, then an **`alert box of "p"`** , and finally **`an alert box of "div"`** will appear on the browser screen.

However, to intentionally use the **capturing** event propagation, we need to use JavaScript standard **`addEventListener()`** function. So, after we put the **`<div id='div2'>`** component and its child components, **`<p>`** and **`<span>`**, into the HTML Body, we then add a simple **`<script>...</script>`** JavaScript block, which automatically defines the **click** event listeners for us.

```
ele.addEventListener(
                  "click",
                  event => console.log(event.currentTarget.tagName),
                  true
```

```
            );
```

By default, the optional third parameter's value of the **`addEventListener()`** function is **false**. However, when we intentionally determine it to be **true**, the event propagation becomes **capturing**.

So, consequently, when we click the **`Click me for 'capturing'!`** text, we will see **`DIV, P`** and **`SPAN`** in the browser console:

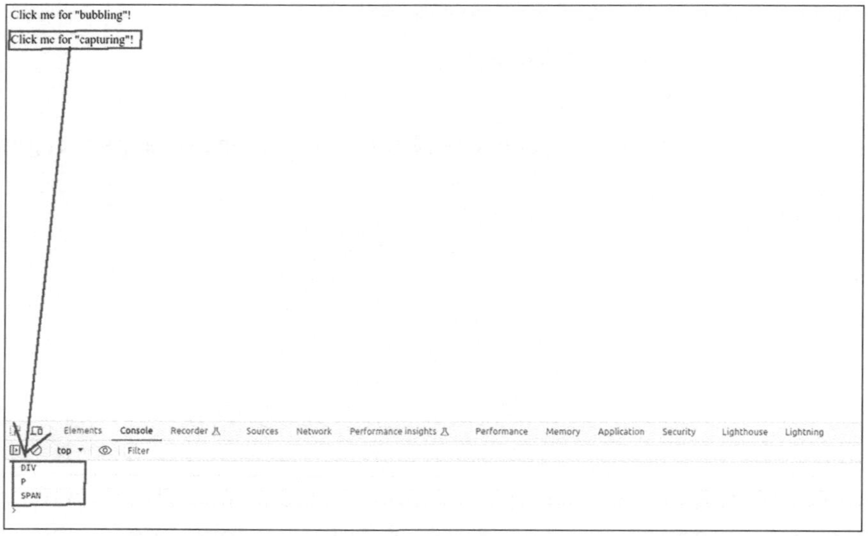

***Figure 5.5:** When we click the "Click me for 'capturing'!" text, the click event is propagated as "capturing"*

Note: When we try to run the HTML file (~ **`js-propagation-examples.html`**) from our previous example, we need to be aware that some browsers, such as Mozilla Firefox, may not allow running JavaScript blocks locally. In contrast, when we run this example in a Google Chrome browser, as shown in *Figure* 5.5, we didn't encounter any issue. However, when you are using this HTML file on your local computer, you need to be sure that the browser security settings allow "local JavaScript executions". (Or even better, you should run this HTML file in a local web server like IIS or Apache Web Server.)

Okay, this covers the standard JavaScript! However, when we return to the LWC Framework, it's important to mention that **capturing** is not allowed. So, for LWC, there is only one way of event propagation, which is **bubbling**.

Event propagation in LWC

While concluding the previous section, we stated that **bubbling** is the only event propagation type supported by the LWC Framework. However, **it is switched off by default** because, with respect to the initial security configuration, Salesforce wants to maintain the encapsulation of nested components in a shadow DOM. This means that a parent component will not be able to listen for a child component's event unless the event is explicitly created by using **`bubbles: true`**.

In brief, when we use the **`addEventListener()`** function programmatically in a parent component, we can expect to catch only the events that are explicitly created with **`bubbles: true`** by the child components.

Child controller - eventChildComponent.js:

```
import { LightningElement } from 'lwc';
export default class EventChildComponent extends LightningElement {
    sendCustomEvent() {
        this.dispatchEvent(new CustomEvent('mycustomevent'));
        this.dispatchEvent(new CustomEvent('mycustomevent2',
{bubbles:true}));
    }
}
```

Parent controller - eventParentComponent.js:

```
import { LightningElement } from 'lwc';
export default class EventParentComponent extends LightningElement {
    constructor() {
     super();
     this.template.addEventListener('mycustomevent2',this.handle
CustomEventProgrammatically);
    }

    handleCustomEventProgrammatically() {
        console.log("We caught the child component's event
programmatically");
    }
```

```
    ...
}
```

Here, for the parent component to listen to the `mycustomevent2` event, the child component should create it with `bubbles: true`.

However, if we define the **event-listener** and the **event-handler** directly in the child component as follows:

Parent template - eventParentComponent.html:

```
<template>
    <c-event-child-component onmycustomevent={handleCustom
Event}></c-event-child-component>
</template>
```

Then we see that the parent will be able to listen to the `mycustomevent` event and handle it as soon as it is caught. (This doesn't mean that the `mycustomevent` will propagate throughout the parent component's shadow DOM component hierarchy, but it should be seen basically as a shortcut to capture and handle the child's events without bothering other components in the parent's template. However, if we do want to make it propagate throughout the parent component's shadow DOM, we can always define it with `bubbles: true`.

Tip: While handling events, `event.target` will always show the initial source of the event for a shadow DOM. For LWC Framework, where **bubbling** is the only type of event propagation, the initial source of an event means always the child (at the deepest level of the component hierarchy, in a shadow DOM) that starts the event.

However, during **bubbling** propagation, if we need to capture the current component in the hierarchy, where the event reaches at a specific time, we need to use `event.currentTarget`.

As seen in previous sections, it is possible to create and dispatch event by using the tags that exist in the shadow DOM of a component by using `this.template.querySelector()` for selecting the tag:

JS controller of component:

```
import { LightningElement } from 'lwc';
export default class EventChildComponent extends LightningElement {
…

this.template.querySelector('lightning-formatted-text').
dispatchEvent(new CustomEvent('tag_dispatch', {bubbles:true}));

…
}
```

HTML template of the same component:

```
<template>
    ...
    <lightning-formatted-text value="Initial value"></
lightning-formatted-text>
</template>
```

Here, we define the event as **`bubbles: true`**. This event will propagate throughout the component's hierarchy (**~ `shadow`** DOM), but won't be listenable by its parent component.

However, as previously shown in this section, when we use **`this.dispatchEvent(new CustomEvent(...))`**, we define and dispatch the event directly from the component itself. In this case, when we do **`bubbles: true`**, the parent component of this component will have the chance to listen and handle the event.

In summary, we believe that bubbles propagation is clear now. It is used for propagating events in a shadow DOM of a component itself or for propagating in its parent component's shadow DOM.

However, if we want to allow the event to propagate through the components' borders in the hierarchy (from one component's shadow DOM to its parent component's shadow DOM) until it is explicitly stopped (using the **`event.stopPropagation()`** function in an event handler method of one of the parent components), what could we use? The answer lies in a property that is called **`composed`**.

```
this.dispatchEvent(new CustomEvent('mycustomevent3', {bubbles:true,
composed: true}));
```

By default, **`composed`** is also **`false`**, similar to **`bubbles`**.

If we make a resume of all the available options for event propagation in LWC:

- **"`bubbles: false`" and "`composed: false`"** → This is the default propagation. You don't need to explicitly add the "`bubbles`" and "`composed`" properties while creating the custom event to have this propagation type.
- **"`bubbles: true`" and "`composed: false`"** → As already explained in this section, if the event is dispatched by the component itself, then it will propagate throughout its parent component's shadow DOM. However, if it is dispatched by a sub-tag of the component, then the event propagation will be limited to the component's own shadow DOM.
- **"`bubbles: true`" and "`composed: true`"** → In this case, the event will become a "`public API`" of the component and all of its ancestors. So, we should really be careful to have a unique name throughout the LWC application for this type of event. Unless it is explicitly stopped by using the "`event.stopPropagation()`" method, the event will propagate throughout the entire DOM document.
- **"`bubbles: false`" and "`composed: true`"** → It is not possible in the LWC Framework.

Publish-Subscribe events (pubsub module)

Until now, we focused on communication through the hierarchy of the components in an LWC application. Nevertheless, while providing solutions for the needs of our customers, we will surely encounter some scenarios in which we need to ensure that independent LWCs can communicate via events without needing to be in the same hierarchy, across the DOM.

There are two ways to achieve this type of communication:

- pubsub module
- Lightning Message Service

Using **Lightning Message Service** is far better than the **pubsub module** because it also supports **Visualforce pages** and **Aura components**, which means it is possible to pass data between LWCs, Aura components, and Visualforce pages with the help of Lightning Message Service. Nonetheless, unfortunately,

Lightning Message Service does not support every container; it supports the following experiences:

- Lightning Experience standard navigation
- Lightning Experience console navigation
- Salesforce mobile app for Aura components and LWCs but not for Visualforce pages
- Lightning components are used in Aura and LWR-based Experience builder sites.

Note: LWR-based: Lightning Web Runtime-based

Lightning Message Service doesn't work with **Salesforce tabs + Visualforce sites** or with **Visualforce pages in Experience Builder sites.** So, when it comes to these types of containers that don't support "Lightning Message Service", we need to use the `pubsub module.`

In this pubsub module, the mechanism is as intuitive as its name sounds: some LWCs will **publish** events for the page, and others will **subscribe** to those events in order to consume them.

The pubsub module is basically a JavaScript file created by Salesforce. It can be downloaded for https://github.com/developerforce/pubsub". To use its functions to publish and subscribe to events, we need to import it as a module to our LWCs. Hence, we need to define it in our project as an LWC. After downloading the code from its GitHub repo", we need to copy-paste it into the JavaScript controller of our newly created LWC.

Note: After we create the pubsub LWC, we shouldn't forget to deploy it to our Salesforce org before starting using it.

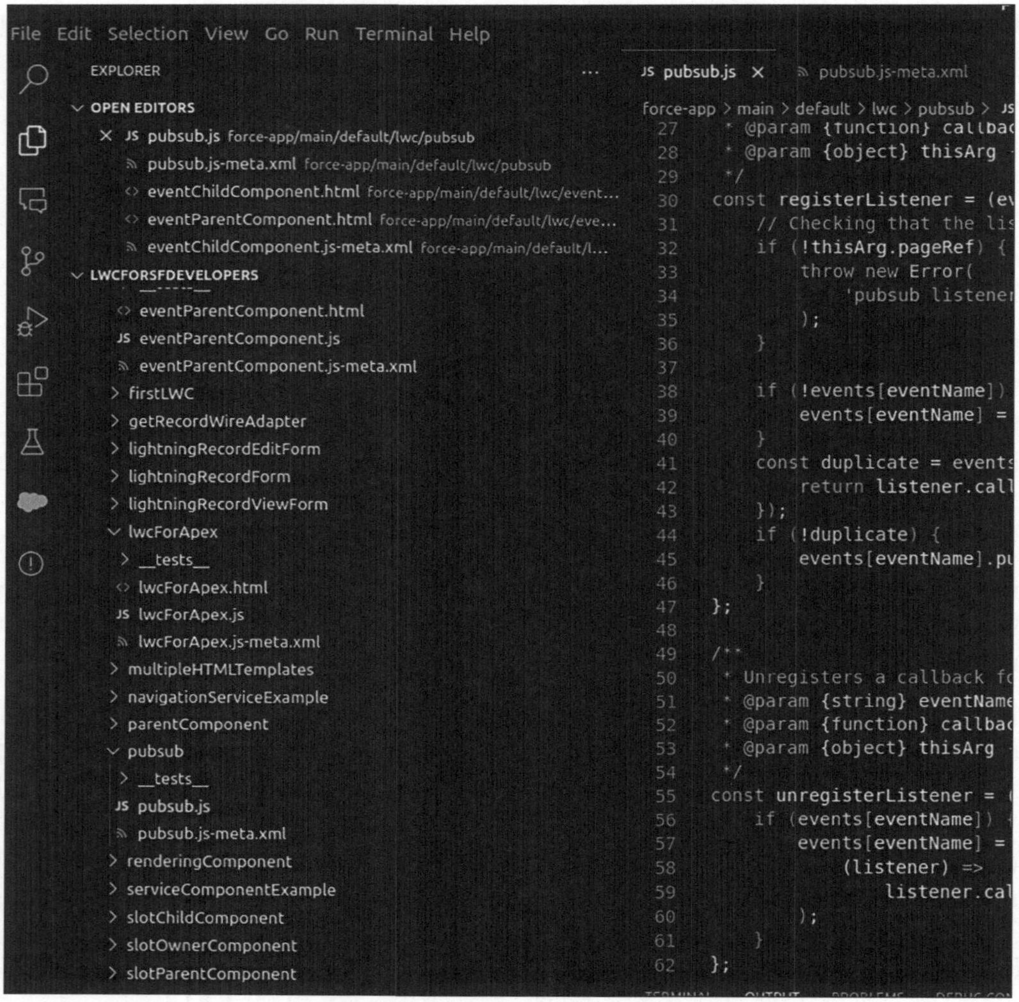

Figure 5.6: *pubsub.js file is downloaded from its GitHub repo and is used to create an LWC in our project*

After we have the pubsub module, we are now ready to implement an example that uses this pubsub module.

First, let's create our **publisher component:**

eventPublisher.js:

```
import { LightningElement, wire } from 'lwc';
import { fireEvent } from 'c/pubsub';
import { CurrentPageReference } from 'lightning/navigation';
```

```
export default class EventPublisher extends LightningElement {
    @wire(CurrentPageReference) pageRef;
    message = "This message is sent from the publisher!";
    publishEvent() {
        fireEvent(this.pageRef, "myPubSubEvent", this.message);
    }
}
```

eventPublisher.html:

```
<template>
 <h1>Publisher Component:</h1>
 <lightning-button variant="brand" label="Publish Event" onclick=
{publishEvent}>
 </lightning-button>
</template>
```

The publisher components should use the **`fireEvent()`** method of the pubsub module to publish the event. Initially, we import this method. While working with the pubsub module, we need to have a reference for the current page, so we also import the **`CurrentPageReference`** from **`lightning/navigation`**.

Note: The pubsub module is restricted for the communication of the LWCs (and Aura components), which reside on the same page. This is why we always need to import **`CurrentPageReference`** in both publisher and subscriber components.

The **`fireEvent()`** method takes three parameters: the current page reference, the name of the event (which should be unique for the page), and the payload (which is basically the data we're going to send). In our example, the payload is a simple text held by the **`message`** property.

And that's all for the controller of the **publisher** component. When we look at its template, we see a basic template with one header and one button. When we click the `Publish Event` button, it will directly publish the event, which will transfer the text **`This message is sent from the publisher!`** to all the components of the page subscribed to this event.

So, now, let's create a simple subscriber component that will consume our publisher's event:

eventSubscriber.js:

```
import { LightningElement, wire } from 'lwc';
import { registerListener, unregisterAllListeners, } from 'c/pubsub';
import { CurrentPageReference } from 'lightning/navigation';

export default class EventSubscriber extends LightningElement {

    @wire(CurrentPageReference) pageRef;

    receivedData = "We're expecting data from the publisher
component...";

    connectedCallback() {
        registerListener("myPubSubEvent", this.handleData, this);
    }

    handleData(data) {
        this.receivedData = data;
    }

    disconnectedCallback() {
        unregisterAllListeners(this);
    }
}
```

eventSubscriber.html:

```
<template>
```

```
    <h1>Subscriber Component:</h1>
    <p>{receivedData}</p>
</template>
```

This time, we import the **registerListener()** and **unregisterAllListeners()** methods from the pubsub module. There is also another method for unregistering events called **unregisterListener()**, which is used for unregistering from just one event. However, to keep our example simple, we basically unregister from all events using the **unregisterAllListeners()** method.

Although we don't use the **CurrentPageReference** anywhere through the subscriber component, we must import it anyway. If we don't import it, the pubsub module method won't work.

To register and unregister events, we use the **connectedCallback()** and **disconnectedCallback()** lifecycle hooks. The **registerListener()** method needs three parameters: the name of the event to which we subscribe, a handler callback method to control what to do when the publisher's event is received, and the subscriber component itself. The **unregisterAllListeners()** method needs only one parameter: the subscriber component itself.

At the beginning, this subscriber component will display the text: **We're expecting data from the publisher component...**, and when the event is fired from the publisher component, this text will become: **This message is sent from the publisher!.**

After we deploy these two components to our Salesforce org, initially, the screen will look like this:

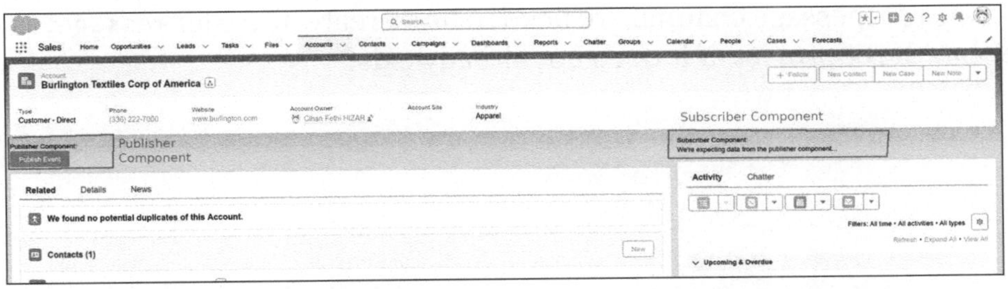

Figure 5.7: *Initial look of the components that are placed independently on the same page*

When we click the **Publish Event** button, we see that the payload is received by the subscriber component:

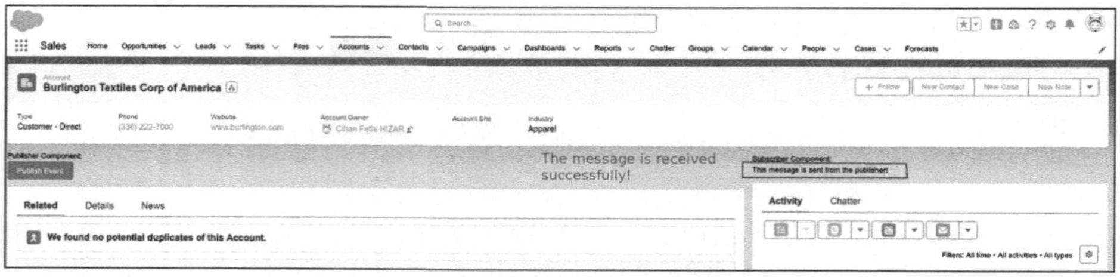

Figure 5.8: *When we click the "Publish Event" button, the message is transferred to the subscriber*

Lightning Message Service

In the pubsub module, the communication between independent components happens without any mediation, which causes the communication to be highly restricted. And, Salesforce already stopped the further developments to the pubsub module. On the other hand, in the Lightning Message Service structure, we first define an independent metadata entity: **message channel**. With the help of this entity and many independent components, Visualforce pages can publish an event with the configured payload. Correspondingly, many other components and Visualforce pages can receive these payloads by subscribing to this "manage channel".

Briefly, a **message channel** is an XML configuration file that holds the name of the event and the types of data that this event will contain. With this information, any component in different active areas can transfer and receive data with ease.

Creating and deploying a Message Channel

For creating a message channel, we need to first create its folder `messageChannels` under our SFDX project, if it does not already exist:

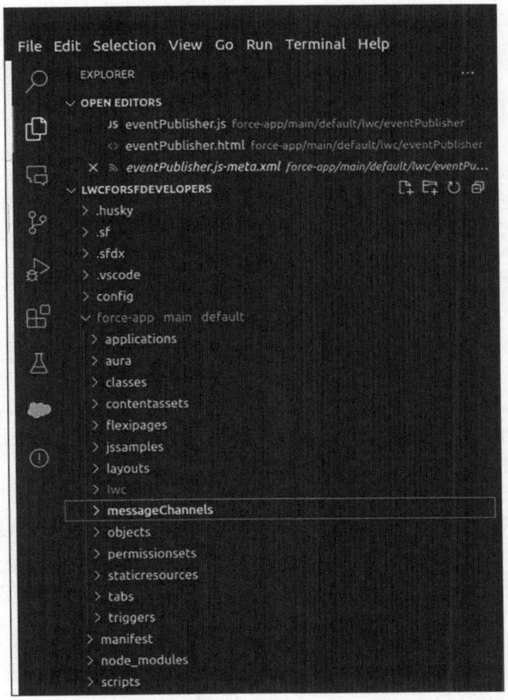

Figure 5.9: *First, we create the folder that will hold the message channels*

Then, we can create our first message channel, which is basically an XML file, as mentioned earlier:

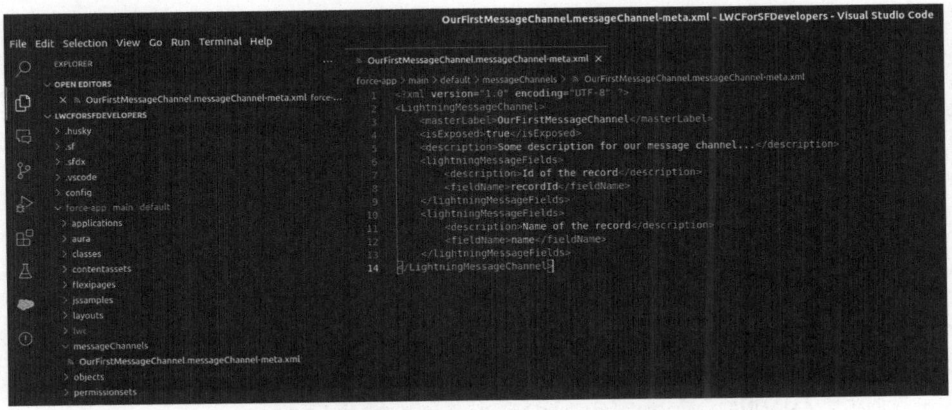

Figure 5.10: *Our first message channel*

The tags in this XML file are self-explanatory, but let us touch on them anyway:

- **masterLabel** → Name of the message channel.
- **isExposed** → Indicates whether this message channel is exposed to components in other namespaces.
- **description** → Description of the message channel.
- **lightningMessageFields** → Used to define a payload (which represents basically the data that will be transferred via this message channel).
    - **description** of the **lightningMessageFields** → Description of the payload.
    - **fieldName** of the **lightningMessageFields** → Unique name of the payload.

We can define as many **lightningMessageFields** as required in the message channel for our application.

When we're done with the message channel's XML configuration, we can easily deploy it by right-clicking it and selecting the SFDX**: Deploy Source to Org** option from the menu that appears.

Creating a publisher component

Now that our message channel is created and deployed, we can start creating an example component that can publish on it:

publisherMessageChannel.html:

```
<template>
  <h1><b>Publish on a Message Channel:</b></h1>
<lightning-button variant="brand" label="Send Message" onclick=
{sendMessage}> </lightning-button>
</template>
```

publisherMessageChannel.js:

```
import { LightningElement, wire } from 'lwc';
import { publish, MessageContext } from 'lightning/messageService';
import FIRST_CHANNEL from '@salesforce/messageChannel/
OurFirstMessageChannel__c';

export default class PublisherMessageChannel extends LightningElement {
```

```
    @wire(MessageContext) mesCon;

    sendMessage() {
        const message = {
            recordId: '12345678',
            name: 'Test name'
        }
        publish(this.mesCon, FIRST_CHANNEL, message);
         console.log('Message is sent to the channel...');
    }
}
```

As usual, we start by making the needed imports: we import the **`publish()`** method and **`MessageContext`** from **`lightning/messageService`**. To use the **`MessageContext`**, we need to wire it to a local variable. In this example, we wire it to **`mesCon`**.

The **`sendMessage()`** method is called when the user clicks the **`Send Message`** button. It first creates an example data object using the **`recordId`** and **`name`** field names (which were defined previously in our message channel XML configuration file).

Finally, we call the **`publish()`** method by using three parameters: the message context, the name of our message channel, and the payload.

Creating a subscriber component

Our publisher component is ready, now it is time to create a subscriber component that will consume the publisher component's event via the message channel:

subscriberMessageChannel.html:

```
<template>
<h1><b>Subscribe/Unsubscribe to/from a Message Channel:</b></h1>

<lightning-button variant="brand" label="Subscribe" onclick={subscribeT-
oMessageChannel}>
</lightning-button> 

<lightning-button label="Unsubscribe" onclick={unsubscribeFromMes-
```

```
sageChannel}>
</lightning-button>

</template>
```

subscriberMessageChannel.js:

```
import { LightningElement, wire } from 'lwc';
import { subscribe, unsubscribe, MessageContext } from 'lightning/
messageService';
import FIRST_CHANNEL from '@salesforce/messageChannel/OurFirstMes-
sageChannel__c';

export default class SubscriberMessageChannel extends LightningElement {
    @wire(MessageContext) mesCon;
    subscription = null;

    subscribeToMessageChannel() {
        console.log('Subscribing...');
        if(this.subscription) return;
        this.subscription = subscribe(this.mesCon, FIRST_CHANNEL,
(message) => {
            console.log(message);
        });
    }

    unsubscribeFromMessageChannel() {
        console.log('Unsubscribing...');
        unsubscribe(this.subscription);
        this.subscription = null;
    }
}
```

The imports are very similar to the ones of the publisher component. The only difference is that, instead of the **`publish()`** method, this time we import the **`subscribe()`** and **`unsubscribe()`** methods from **`lightning/messageService`**.

To allow the user to unsubscribe from the message channel, we need to keep the subscription info. For this purpose, we use a local property **`subscription`**, which has a **`null`** value by default. However, whenever the subscription is successful, it starts to hold the subscription details. This allows us to unsubscribe from the correct message channel in the **`unsubscribe()`** method. In addition, using this **`subscription`** property, it is also possible to prevent multiple subscription attempts by using this simple condition:

```
if(this.subscription) return;
```

`in the "subscribeToMessageChannel()" method.`

Components in action

When we deploy the **`publisherMessageChannel`** and **`subscriberMessageChannel`** components to our Salesforce org, the initial look will be as follows:

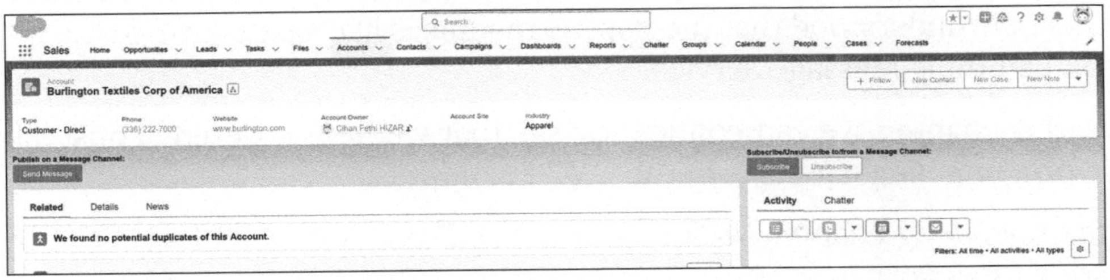

Figure 5.11: *Initial look of the publisher and subscriber components*

As soon as we click the **`Subscribe`** button, the subscriber component starts to listen to the message channel. Thus, it receives data each time we click the **`Send Message`** button of the publisher component. As expected, when we click the **`Unsubscribe`** button, the subscriber component stops listening to the message channel.

Here is the screenshot of how they are in action:

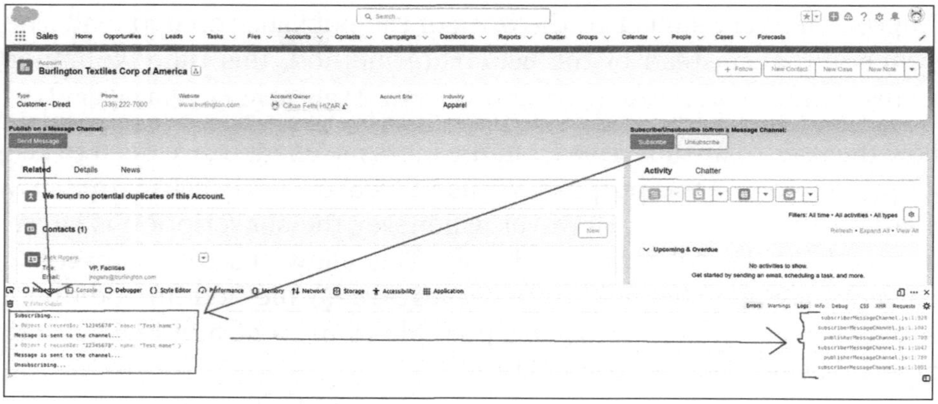

Figure 5.12: *Lightning Message Channel in action*

Conclusion

In this chapter, we learned all the details related to communication between LWCs. We started by looking at the interactions and propagations between the parent and the child components. Then, we dive into how the independent components can interact with each other in an application. We found that, for this purpose, there are two options: pubsub module and Lightning Message Service. We understood that the pubsub module is like a patch, while the future lies in Lightning Message Service.

With this chapter, we can confidently say that we have covered almost all the core programming concepts of the LWC Framework.

In the upcoming chapter, we'll continue our LWC journey by looking at other exciting aspects.

References

- Introduction to JavaScript events - https://developer.mozilla.org/en-US/docs/Learn/JavaScript/Building_blocks/Events
- Standard DOM Events Reference - https://developer.mozilla.org/en-US/docs/Web/Events
- Salesforce JavaScript pubsub file - https://github.com/developerforce/pubsub
- Metadata API Developer Guide: LightningMessageChannel - https://developer.salesforce.com/docs/component-library/documentation/en/lwc/lwc.use_message_channel_intro

- Lightning Message Service (Developer Preview) - https://developer.salesforce.com/blogs/2019/10/lightning-message-service-developer-preview

CHAPTER 6
LWC and FLOWS

Introduction

Salesforce Flow is one of the automation tools of Salesforce along with Process Builder and Workflow Rules. However, like LWC being the future of UI development for Salesforce (by replacing Aura components and Visualforce pages), Flow is the future of automation tools (which is currently replacing Process Builder and Workflow Rules). In fact, Salesforce already stopped supporting Workflow Rules and Process Builder at the end of 2022. Besides, starting with the past Winter'23 release, Salesforce blocked the creation of new Workflow Rules. Similarly, with the past Summer'23 release, it is not possible anymore to create new business processes by using Process Builder. Nowadays, if one needs to build a low-code automation in Salesforce, Flow is the only recommended way to move forward.

Salesforce Flow is not a topic of this book; actually, an entire another book on this subject can be written. However, we want to mention how to use Salesforce Flow with LWC in this chapter to show how to build solutions that can use flows as a Salesforce backend controller for LWCs, without needing to write an Apex Class. Salesforce is largely investing in flows, not only for building automations but also to minimize the needs for using backend Apex codes.

Structure

In this chapter, we will discuss the following topics:

- A simple flow in action
- Call LWCs from flows
- Launch flows from LWCs

A simple flow in action

As mentioned, Salesforce Flow is a vast topic that should be studied in its own book. There are already many different flow types as follows:

- Screen flow
- Record-triggered flow
- Schedule-triggered flow
- Platform event-triggered flow
- Autolaunched flow (without trigger – it is launched in the background when invoked by Apex, processes, REST API, etc.)
- and so on

In this book, we'll work with screen flows, which basically allow us to build **wizards** on the user interface. To create a flow, we should open `Setup → Flows` menu and then we should click on the `New Flow` button:

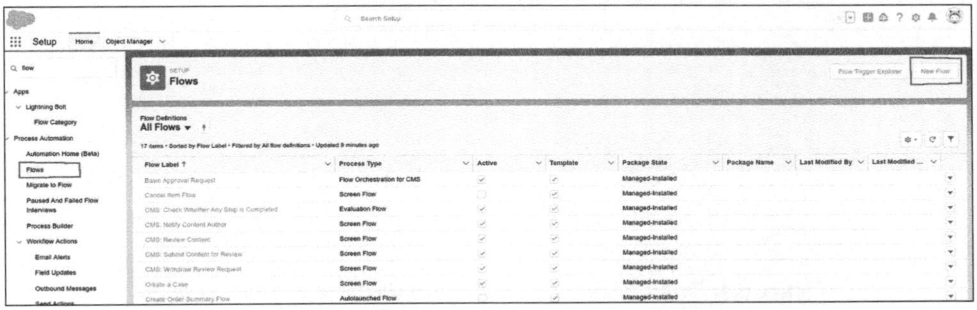

***Figure 6.1**: Creating a flow from scratch*

After we select `Screen Flow` flow type, the empty `Flow Builder` is opened to allow us to build our flow:

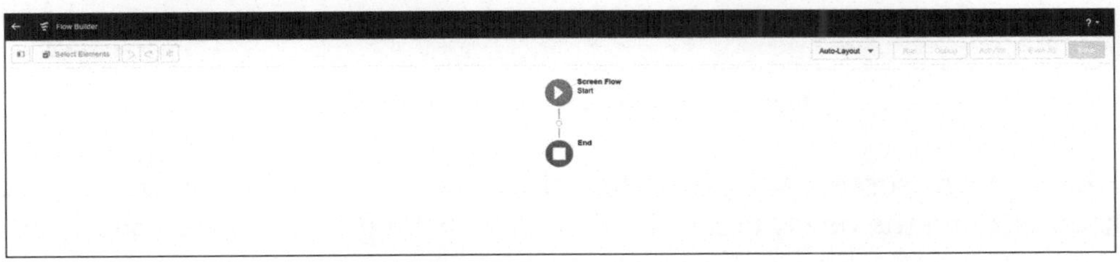

***Figure 6.2**: Empty Flow Builder screen*

In this flow, we build a custom form that'll get first name, last name, phone, and email data to save a contact for a selected account:

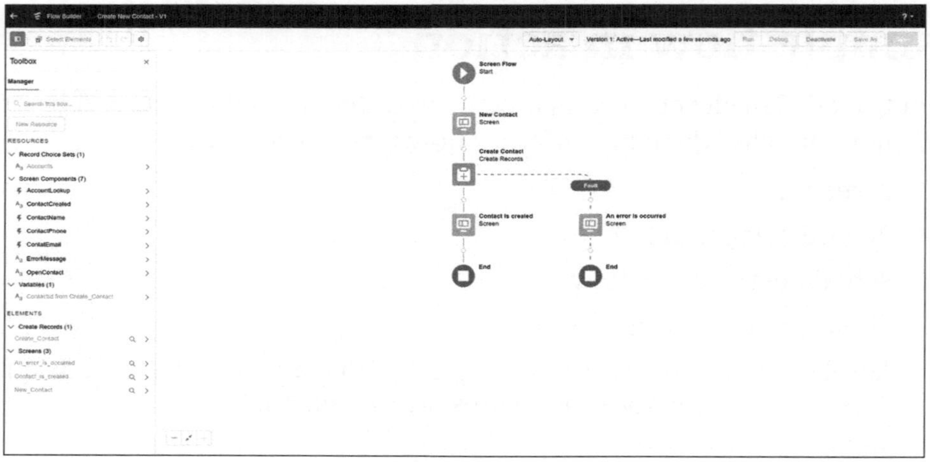

Figure 6.3: *Flow is created*

Here, when we run the flow, we first show a **`New Contact`** screen where we ask for **`Account, First Name, Last Name, Phone,`** and **`Email`** of the new contact:

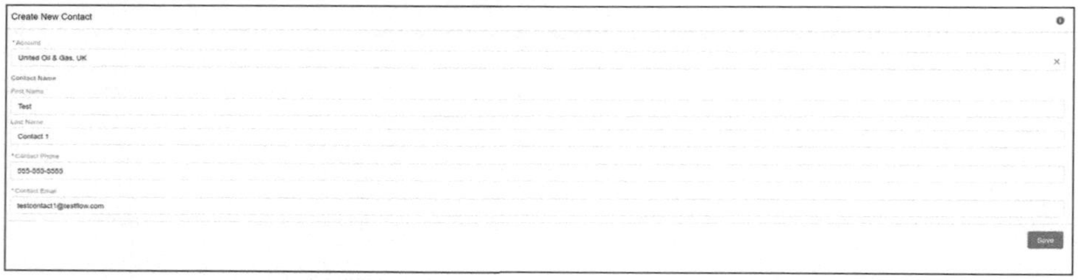

Figure 6.4: *Our screen flow starts with the New Contact screen*

When the user clicks on the **`Save`** button after entering all the values, the contact is created:

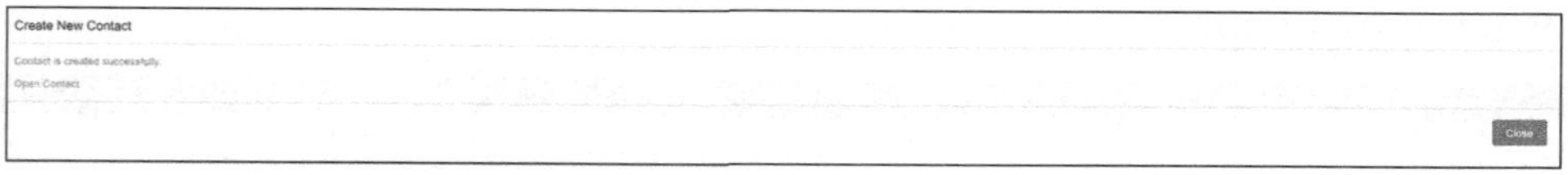

Figure 6.5: *Contact is created successfully*

In this success screen, we can either close the flow by clicking on the **`Close`** button or open the newly created contact by clicking on the **`Open Contact`** link:

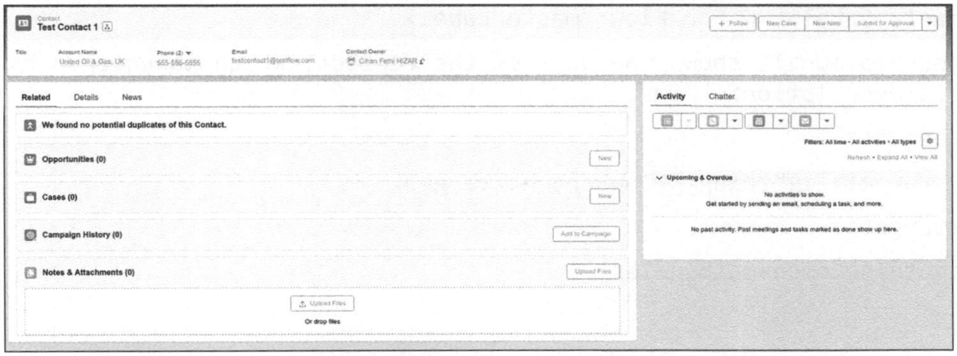

Figure 6.6: *Newly created contact*

However, if the user forgets to fill in a required field (like the **`Last Name`**), then instead of creating a contact, an error message is shown to the user:

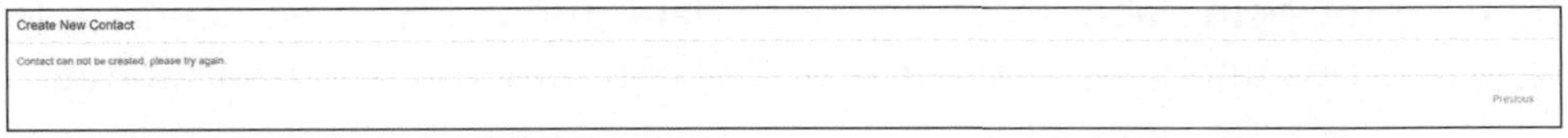

Figure 6.7: *Error message is shown when a contact cannot be created*

This was a very simple flow in action. In the next section, we'll develop this flow by adding a read-only LWC, which shows all the data entered by the user.

Note: We share the code (~ the metadata) of this flow **Create New Contact** in the **book39-chapter6-codes** folder of this book. By using it the reader can deploy the flow directly to any Salesforce org (s)he wants.

Call LWCs from flows

In *Chapter 2, Creating Your First LWC*, we mentioned what is a component configuration file of an LWC and how we can use it to define supported targets. Basically, as flows are just another type of target for LWCs, in order to use an LWC in a flow, we need to have a component configuration file similar to the following:

lwcForFlow.js-meta.xml component configuration file:

```
<?xml version="1.0" encoding="UTF-8"?>
<LightningComponentBundle xmlns="http://soap.sforce.com/2006/04/metadata">
  <apiVersion>57.0</apiVersion>
  <isExposed>true</isExposed>
```

```
  <masterLabel>LWC For Flow</masterLabel>
  <description>It shows the data of the contact, which is entered by the
user.</description>
  <targets>
    <target>lightning__FlowScreen</target>
  </targets>
</LightningComponentBundle>
```

Here, as we can see, the only thing that needs to be done is to define `lightning__FlowScreen` as a supported target for the LWC.

In the previous section, we've defined a screen flow where we were getting the inputs for `account, first name, last name, phone, email` in order to create a contact. So for being able to show those data in our LWC, we need to define those properties under `targetConfigs` of this component configuration file:

lwcForFlow.js-meta.xml component configuration file:

```
<?xml version="1.0" encoding="UTF-8"?>
<LightningComponentBundle xmlns="http://soap.sforce.com/2006/04/
metadata">
  <apiVersion>57.0</apiVersion>
  <isExposed>true</isExposed>
  <masterLabel>LWC For Flow</masterLabel>
  <description>It shows the data of the contact, which is entered by the
user.</description>
  <targets>
    <target>lightning__FlowScreen</target>
  </targets>
  <targetConfigs>
    <targetConfig targets="lightning__FlowScreen">
      <property name="accName" label="Account Chosen" type="String"
role="inputOnly" />
      <property name="firstname" label="Contact First Name" type="String"
role="inputOnly"/>
      <property name="lastname" label="Contact Last Name" type="String"
role="inputOnly" />
```

```
        <property name="phone" label="Contact Phone" type="String"
role="inputOnly" />
        <property name="email" label="Contact eMail" type="String"
role="inputOnly" />
      </targetConfig>
   </targetConfigs>
</LightningComponentBundle>
```

The rest of the LWC is left as simple as possible for the sake of this example:

lwcForFlow.js:

```
import { LightningElement, api } from 'lwc';

export default class LwcForFlow extends LightningElement {
    @api accName;
    @api firstname;
    @api lastname;
    @api phone;
    @api email;
}
```

lwcForFlow.html:

```
<template>
    <p><strong>Account Chosen = </strong>{accName}</p>
    <p><strong>Contact First Name = </strong>{firstname}</p>
    <p><strong>Contact Last Name = </strong>{lastname}</p>
    <p><strong>Contact Phone = </strong>{phone}</p>
    <p><strong>Contact eMail = </strong>{email}</p>
</template>
```

Briefly, when deployed into the flow, this LWC will show the values which are entered by the user, for "review" purposes:

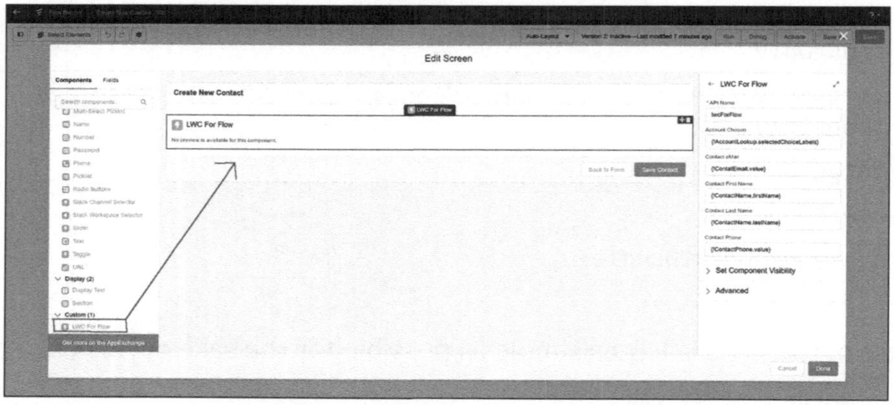

Figure 6.8: *Our newly created LWC is ready to be used in the flow*

After we add this new `Review Contact Data` screen (which consists of our `lwcForFlow` component) into our flow, the flow is updated as follows:

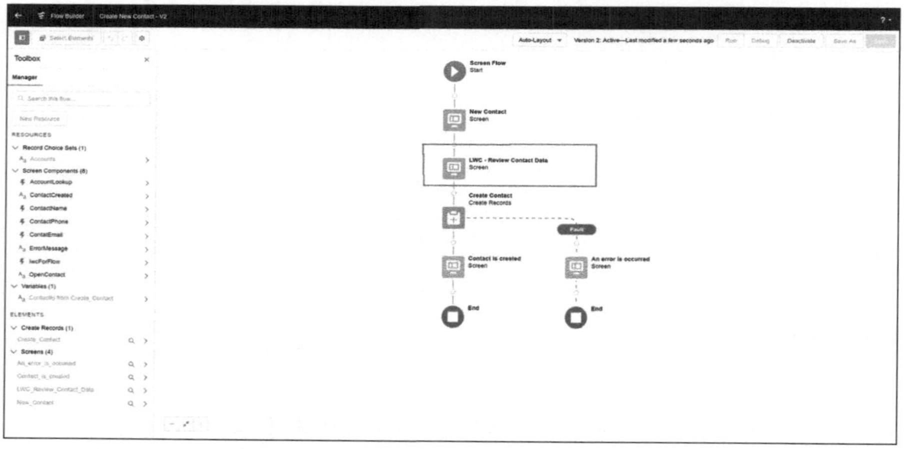

Figure 6.9: *LWC – Review Contact Data" screen is added to the flow*

When we run the flow, after we enter the contact data, we click on the `Review` button:

Figure 6.10: *Before we click on the Review button*

Then, we see that our LWC is showing the entered contact data as expected:

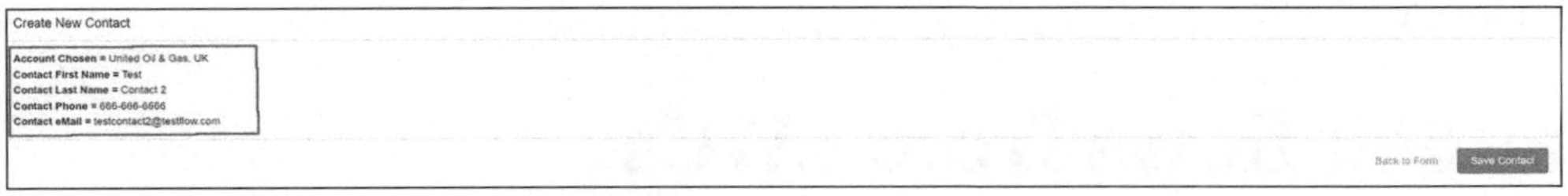

Figure 6.11: *LWC in action in the flow*

The rest of the flow is functioning similarly as explained in the previous section: when we click on the `Save Contact` button, the new contact is saved, or we can return to the form by clicking on the `Back to Form` button.

In this example, we see that our LWC is able to show the data of the flow without needing to call an Apex class or to use Lightning Data Service. This means that when combined with flows, we can build LWCs that are able to use backend data and functionalities without having an Apex controller or without using a Wire service.

Flows have elements like `Get Records`, `Update Records`, `Create Records`, `Loop`, `Assignment`, `Decision`, etc., and many actions, including `email alert`, `http callout`, `submit for approval`, etc. These elements and actions allow us to build any logic we want by communicating with the Salesforce database and by calling standard Salesforce actions without the need to write any Apex code. They can even call other flows as subflows, which give us the ability to divide-and-conquer functionalities via smaller flows.

When the existing standard actions are not sufficient, we can even define our custom Apex classes to be invoked in the flows as custom Apex actions: vice-versa is also true, which means Apex classes can also invoke **autolaunched flows** in the background during their execution.

Tip: In our LWC of the previous example, we define all the properties' roles as `inputOnly`, one example:

```
<property name=”accName” label=”Account Chosen” type=”String”
role=”inputOnly” />
```

That's why the LWC receives the values from the flow. Here if we defined the role as `outputOnly` then this time it would be possible to send the data from LWC to flow.

However, if we don't specify the `role` attribute at all, by default the property will become usable for input and output.

So, we see how to call an LWC inside a flow. Now let's see how to invoke a flow from an LWC.

Launch flows from LWCs

When a screen flow is defined, it can be called from a `Quick Action` button. In this case, the flow will be called in a popup:

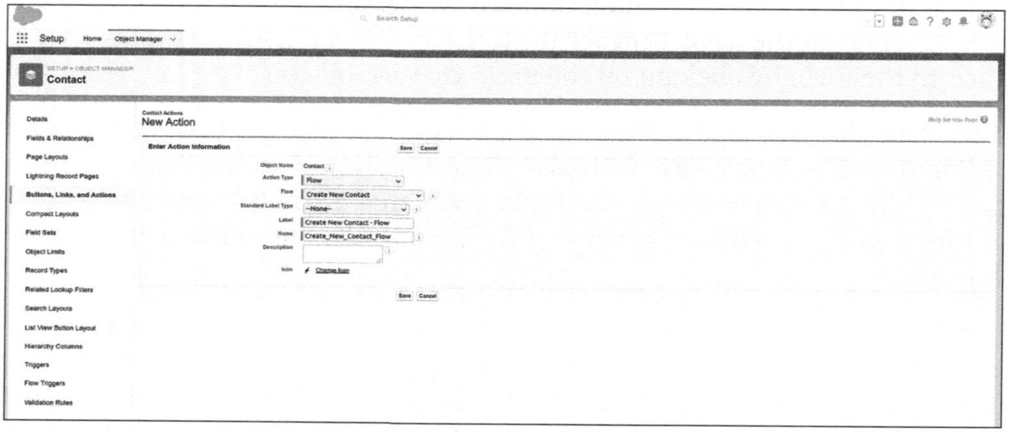

Figure 6.12: *We define our flow as a quick action*

We update the page layout to include the new button:

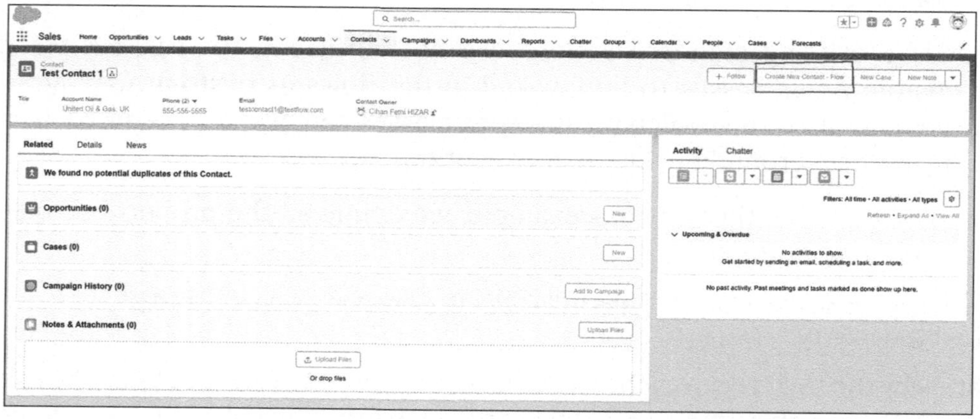

Figure 6.13: *Quick action button for our flow is on the layout*

When we click on it, the flow is opened in a popup window as expected:

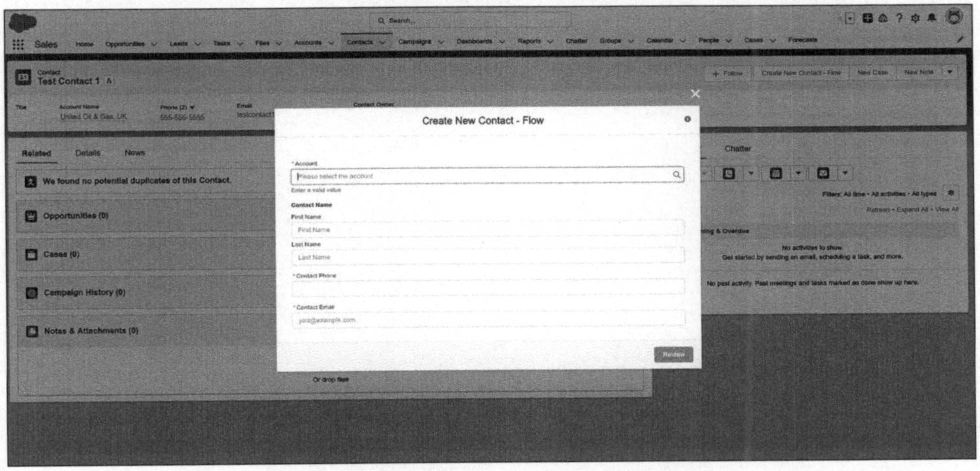

***Figure 6.14**: Flow running in a popup window*

However, we can easily put our flow in an LWC, and then it would be possible to use our flow inline, directly on the page:

lwcCallsFlow.js:

```
import { LightningElement } from ‘lwc’;
export default class LwcCallsFlow extends LightningElement {}
```

lwcCallsFlow.html:

```
<template>
    <lightning-flow flow-api-name=”Create_New_Contact”></lightning-flow>
</template>
```

To run our flow in an LWC, the only thing to do is to call it by using a standard `lightning-flow` tag. Here is the result, when we deploy this `lwcCallsFlow` LWC:

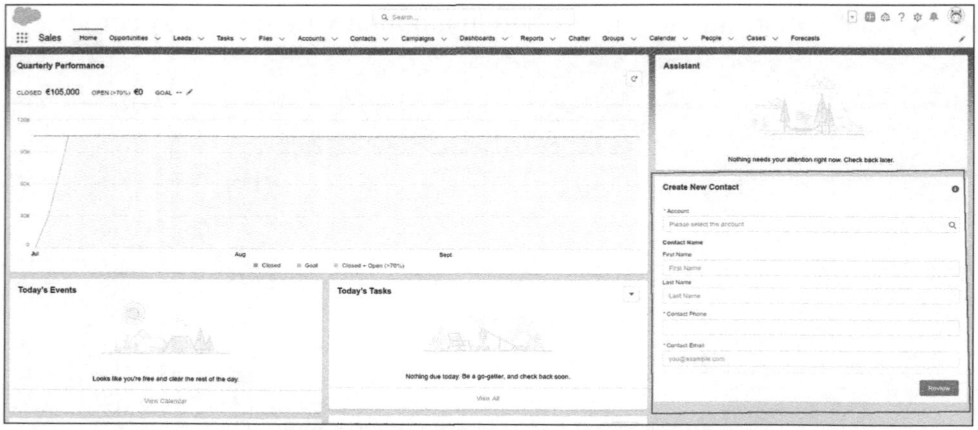

Figure 6.15: *Flow is launched directly in the LWC*

Conclusion

Salesforce Flow has now become a very important tool for the low-code strategy of the Salesforce, not only by replacing the old school Process Builder and Workflow Rules but also by having the enhanced capabilities to replace the Apex triggers and callouts in many scenarios.

Any investment in Salesforce Flow, by allowing time to study it, would not go to waste. On the contrary, when combined with LWC knowledge, it would be easily possible to provide highly maintainable solutions for clients.

Until now, we mostly worked inside Salesforce Platform, but as mentioned in *Chapter 1*, LWC was developed by Salesforce as an open-source JavaScript framework. This means it is possible to write LWCs outside of Salesforce, directly in other web applications. In the following chapter, we'll focus on how to achieve this.

References

- Lightning Flow Support - https://developer.salesforce.com/docs/component-library/bundle/lightning-flow-support/documentation
- LWC Best Practices for Screen Flows - https://developer.salesforce.com/blogs/2023/02/lwc-best-practices-for-screen-flows
- Build Flows with Flow Builder - https://trailhead.salesforce.com/content/learn/trails/build-flows-with-flow-builder

- Automate Your Business Processes with Salesforce Flow - https://trailhead.salesforce.com/content/learn/trails/automate_business_processes
- Go with the Flow: What's Happening with Workflow Rules and Process Builder? - https://admin.salesforce.com/blog/2021/go-with-the-flow-whats-happening-with-workflow-rules-and-process-builder

CHAPTER 7
Lightning Out

Introduction

Lightning Out is a feature of the Salesforce Platform that allows you to run LWCs (and/or Aura components) outside of Salesforce servers. Wherever our custom web application is hosted, we can easily run our LWCs (and/or Aura components) through a standalone Aura dependency app, which is embedded into the web application. `Lightning Out` is different than the `LWC Open Source`, which is a third-party JavaScript Framework (as demonstrated in *Chapter 1, Introduction*). Unlike `LWC Open Source`, `Lightning Out` enables to build Salesforce applications that can connect to the Salesforce database (via an active, valid Salesforce session ID), despite the fact that they are running within our custom web applications that are hosted outside of the Salesforce servers.

`Lightning Out` was first available for running Aura components; however, currently, it is also used to run LWCs. In this book, we'll focus only on its usage with LWCs.

We'll first start by investigating the differences between `Lightning Out` and `LWC Open Source`. Then, we'll build our first `Lightning Out` application for a Visualforce page. Finally, we'll show how to build a more complete `Lightning Out` application for a third-party custom web application hosted outside of Salesforce org.

Structure

In this chapter, we will discuss the following topics:

- Lightning Out vs LWC Open Source
- A simple Lightning Out to a Visualforce page
- Lightning Out to a third-party web application

Lightning Out vs LWC Open Source

In *Chapter* 1, we demonstrated how to install and use `LWC Open Source` to build a simple hello world site. `LWC Open Source` is open to the World (namely, to everyone), and we don't need to have a Salesforce subscription to use it. We can use it as a cutting-edge JavaScript Framework, much like we would with Angular.js, Vue.js, etc., in our custom web projects.

Similar to `LWC Open Source`, `Lightning Out` also lets us run LWCs outside of Salesforce, but with one big difference: we can directly access our Salesforce data while using `Lightning Out`.

Tip: It is also technically possible to access Salesforce data by using LWC Open Source. However, for achieving this, we need to use standard XHR requests in our JavaScript code (or any third-party npm packages will facilitate the process for us).

Briefly, LWC Open Source has no Salesforce-specific data access features like Lightning Data Service, instead we should build a custom connection with pure JavaScript codes.

`Lightning Out` uses `Salesforce Lightning Platform LWC`. The code in `LWC Open Source` is ahead of `Salesforce Lightning Platform LWC`. For `LWC Open Source`, there is a release approximately every week, but for the Salesforce Lightning Platform, there are three releases per year. In addition, Salesforce does not guarantee to support all `LWC Open Source` features.

Note: `Salesforce Lightning Platform LWC` is the managed version of `LWC Open Source`. Basically, the progress in `LWC Open Source` Salesforce takes what it needs from the open source project.

Both are using the same LWC engine but their configurations are different at the compiler level and runtime.

Throughout this book, we study `Salesforce Lightning Platform LWC`.

A simple Lightning Out to a Visualforce page

We'll start our "Lightning Out" journey by using a Visualforce page as the third-party application container. Despite being run by Salesforce org, Visualforce pages are treated differently than the LWCs, Aura components, Apex classes, etc. This example will give us the chance to understand how to expose an LWC by using `Lightning Out` without losing time for authentication matters (and for creating a "connected app") because while working with a Visualforce page, we don't need to manually capture the Salesforce session.

Note: `Lightning Out` does not have features for managing authentication and capturing Salesforce sessions. to simply the authentication token that is provided. So it is up to us to capture the **`session ID`** or **`OAuth token`** in our custom web application.

Let's start by defining a simple LWC that uses the wire service to capture all accounts and then prints these accounts' details on the screen:

lwcForLghtOutVFPage.js Controller:

```
import { LightningElement, wire } from 'lwc';
import getAccounts from '@salesforce/apex/simpleApexClass2.
getAllAccounts';
export default class LwcForLghtOutVFPage extends LightningElement {
    accounts;
    @wire(getAccounts, {}) wiredFunction({error, data}) {
        if(data) {
            this.accounts = data;
            console.log(this.accounts);
        }
        else if(error) {
            console.log("Error occurred while decorating the
'wiredFunction'.");
            console.log(error);
        }
```

```
    }
}
```

Wire service is a specific feature of the Salesforce Platform. This is why `Lightning Out` is the solution that we need to use here instead of `LWC Open Source`.

lwcForLghtOutVFPage.html Template:

```
<template>
    <h1><b>List of Accounts:</b></h1>
    <template for:each={accounts} for:item="acc">
        <p key={acc.Id}>{acc.Name}, {acc.Phone}</p>
    </template>
</template>
```

The Apex class that is used to query the accounts' data:

simpleApexClass2.cls Apex Class:

```
public with sharing class simpleApexClass2 {
    @AuraEnabled(cacheable=true)
    public static List<Account> getAllAccounts() {
        return [SELECT Id, Name, Phone FROM Account];
    }
}
```

To expose this LWC to a Visualforce page, we must first place it in an Aura dependency app. We can define one by using the "Developer Console" as follows:

1. In **`Developer Console`**, first select **`New → Lightning Application:`**

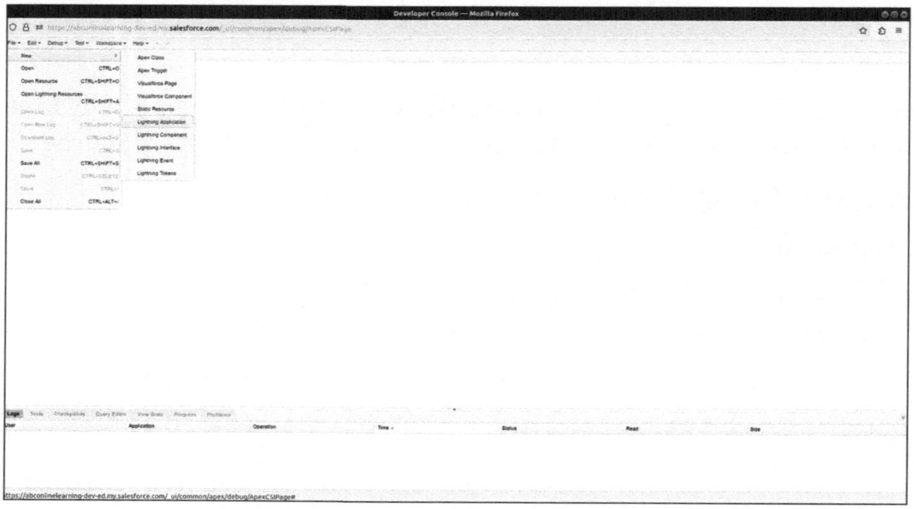

Figure 7.1: *Selecting the Lightning Application menu*

2. Then, provide a name and check the **`Lightning Out Dependency App`** checkbox:

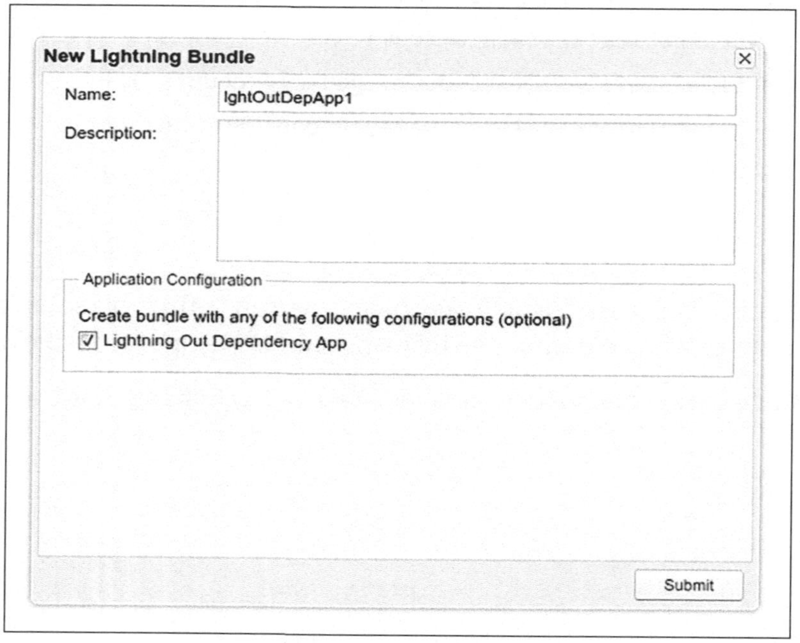

Figure 7.2: *Checking the Lightning Out Dependency App checkbox*

3. As we created it directly via **`Developer Console`**, it is already deployed in the Salesforce org; so, we can simply edit it in **`Developer Console`**:

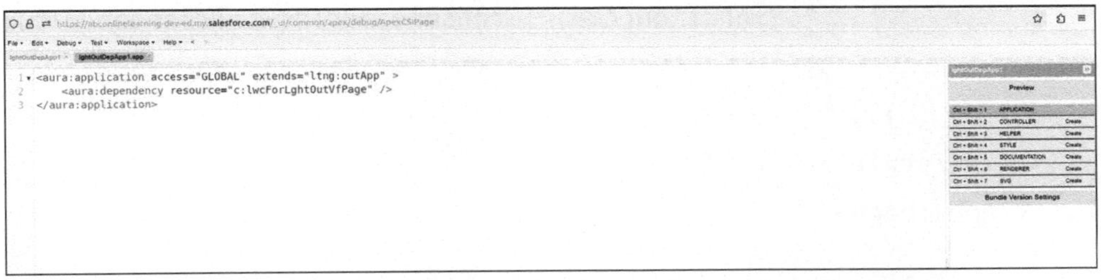

Figure 7.3: *Creation of Aura dependency application and editing it to include our LWC as a dependency*

Here, in this application, the access should be defined as `GLOBAL`. Currently, the application is extended as `ltng:outApp`, which means we will use the standard

Lightning Design System for the styling of the components. If we want to use our own CSS styling instead of the standard Lightning Design System, we should use `ltng:outAppUnstyled` instead of ltgn:outApp.

Note: We'll investigate the Lightning Design System in detail in *Chapter 8, Salesforce Lightning Design System.*

In the application, we have added only one `aura:dependency` tag, because in this example, we only have one LWC that we want to expose via `Lightning Out`. However, it is possible to add as many `aura:dependency` tags as we want according to our needs in a real-life application.

Now, we're ready to expose our LWC to a Visualforce page:

lghtOutContainer.page Visualforce Page:

```
<apex:page>
    <apex:includeLightning/>

    <div id=”lwc2Here” />

    <script type=”text/javascript”>
        $Lightning.use(“c:lghtOutDepApp1”, function() {
            $Lightning.createComponent(
                “c:lwcForLghtOutVFPage”,
                {},
                “lwc2Here”,
```

```
                function(cmp) { console.log("LWC is created!"); }
            );
        });
    </script>
</apex:page>
```

Here, `<apex:includeLightning/>` takes care of all the JavaScript imports and session management for running the `Lightning Out` in the Visualforce page.

The `<div id="lwc2Here"/>` is the placeholder for our LWC. This allows us to mark the place where "`lwcForLghtOutVFPage`" component should be added when the page is loaded.

`$Lightning.use` and `$Lightning.createComponent` functions are where the magic happens:

- Both functions can be used more than once within the same page, but they should always refer to the same Aura dependency app and its components.
- **`$Lightning.use`** is used to specify the Aura dependency app that we've created in **`Developer Console`**. It can take four arguments as follows:
    - **`appName`**: Its type is string and it is required. This refers to the name of the Aura dependency app. In our example, we assign `c:lghtOutDepApp1` as its value.
    - **`callback`**: Its type is function. It is the callback function that is called when our Aura dependency app is fully loaded, and it takes no arguments. It is generally used (as also seen in our example) to call `$Lightning.createComponent` function, which is responsible for adding and running LWCs.
    - **`lightningEndPointURI`**: Its type is string. It is the URL for the Lightning domain on our Salesforce instance. In our example, as we are not using a third-party application but a Visualforce page, we didn't need to use it.
    - **`authToken`**: Its type is string. It is the session ID (or OAuth access token) for a valid, active Salesforce session. As mentioned previously, `Lightning Out` does not have mechanisms to automatically capture authorization tokens for us, so before adding this argument, we need to obtain tokens first. Again, in our example, as we are not using a Visualforce page for the container custom web application page, we don't need to use this argument either.

- As mentioned above, **`$Lightning.createComponent`** function is responsible for adding and activating the LWCs on the page. It can take four arguments as follows:
    - **`componentName`**: Its type is string and it is required. It refers to the name of the component that we want to add. In our example, we assign `c:lwcForLghtOutVFPage` as its value.
    - **`attributes`**: Its type is object and it is required. It defines the attributes of the component. If the component does not have any attribute, then we can define empty `{}`, as we did in our example.
    - **`domLocator`**: Its type is string (or DOM element) and it is required. It holds the DOM element or the element ID under which we want to add our component. In our example, we assign `lwc2Here` as its value.
    - **`callback`**: Its type is function. It is the callback function that is called when the component is added and is activated on the page. It takes the created component as the only argument. In our example, we define it to log a `LWC is created!` message on the console.

Tip: Lightning components through `Lightning Out` set cookies in users' browsers as they are served from different domains than the container web pages (even if container pages are Visualforce pages), users must allow third-party cookies in their browsers.

For Safari browsers, it is also needed to disable **`prevent cross-site tracking`** setting.

Consequently, when we deploy and run this Visualforce page, we see that it successfully adds and runs our LWC:

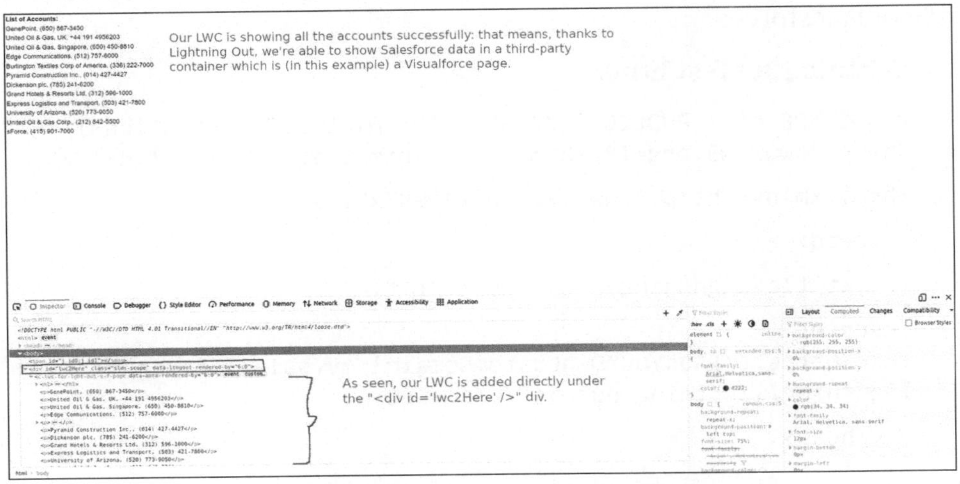

***Figure 7.4:** Visualforce page is working as expected*

Tip: In this example, while working with the components we use `c:` default namespace because none of components belong to a managed package. However, whenever we have a custom namespace for a component, we need to use it instead of `c:` default namespace.

If our `lwcForLghtOutVFPage` component had some child components, all of would be exposed automatically in the Visualforce page without needing to separately call the child components.

Lightning Out to a third-party web application

In the previous section, we used `Lightning Out` to load and use an LWC in a Visualforce page. Despite the Visualforce page is delivered by our Salesforce org from a different domain than our Aura dependency app, as already all the related metadata (Visualforce page, Aura dependency app, and LWC) are published from this same Salesforce org, we didn't need to configure any authentication procedure: the user session was directly active and valid throughout all metadata. However, in this section, we're going to use `Lightning Out` in a third-party web application, which is not hosted in Salesforce servers. Thus, we will have the chance to see how to do the configurations and implementations for capturing an active Salesforce session for a third-party web application to run an LWC via `Lightning Out`.

In this example, we will not be updating our previous Aura dependency app and LWC. Instead, we will focus on creating a new web page that will be hosted outside of Salesforce:

lightningOutTest.html:

```
<!DOCTYPE html PUBLIC "-//W3C//DTD XHTML 1.0 Transitional//EN"
"http://www.w3.org/TR/xhtml1/DTD/xhtml1-transitional.dtd">

<html xmlns="http://www.w3.org/1999/xhtml">

  <head>

    <title>Lightning Out - Test</title>

 <script
src="https://[AddYourOwnCustomDomain].my.salesforce.com/
lightning/lightning.out.js"></script>

  </head>
```

```
<body>
  <div id="lwc2Here" />
  Lightning Out - Testing...
  <script type="text/javascript">
      $Lightning.use("c:lghtOutDepApp1", function() {
          $Lightning.createComponent(
              "c:lwcForLghtOutVFPage",
              {},
              "lwc2Here",
              function(cmp) { console.log("LWC is created!"); }
          );
      },
      "https://[AddYourOwnCustomDomain].lightning.force.com]",
      "[AddYourOwnSESSIONID]");
  </script>
 </body>
</html>
```

This web page (`lightningOutTest.html`) is almost the same as our previous Visualforce page (`lghtOutContainer.page`), with only two differences:

1. In the previous Visualforce page, we've called the `Lightning Out` JavaScript library by using the standard Visualforce page tag: `<apex:includeLightning/>`. However, in this case, we directly call this JavaScript library by using the following explicit script tag:

   ```
   <script src="https://[AddYourOwnCustomDomain].my.salesforce.com/
   lightning/lightning.out.js"></script>
   ```

2. In the previous Visualforce page, as no authentication was required, the `$Lightning.use()` function had only two parameters: the name of the Aura dependency app and the function for creating our LWC `lwcForLghtOutVFPage`. However, in this third-party web page, we added the third `lightningEndPointURI` and the fourth `authToken` parameters into it.

```
   "https://[AddYourOwnCustomDomain].lightning.force.com]",
//lightningEndPointURI
      "[AddYourOwnSESSIONID]" // authToken
```

Note: Throughout this book, we're using a Salesforce developer edition org has a custom my domain **`abconlinelearning-dev-ed`**. So, in our working copy of `lightningOutTest.html` web page, the script of the `lightning.out.js` is called as:

```
                    <script src= "https://abconlinelearning-dev-ed.
      my.salesforce.com/lightning/lightning.out.js"></script>
```

And respectively the third parameter `lightningEndPointURI` of the `$Lightning.use()` function is defined as follows:

```
                    https://abconlinelearning-dev-ed.lightning.force.com
```

Henceforth, before deploying and running `lightningOutTest.html` in a web server, **`[AddYourOwnCustomDomain]`** parts of the code should be replaced with the custom **`my domain`** of the current Salesforce org.

Tip: To define and/or see **`my domain`** of a Salesforce org, we can visit

`Setup → Company Settings → My Domain` page.

The fourth parameter of the `$Lightning.use()` function is `authToken`, as previously discussed. We can have an `authToken` via two ways: either as the `session ID` of the current user or as an `OAuth access token` that can be captured via a connection to an **OAuth Connected App.**

In this chapter, for the sake of simplicity, we run our example by using the hard-coded `session ID` of the connected active user instead of a dynamic `OAuth access token`. For capturing dynamically an `OAuth access token`, first we need to create a **Connected App** in Salesforce Setup. And then we need to add backend code to our web application to capture `OAuth access token` by following the same process that we would use to obtain an authenticated session to use with the REST API.

As mentioned, here we want to keep our third-party web page (`lightningOutTest.html`) simple, without having any backend code; namely, a one-pager application that is just formed of pure HTML and JavaScript. For this reason, in this example, we use a hard-coded `session ID` for an `authToken` parameter of the `$Lightning.use()` function.

Similar to **`my domain`** of a Salesforce org, the `session ID` is also specific to the Salesforce org, frankly to the logged-in active user. Therefore, before running this example on a third-party web server, the `session ID` of the current Salesforce user should be obtained.

Note: We can obtain the `session ID` of our current user by running code line in the **Execute Anonymous Window** of our Developer Console:

```
System.debug(UserInfo.getOrganizationId()+UserInfo.
getSessionId().substring(15));
```

(refer to *Figure 7.5*)

Figure 7.5: *Code line for obtaining the current session ID*

Once the current `session ID` is obtained, we need to replace **`[AddYourOwnSESSIONID]`** part of the `lightningOutTest.html` web page with this `session ID`.

Note: The **`[AddYourOwnCustomDomain]`** and **`[AddYourOwnSESSIONID]`** parts as explained, before starting to test this html page (`lightningOutTest.html`), we need to deploy it to a third-party hosting. his requirement is the scope of this book and should be accomplished by the reader.

In our example, we deploy it to `https://www.abccloudservices.co.uk` domain's root folder in order to call it by using `https://www.abccloudservices.co.uk/lightningOutTest.html` address.

When we deploy and then open the (`lightningOutTest.html`) page in our browser, an error is encountered: **`...the same origin policy disallows reading the remote resource....`**Due to security restrictions, Salesforce delivers its functions and runs them only in the allowed origins. So here, we need to add our third-party web server's domain under **`Setup → CORS`** to show Salesforce that this domain is trusted by us.

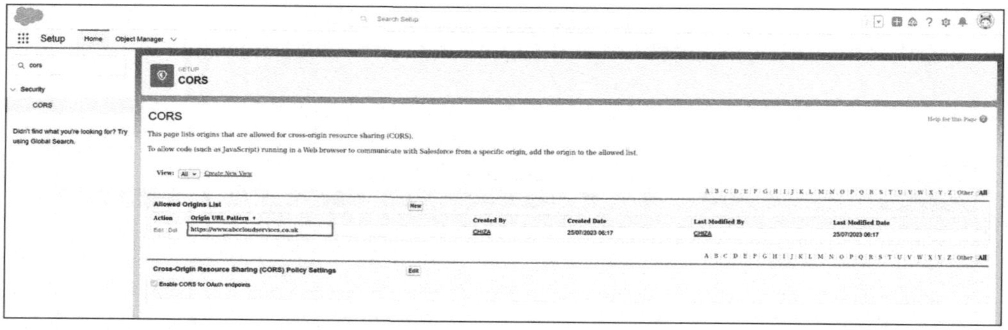

Figure 7.6: *Adding our third-party domain into Cross-Origin Resource Sharing (CORS)*

And when we reload the page, bingo! All the accounts are now visible.

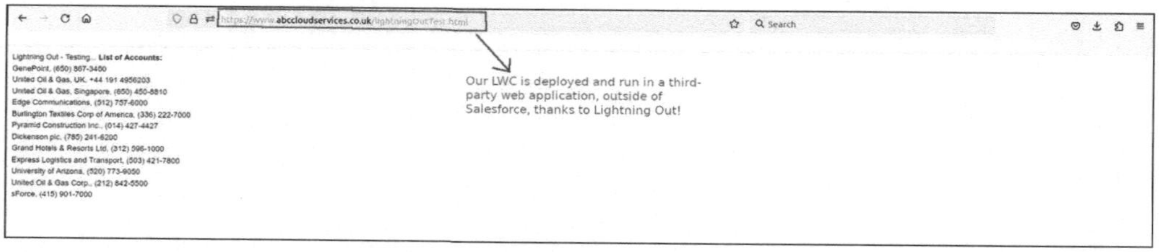

Figure 7.7: *Our LWC, hosted on a third-party domain, is showing our Salesforce data*

One thing to note is that the listed data of this LWC will be dependent on the `session ID` of the user. So, only the records that this user has access will be shown on the screen. Similarly, if we have used `OAuth Access Token` instead of `session ID`, then the records that will be listed here would be determined according to the `OAuth scope` of the **Connected App.**

Share Lightning Out with Guest Users

By default, `Lightning Out` delivers components for authenticated users. However, if we do a small update in our Aura dependency app, it is also possible to publish components via Lightning Out to **unauthenticated** guest users:

```
<aura:application access="GLOBAL" extends="ltng:outApp"
implements="ltng:allowGuestAccess">
    <aura:dependency resource="c:lwcForLghtOutVFPage" />
</aura:application>
```

Briefly, as seen previously, the only thing we need to do is to implement the `ltgn:allowGuestAccess` interface in our Aura dependency app.

We can have **guest users** in our Salesforce org only if we use Experience Cloud sites. Thus, this feature can only be used when we have Experience Cloud sites. However, we need to be cautious with this feature because when the apps are shared with guest users, even if the Experience Cloud sites are not enabled for public access, any guest user, who (by chance) knows the URL of the `Lightning Out` page, can open it. Furthermore, the apps that are enabled for guest access will bypass object and field-level security. Briefly, we need to be extremely cautious and must test the apps very well when they're published to the outside world.

Conclusion

At the time of writing this book (Winter '24 release), `Lightning Out` continues to be in **Beta** version. However, as seen in this chapter, despite not yet being generally available, it is already a very powerful feature, opening doors for diverse use cases as follows:

- We can build custom web pages in our intranet, which will be able to use Salesforce data.
- We can partially add custom LWCs into our custom web applications.

- We can create custom pages for outside guest users by using our custom LWCs.
- If it is hard to upgrade our Visualforce pages for some technical and/or business reasons in our Salesforce org, we can use `Lightning Out` to integrate LWCs into our Visualforce pages to quickly modernize them.
- And many other use cases that involve building outside applications that can easily use Salesforce data.

In addition to its modern JavaScript features, LWCs' design is also newsworthy. In the next chapter, we'll focus on the Lightning Design System, which is the modern design system behind the Salesforce Lightning interface.

References

- Lightning Web Components: Open Source - https://developer.salesforce.com/docs/component-library/documentation/en/lwc/lwc.get_started_oss
- Differences Between Building Lightning Web Components on Lightning Platform and Open Source - https://developer.salesforce.com/blogs/2019/06/differences-between-building-lightning-web-components-on-lightning-platform-and-open-source
- Use Components in Visualforce Pages - https://developer.salesforce.com/docs/platform/lwc/guide/use-visualforce.html
- Lightning Out Supports Lightning Web Components (LWC) – Explained! - https://eltoroit.medium.com/lightning-web-components-support-lightning-out-5a79c513302f

CHAPTER 8

Salesforce Lightning Design System

Introduction

Salesforce Lightning Design System (SLDS) is the design system of Salesforce that is used both internally and externally. It is a system that was created to standardize the look and feel of the Lightning interface for standard Salesforce applications and components that are developed internally by Salesforce, as well as for any custom applications and components that are developed by external Salesforce development experts. Briefly, if we develop for the Salesforce Lightning interface, this is the standard design system that we use for styling our applications, components, and so on.

We call it a design **system** rather than a **CSS framework** because it also includes various design guidelines to help developers in creating pages and apps like the existing pages and apps of Salesforce, ensuring consistency in end users' experiences.

We begin this chapter by overviewing the features of SLDS. Then, we'll proceed to learn how to use SLDS in our LWCs. Before concluding the chapter, we'll also look at the mobile app design principles to have a complete 360-degree view for every aspect of designing applications.

Structure

In this chapter, we will discuss the following topics:

- SLDS overview
- SLDS in action
- Mobile application design principles

SLDS overview

Salesforce Lightning Design System (SLDS) is a living, open-source, enterprise, accessible, and framework-agnostic design system. It is considered living because it is continuously updated, three times per year, with Salesforce releases. It is open-source; its codebase is publicly available on GitHub at https://github.com/salesforce-ux/design-system. We describe it as enterprise because it is scalable, testable, reliable, and compatible with the latest technologies. Nevertheless, accessibility is the core strength of SLDS, as it is developed keeping all the users in mind, regardless of any disadvantages they may have. Last but not least, it is built as framework-agnostic, which means it can be used not only with the LWC framework but also with any other JS framework, such as `React.js`, `Angular.js`, and more in their applications.

There are four principles behind SLDS as follows:

- Clarity
- Efficiency
- Consistency
- Beauty

They are self-explanatory, so we don't need to provide much explanation here. However, we can briefly mention that Salesforce is improving SLDS in each release by taking into account these four principles.

The main features of SLDS are as follows:

- Design guidelines, patterns, accessibility
- Component blueprints
- Utility classes
- Design tokens
- Ready-to-use resources like icons

Let's examine each one of them.

Design guidelines, patterns, and accessibility

Design guidelines are the patterns that aim to ensure a common experience for repeatable design needs. They are important for Salesforce to maintain a consistent look and feel, even for custom applications, regarding the end users' experiences. During the writing of this book, SLDS contains twenty guidelines:

- **Builder:** This is the pattern for showing how to fulfill the needs when developing applications that are used to create wizards, flows, and more. Some examples of standard builder applications are Lightning App Builder, Flow Builder, and Experience Builder.
- **Color:** It focuses on how to use colors in an application, based on Color Theory.
- **Conversation design:** This is the pattern for designing chat popups.
- **Data entry:** This is the pattern for various input fields.
- **Data visualization:** It shows how to work with visual charts.
- **Displaying data:** This is the pattern for working with data tables and feeds.
- **Empty state:** This is the pattern for empty result pages.
- **Iconography:** It focuses on the usage of icons and their different states.
- **In-app feedback:** It explains how to get user feedback in an application.
- **Layout:** It focuses on different layout types for various needs.
- **Loading:** It describes the needed experience while users are waiting for data to load.
- **Localization:** This is the pattern for resolving internationalization needs in an application.
- **Markup and style:** It shows the best practices for working with CSS markups.
- **Messaging UI:** We can say that this is the parent pattern of the previously mentioned `conversation design` pattern. It focuses more generally on business user–customer messaging needs.
- **Navigation:** It shows how to implement different navigation types like tabs, breadcrumbs, modals, and more.
- **Notifications:** It is related to how to notify users.
- **Rules, Filters, and Logic:** It is about how to design filtering mechanisms and data rules for providing the best experience to users dealing with large data sets.
- **Search:** It is all about the usage of the search box, whether it is a global search or a local search.
- **User engagement:** it is a very important pattern that deals with the fast and reliable adaptation of the Salesforce end users.
- **Voice and tone:** It is for ensuring that the custom applications have also a similar voice and tone as existing standard Salesforce applications.

Here, we have shared brief information for each of them, as this book is for the developers rather than the designers. However, one can find all the details on the official SLDS website. Please refer to the *References* section of this chapter for its web address.

Note: In design guidelines, only theoretical information but also a chance to design screens by implementing those patterns via design kits reside Figma platform: https://www.figma.com/@salesforce

By creating a Figma account, we can directly open various design kits added by Salesforce and utilize them as the basis for our own designs.

As mentioned previously, accessibility is very important for Salesforce. Currently, SLDS comprehends all aspects of accessibility as follows:

- Use of ARIA roles in components, based on W3C standards
- Keyboard navigation patterns
- Appropriate use of color
- Accessible forms
- How the different components should behave

Salesforce has also developed **`Build with Intention`** workshops to assure that any of the products and applications that are developed by Salesforce do not unintentionally harm or negatively affect people in areas like inclusion, accessibility, and ethics.

So, being Salesforce experts, we also need to do our part and ensure that our custom applications include all the accessibility patterns to cover the maximum number of users. To validate whether our application is accessible or not, we can use the **sa11y** tool, which was created by Salesforce. It is a set of JavaScript libraries, which are delivered as an open-source project on GitHub. (For the links, please refer to the *References* section of this chapter.)

Component blueprints

Component blueprints are the HTML–CSS implementations for almost all the UI elements that a website would need. We can divide them into two categories:

- **Base components:** The smallest atomic re-usable piece of the UI like buttons, icons, input elements, and more. Base components can be used either independently or in the experience components.

- **Experience components:** A composition of many base components, solving specific problems like color picking, app launching, text editing, and more.

The current list of component blueprints is as follows:

- **Accordion:** It allows a user to toggle the display of a section of content.
- **Activity Timeline:** It displays each of the user's upcoming, current, and past activities.

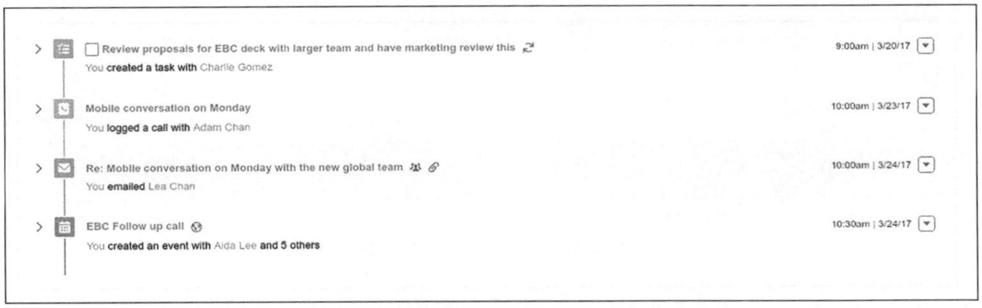

Figure 8.1: *Activity Timeline*

- **Alert:** it is a banner type that communicates a state (like info, warning, error, and more) that affects the entire system, not just a feature or page.

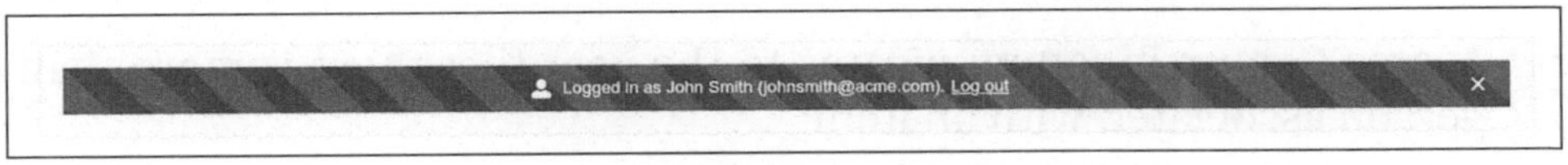

Figure 8.2: *Alert*

- **App Launcher:** it allows the user to quickly access all the apps and functionalities within the organization.

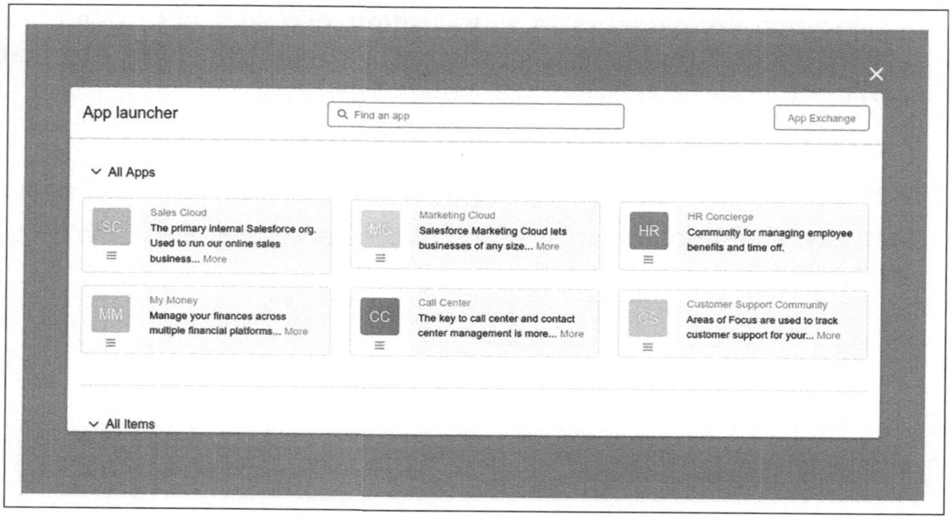

Figure 8.3: *App Launcher*

- **Avatar:** It represents an object or entity.

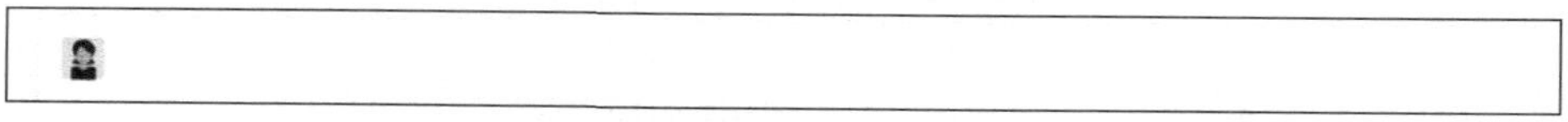

Figure 8.4: *Avatar*

- **Avatar Group:** It communicates to the user that there is more than one person associated with an item.

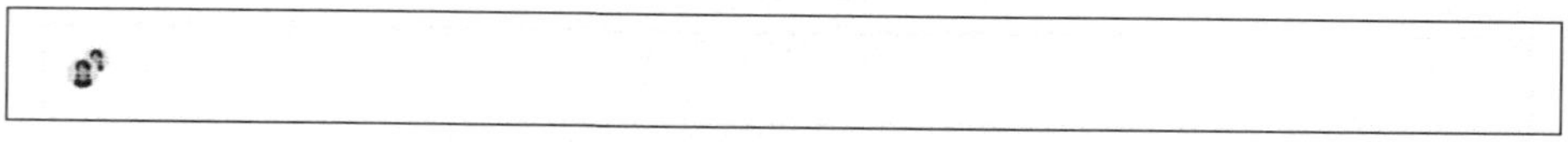

Figure 8.5: *Avatar Group*

- **Badge:** It is a label that holds small amounts of information.
- **Brand band:** It provides theming capability and improves contrast.

Figure 8.6: *Brand Band*

- **Breadcrumbs:** A navigation component to note the path of the current page.
- **Builder Header:** A header of builder applications. It contains basic navigation elements, builder type, and content name.

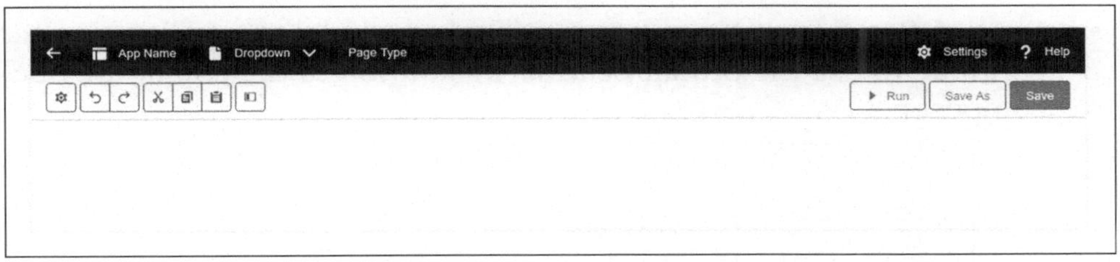

Figure 8.7: *Builder Header*

- **Button Group:** A group of buttons with similar actions.
- **Button Icon:** A button without text with visual iconography.
- **Button:** A clickable item to perform an action.
- **Card:** A container around a related grouping of information.

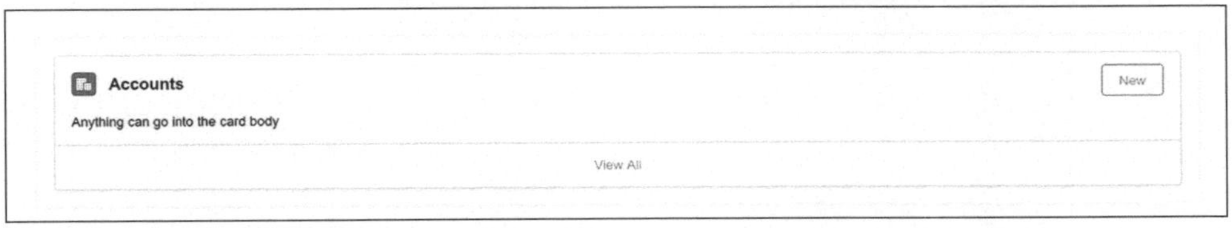

Figure 8.8: *Card*

- **Carousel:** A multiple pieces of featured content like images, videos that occupies an allocated amount of space.
- **Chat:** For displaying real-time and past chat logs between users and customers.
- **Checkbox:** A standard checkable input field.
- **Checkbox Button:** A checkbox in button format that changes images or colors when clicked.
- **Checkbox Button Group:** A group of similar checkbox buttons.
- **Checkbox Toggle:** A checkbox that is like a toggle switch.
- **Color Picker:** An interface for color selection.
- **Combobox:** An input field that is accompanied by a listbox of options, where a user can select one option or filter the option list by entering text in the input field.
- **Counter:** It allows a user to increase or decrease a numerical value.

- **Data Table:** An enhanced version of an HTML table that is used to display tabular data.
- **Date Picker:** It is a text input to capture a date.
- **Datetime Picker:** It is used to select a day and a time.
- **Docked Composer:** A persistent utility bar window that allows a user to continue to use the primary canvas in addition to the app in the docked composer.

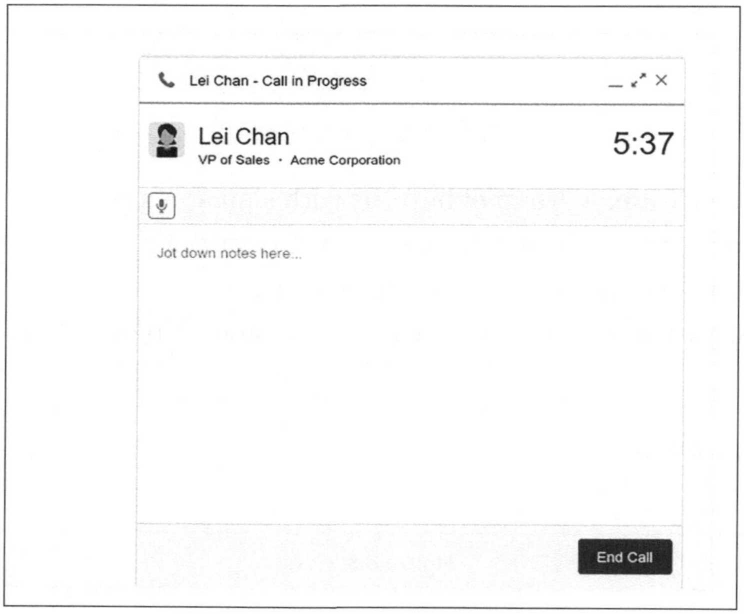

Figure 8.9: *Docked Composer*

- **Docked Form Footer:** It is used to dock form actions to the bottom of the viewport.

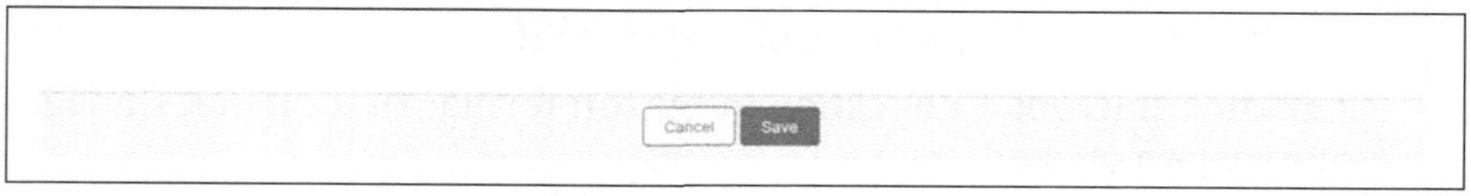

Figure 8.10: *Docked Form Footer*

- **Docked Utility Bar:** A persistent bar that allows the expansion/collapse of different docked composers.

Figure 8.11: *Docked Utility Bar*

- **Drop Zone:** For dragging and dropping components onto a page.
- **Dueling Picklist:** It is used to move options between two lists and is often referred to as a multi-select.
- **Dynamic Icon:** Animated icon.
- **Dynamic Menu:** A menu item that includes a number of actions to take.
- **Expendable Section:** It toggles the visibility of section content.
- **Expression Builder:** It helps the user to declaratively construct logical expressions.

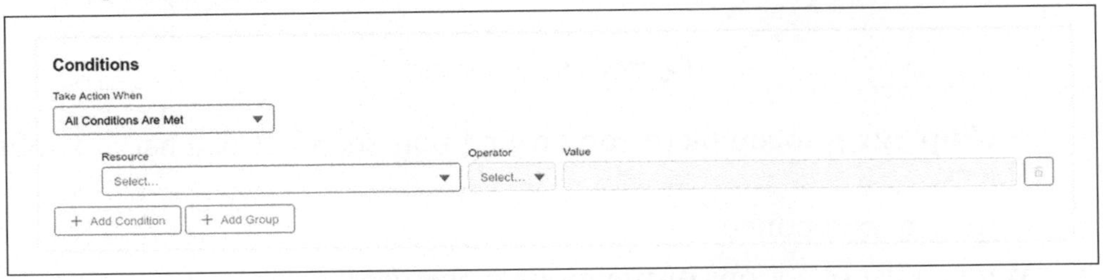

Figure 8.12: *Expression Builder*

- **Feed:** A list of recurring elements of similar types like a discussion feed.
- **File Selector:** It allows the user to select file(s) from the computer's file system.
- **File:** A representation of content uploaded as an attachment.

- **Form Element:** It contains an HTML input element paired with a label.
- **Global Header:** A header that is shown in every application of the organization.
- **Global Navigation:** A navigation component that is used in every application of the organization.
- **Icons:** They provide visual context and enhance usability.
- **Illustration:** It is an image and inline text that communicates a state in a more friendly way (for example, `Page not found` page.)
- **Input:** For freeform data entry.
- **List Builder:** A quick, visual, and efficient approach to adding multiple items to a parent object.

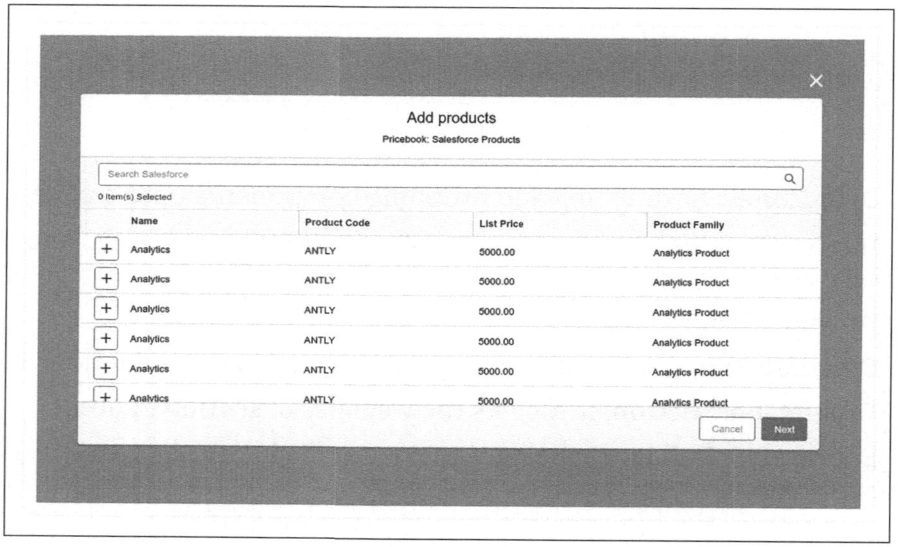

Figure 8.13: *List Builder*

- **Lookup:** An autocomplete combo-box that searches against a database object.
- **Map:** Map component.
- **Menu:** A list of actions or functions that a user can access.
- **Modal:** Popup windows to display content in a layer above the app. They can have various types, such as static texts, wizards, and more.
- **Notification:** It serves as a feedback and confirmation mechanism.
- **Page Header:** It is used at the top of several page types and contains the title of the page.

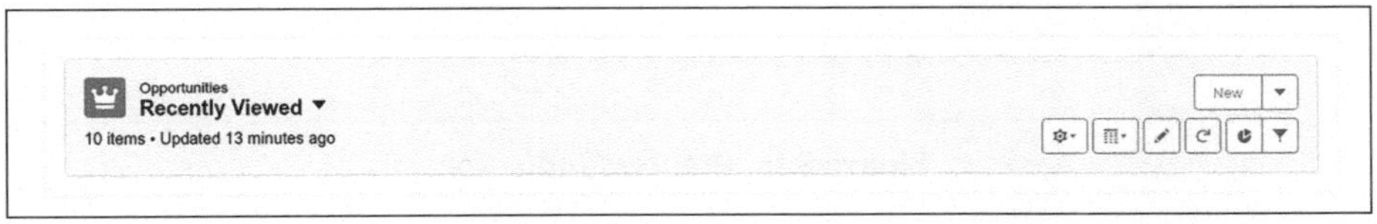

Figure 8.14: *Page Header*

- **Panel:** It is used to provide supplemental information or form inputs related to the primary canvas.

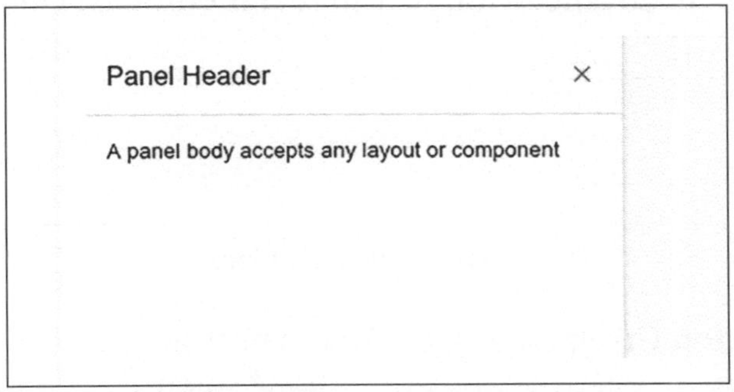

Figure 8.15: *Panel*

- **Path:** It communicates the progress of a particular process in a discrete way.

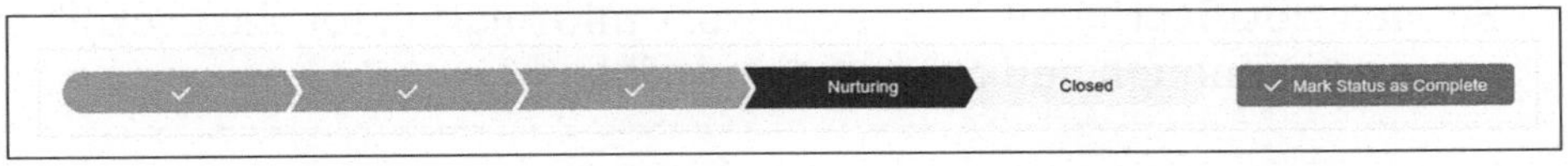

Figure 8.16: *Path*

- **Picklist:** A similar component to an HTML select element. It can have either a single or multi-select pattern.
- **Pill:** It represents an object, used mostly as selected tags or for communicating the selected items/filters/options on the page.

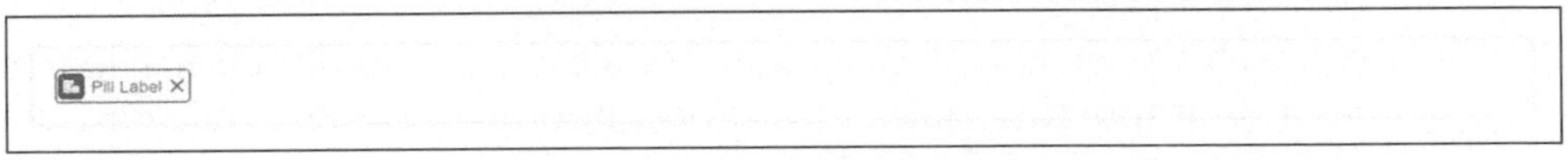

Figure 8.17: *Pill*

- **Popover:** It is used to display contextual information.
- **Progress Bar:** It communicates the progress of a particular process in a continuous way.
- **Progress Indicator:** It communicates the progress of a particular process of a wizard.

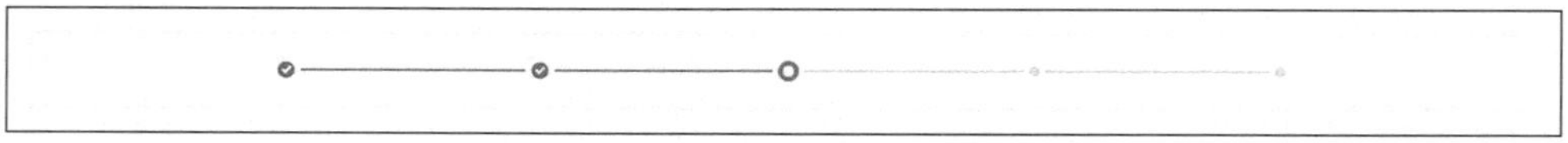

Figure 8.18: *Progress Indicator*

- **Progress Ring:** A circle version of a progress bar.
- **Prompt:** It is a popup to grab the attention of the user for alerting him/her about a system-related issue.
- **Publisher:** An advanced long-form text input form element.

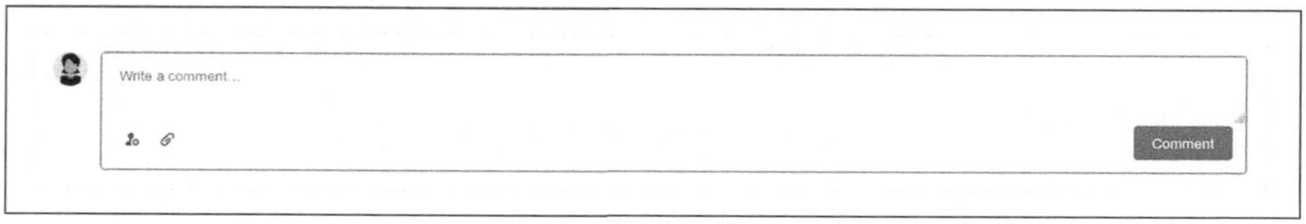

Figure 8.19: *Publisher*

- **Radio Button Group:** A group of radio buttons.
- **Radio Group:** A group of radio inputs, where only one option can be selected.
- **Rich Text Editor:** It is a text area with added capabilities for use in various publishers.
- **Scoped Notification:** It serves advisory information for the user. They are important enough and are not dismissible.

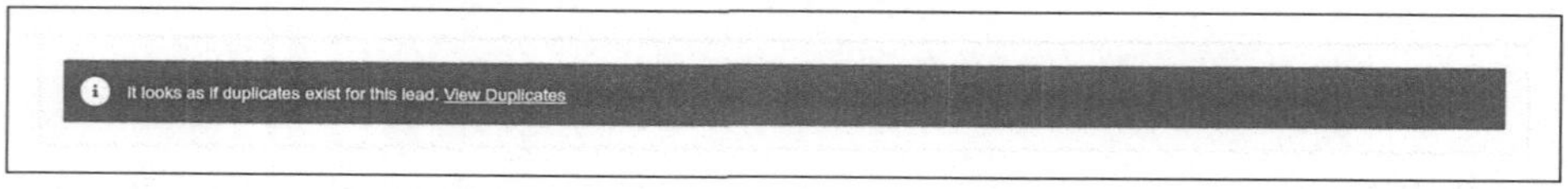

Figure 8.20: *Scoped Notification*

- **Scoped Tab:** A tab in which the content of the selected tab is bordered.
- **Select:** HTML select element.
- **Setup Assistant:** It is a large panel consisting of guidance for learning, configuring, importing data, and more, about a process that can take a considerable amount of time (hours to days).

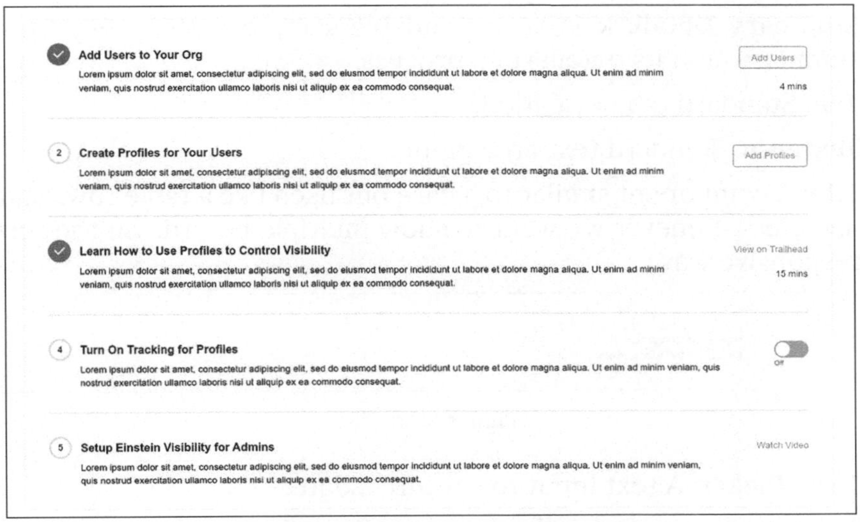

Figure 8.21: *Setup Assistant*

- **Slider:** An input slider that lets the user specify a numeric value between a min and a max value.
- **Spinner:** A CSS loading indicator.
- **Split View:** It is a panel on the left and the main page on the right layout, which permits the user to navigate between records while staying on the same screen.

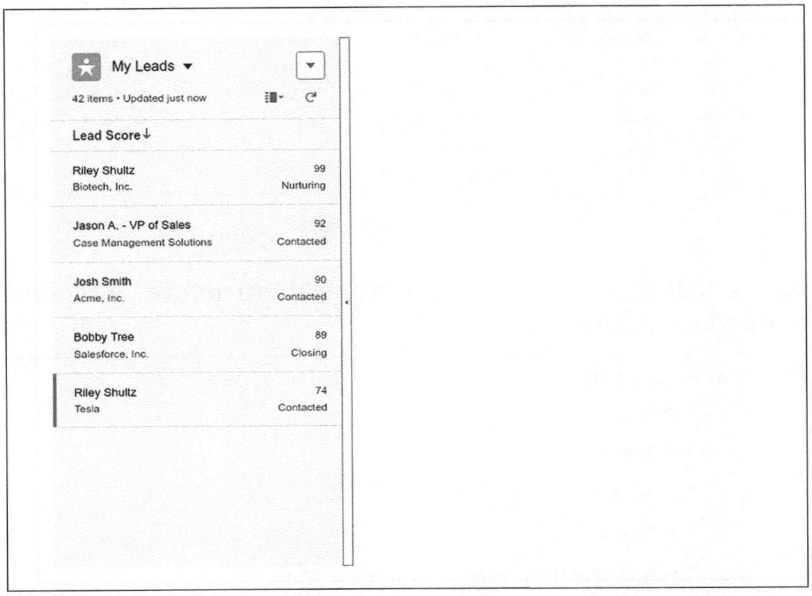

Figure 8.22: *Split View*

- **Summary Detail:** It is an expendable section with a badge to show a summary (and its details) of a process.
- **Tab:** Standard tab navigation.
- **Textarea:** Standard text area input.
- **Tile:** A component similar to a card but used like a table row. Namely, we use tiles whenever we want to show multiple records on the screen in a responsive way.

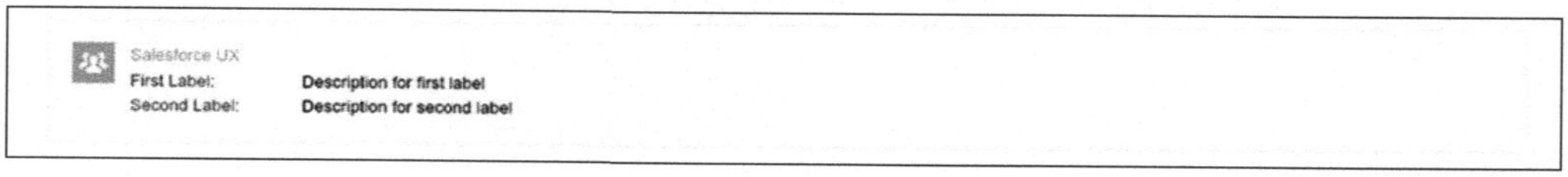

Figure 8.23: *Tile*

- **Time Picker:** A text input to capture a date.
- **Toast:** It serves as a feedback and confirmation mechanism after the user takes action. It is similar to the scoped notification but can be dismissed.
- **Tooltip:** It is a small piece of contextual information about an element on the screen, which is displayed when the user hovers or focuses on the element.
- **Tree Grid:** A visualization of a hierarchical structure, implemented similarly to an HTML table component. Branches can be expanded or collapsed.

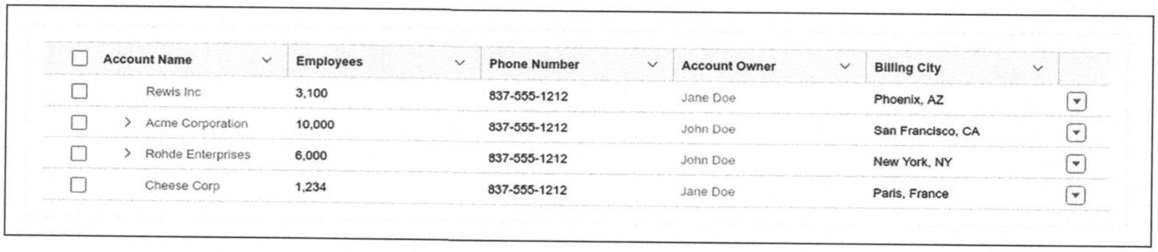

Figure 8.24: *Tree Grid*

- **Tree:** A visualization of a hierarchical structure. Branches can be expanded or collapsed.

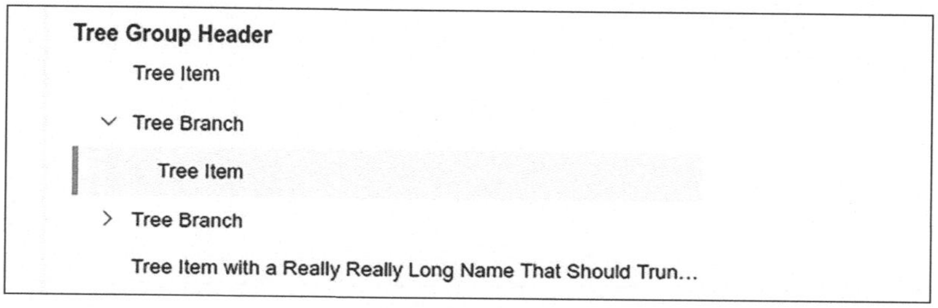

Figure 8.25: *Tree*

- **Trial Bar:** It is used to provide an interactive and educational prospect experience for setup.

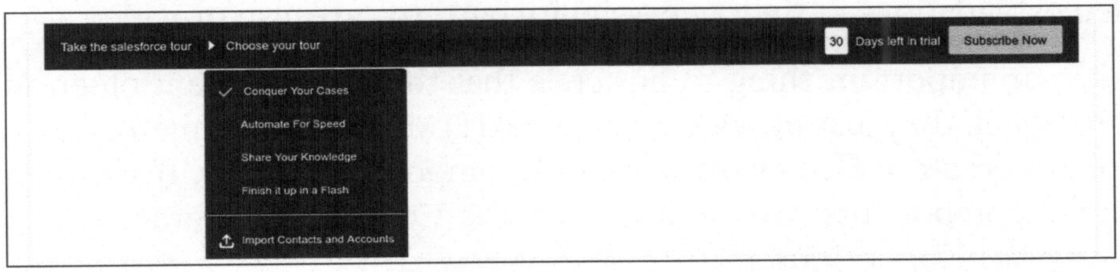

Figure 8.26: *Trial Bar*

- **Vertical Navigation:** A navigation that is designed vertically.
- **Vertical Tab:** A tab navigation that is designed vertically.
- **Visual Picker:** It can be either radio buttons, checkboxes, or links that are visually enhanced.

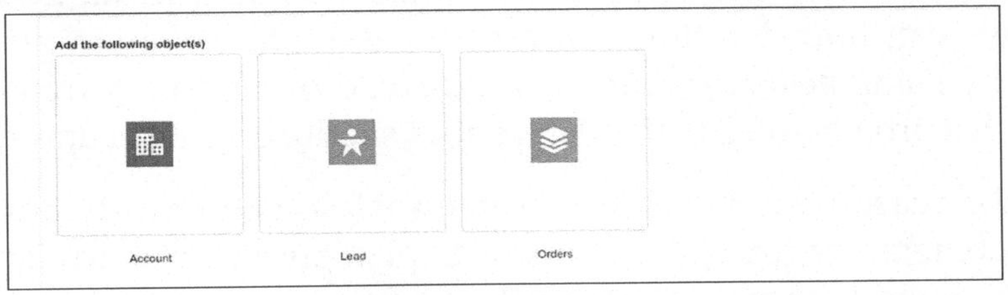

Figure 8.27: *Visual Picker*

- **Welcome Mat:** It provides a series of unordered items that a user can click to learn about a thematic topic.

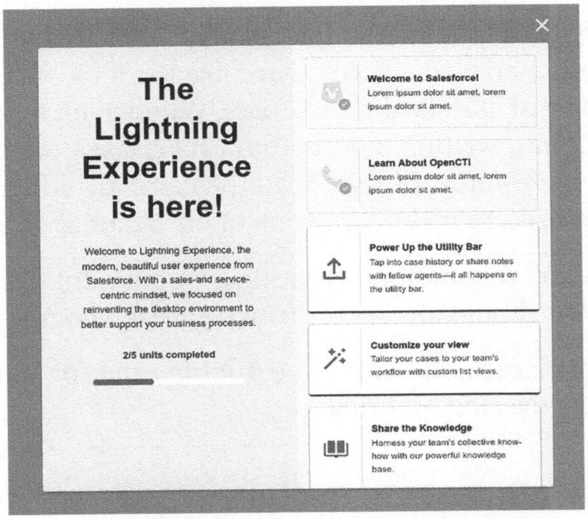

Figure 8.28: *Welcome Mat*

To underscore again, all of these blueprints have the HTML–CSS implementations available on the official Salesforce Lightning Design System website. In addition, detailed explanations of their accessibility patterns are also provided.

However, an important thing to notice is that these component blueprints are not functional; they just provide a universal HTML–CSS implementation to help developers create a framework-agnostic component quickly. If we search for functional components, we need to visit the Component Library page in the Lightning Developer Center:

https://developer.salesforce.com/docs/component-library/overview/components

This page, as we already know, comprehends all the implementation of LWC and Aura standard components.

Note: There is also an another opensource project called **Lightning Design System for React** we can find this time the functional implementation of component blueprints by using `React.js` framework instead of Lightning framework. (For the link of this project, please the References section of this chapter.)

So, that's the reason we mentioned **framework-agnosticwhile** describing the component blueprints can be functionally implemented by Lightning framework `React.js` framework or any other JavaScript framework as they have universal HTML–CSS implementation ready-to-be-used by any JavaScript library.

Utility Classes

Despite the fact that component blueprints may fulfill almost all of our UI needs, there may be times when we need to customize the look of components and/or fine-tune the styling of standard HTML tags. When such a need arises, instead of directly jumping into writing our custom CSS classes, we should first look at SLDS because the Salesforce Design Team has already added many CSS utility classes that can be used to meet almost all of our standard CSS styling needs.

Tip: Salesforce doesn't recommend creating a component from scratch by using the utility classes we should always prioritize existing component blueprints.

Ultimately, utility classes are for fine-tuning and/or customizing HTML components, re-discovering America.

Here is the list of the utility classes, as of the Winter '24 release:

- **Alignment**
  - **slds-align_absolute-center**: It absolutely centers the content
- **Borders**
  - **slds-border_bottom**
  - **slds-border_left**
  - **slds-border_right**
  - **slds-border_top**
- **Box and Themes**
  - **slds-box**: Regular box around the element
  - **slds-box slds-box_small**: Small box
  - **slds-box slds-box_x-small**: Extra-small box
  - **slds-box slds-box_xx-small**: Extra-extra-small box
  - **slds-box slds-theme_default**: Box with white background color
  - **slds-box slds-theme_shade**: Box with gray background color
  - **slds-box slds-theme_inverse**: Box with dark blue background color
  - **slds-box slds-theme_alt-inverse**: Box with darker blue background color
  - **slds-box slds-theme_success**: Box with green background color
  - **slds-box slds-theme_info**: Box with grayish blue background color
  - **slds-box slds-theme_warning**: Box with yellow background color
  - **slds-box slds-theme_error**: Box with red background color
  - **slds-box slds-theme_offline**: Box with black background color
  - **slds-box slds-theme_alert-texture**: Box with striped background
- **Description List**
  - For inline construction:
    - **dl.slds-dl_inline**
    - **dt.slds-dl_inline__label**
    - **dd.slds-dl_inline__detail**
  - For inline construction having 33% space for dt and the rest for dd
    - **dl.slds-dl_horizontal**
    - **dt.slds-dl_horizontal__label**
    - **dd.slds-dl_horizontal__detail**

- **Floats**
    - **slds-float_left**
    - **slds-float_right**
    - **slds-float_none**: It can dynamically be assigned to the element for cancelling the float.
- **Grid and Sizing**: These are the most important set of CSS classes in the utility classes. They allow the designer/developer to build responsive layouts. For its details, please refer to the official documentation at Lightning Design System official website: https://www.lightningdesignsystem.com/utilities/grid/ and https://www.lightningdesignsystem.com/utilities/sizing/
- **Horizontal List**
    - **slds-list_horizontal:** Standard horizontal list
    - **slds-list_horizontal slds-has-block-links**: Horizontal list with links
        - **slds-list_horizontal slds-has-inline-block-links**: Horizontal list with inline block links
    - **slds-list_horizontal slds-has-block-links_space**: Horizontal list with links, and links have space between them
        - **slds-list_horizontal slds-has-inline-block-links_space**: Horizontal list with inline block links, and links have space between them
    - **slds-list_horizontal slds-has-dividers_left**: Horizontal list with dot dividers to the left
    - **slds-list_horizontal slds-has-dividers_right**: Horizontal list with dot dividers to the right
- **Hyphenation**: It is a specific class that allows the text to break (to hyphenate) at the end of the line. Not all browsers support it currently.
    - **slds-hyphenate**
- **Interactions**
    - **slds-text-link_reset**: When assigned to a link, it removes all format related to the linking and shows the link as a normal text (but the text continues to be clickable, namely this class does not remove the linking functionality)
    - **slds-text-link**: Standard link formatting is assigned to the text
    - **slds-has-blur-focus**: When the link text is clicked, it creates a blurred focus

- **span.slds-text-link_faux:** It adds faux link interactions to the span element
- **Magnets**: They are used to vertically attach adjacent card-like components (which are **cards**, **page headers**, and **boxes**).
  - **slds-card slds-has-bottom-magnet:** Pulls the below adjacent element
  - **slds-card slds-has-top-magnet**: Pulls the above adjacent element
- **Line Clamp**: It allows multi-line text truncation. It is useful when you have a long text that you want to truncate automatically to fit it in a limited space. However, not all browsers are supporting it currently.
  - **slds-line-clamp**: by default, it truncates the text after three lines of content, but the number of lines of content can be determined by using "`line-clamp`" token
  - **slds-line-clamp_x-small**: it truncates the text after two lines
  - **slds-line-clamp_small**: it truncates the text after three lines
  - **slds-line-clamp_medium**: it truncates the text after five lines
  - **slds-line-clamp_large**: it truncates the text after seven lines
- **Margin**
  - **slds-m-top_none, slds-m-top_xxx-small, slds-m-top_xx-small, slds-m-top_x-small, slds-m-top_small, slds-m-top_medium, slds-m-top_large, slds-m-top_x-large, slds-m-top_xx-large**
  - **slds-m-bottom_none, slds-m-bottom_xxx-small, slds-m-bottom_xx-small, slds-m-bottom_x-small, slds-m-bottom_small, slds-m-bottom_medium, slds-m-bottom_large, slds-m-bottom_x-large, slds-m-bottom_xx-large**
  - **slds-m-left_none, slds-m-left_xxx-small, slds-m-left_xx-small, slds-m-left_x-small, slds-m-left_small, slds-m-left_medium, slds-m-left_large, slds-m-left_x-large, slds-m-left_xx-large**
  - **slds-m-right_none, slds-m-right_xxx-small, slds-m-right_xx-small, slds-m-right_x-small, slds-m-right_small, slds-m-right_medium, slds-m-right_large, slds-m-right_x-large, slds-m-right_xx-large**
  - **slds-m-horizontal_none, slds-m-horizontal_xxx-small, slds-m-horizontal_xx-small, slds-m-horizontal_x-small, slds-m-horizontal_small, slds-m-horizontal_medium, slds-m-horizontal_large, slds-m-horizontal_x-large, slds-m-horizontal_xx-large**

    - `slds-m-vertical_none`, `slds-m-vertical_xxx-small`, `slds-m-vertical_xx-small`, `slds-m-vertical_x-small`, `slds-m-vertical_small`, `slds-m-vertical_medium`, `slds-m-vertical_large`, `slds-m-vertical_x-large`, `slds-m-vertical_xx-large`
    - `slds-m-around_none`, `slds-m-around_xxx-small`, `slds-m-around_xx-small`, `slds-m-around_x-small`, `slds-m-around_small`, `slds-m-around_medium`, `slds-m-around_large`, `slds-m-around_x-large`, `slds-m-around_xx-large`
- **Media Objects**: These classes help to build publisher-like components from scratch. Namely, components where an image, a video, or others are placed horizontally aligned with the text. For more details, please refer to the official documentation at Lightning Design System official website: https://www.lightningdesignsystem.com/utilities/media-objects/
- **Name Value List**: It provides an alternative to the Description List inline utility classes.
- **Padding:** Their spelling is similar to Margin utility classes, but instead of **m,** we use **p** this time. Some examples: `slds-p-left_xxx-small`, `slds-p-around_none`, and so on
- **Position**
    - `slds-is-static`: for resetting positioning
    - `slds-is-relative`: for relative positioning
    - `slds-is-fixed`: for fixed positioning
    - `slds-is-absolute`: for absolute positioning
    - `slds-is-nested`: used for nested lists
    - `slds-is-collapsed`: for putting the element into "collapsed" behavior
    - `slds-is-expanded`: for putting the element into "expanded" behavior
    - `slds-is-visually-empty`: removes width and hides the element
- **Print**
    - `slds-no-print`: for hiding the element when printing the page
- **Scrollable**
    - `slds-scrollable`: makes the content scrollable if it doesn't fit within its container. It can put horizontal, vertical, or both scrolls according to the placement of the content.
    - `slds-scrollable_x`: for horizontal scrolling
    - `slds-scrollable_y`: for vertical scrolling
    - `slds-scrollable_none`: for forcing the browser not to put any scroll for the content

- **Text**: It contains classes for styling the texts. For details, please refer to the official documentation at Lightning Design System official website: https://www.lightningdesignsystem.com/utilities/text/
- **Truncation**: It contains the classes to truncate long texts with a capability that assures the whole text can be seen when the user hovers over it.
    - **`slds-truncate_container_25`**: for truncating the text at 25% of its parent container
    - **`slds-truncate_container_50`**: for truncating the text at 50% of its parent container
    - **`slds-truncate_container_75`**: for truncating the text at 75% of its parent container
    - **`slds-truncate_container_33`**: for truncating the text at 33% of its parent container
    - **`slds-truncate_container_66`**: for truncating the text at 66% of its parent container
    - **`slds-has-flexi-truncate`**: it is used when truncation is nested in a flexible container in a grid
- **Vertical List:** For styling the unordered and ordered lists with default behavior (= namely placed vertically). For details, please refer to the official documentation at Lightning Design System official website: https://www.lightningdesignsystem.com/utilities/vertical-list/
- **Visibility**
    - **`slds-assistive-text`**: it enables a screen reader to read text that is hidden
    - **`slds-hidden`**: to make the content hidden
    - **`slds-visible`**: to make the content visible
    - **`slds-hide`**: it hides the content from view and from screen readers
        - It can be responsive: **`slds-hide_x-small`**, **`slds-hide_small`**, **`slds-hide_medium`**, **`slds-hide_large`**, **`slds-hide_x-large`**
    - `slds-show`: to undo slds-hide
        - It can be responsive: **`slds-show_x-small`**, **`slds-show_small`**, **`slds-show_medium`**, **`slds-show_large`**, **`slds-show_x-large`**
    - **`slds-transition-hide`**: slowly transitions the content from visible to hidden
    - **`slds-transition-show`**: slowly transitions the content from hidden to visible

Tip: To see code examples for how to use the utility classes, please visit the **Lightning Design System Official Website.**

Design Tokens

A good programming approach always requires using global constants whenever possible. And it is not different when creating a design system like Salesforce Lightning Design System. So, the Salesforce Design Team provides us with some global constants to prevent the usage of hard-coded values for common styling needs: they are called design tokens, or simply tokens. This way, if in future, the Salesforce Design Team decides to update some CSS styling values, our application would be updated automatically and instantly if we use these constants.

There are a good amount of tokens that are defined under sixteen categories, as of the Winter '24 release:

- Colors
- Background Color
- Text Color
- Border Color
- Font
- Font Size
- Opacity
- Line Height
- Spacing
- Radius
- Sizing
- Shadow
- Time
- Touch
- Media Query
- Z-index

Not all tokens are generally available, some of them are for Salesforce internal usage. For the full list, you can refer to the documentation at https://www.lightningdesignsystem.com/design-tokens/

For example, the `brandBackgroundDark` token, under the `Colors` category, is used to define a dark branding blue background-color, which has an hexadecimal value of `#014486`. So, in our code, instead of using `#014486` directly in a hard-coded way, we should use the token directly as:

```
color: var(--lwc-brandBackgroundDark);
```

in the CSS file of our LWC bundle.

The Salesforce Design Team uses an open-source tool to generate design tokens called **Theo.** Its GitHub project address is https://github.com/salesforce-ux/theo.

This **Theo** tool was created (and it is currently used) by Salesforce. Its usage is straightforward. We first define a JSON file as a single source of truth, and then, by using **Theo,** we convert this JSON string to design property constants for each platform, which are as follows:

- Lightning
- Sass
- Less
- Stylus
- JSON (iOS)
- XML (Android)
- CSS Custom Properties
- Color Swatches (Photoshop and Sketch)

For example, if we have the following JSON file:

```
{
  "name": "COLOR_TEXT",
  "value": "#000",
  "category": "text-color",
  "comment": "Body text"
}
```

It is converted by **Theo** as follows:

- **Saas**: `$color-text: #000;`
- **Aura**: `<aura:var name="colorText" value="#000" />`
- **Android**: `<property name="COLOR_TEXT" category="text-color" value="#00000000" />`

In our daily life, we don't need to use **Theo**; we can directly use the exported generally available design tokens as mentioned in the documentation. Nonetheless, being aware of such a tool would always be a plus for us.

Icons

We cannot think of a design system that doesn't have its own icon sets, and Salesforce Lightning Design System is no different. In SLDS, we have four types of icon sets:

- Utility icons
- Doctype icons
- Standard & Custom icons
- Action icons

All of them are shown in the official documentation (https://www.lightningdesignsystem.com/icons/), and it is very easy to use them. The icons' component blueprint is under *component blueprints*, as mentioned previously in this chapter, and if we recall, there is also a specific design guideline for **iconography**.

Here is an example of code for **`utility → archive`** icon:

```
<lightning-icon icon-name="utility:archive" alternative-text="archive"
title="archive" size="medium" aria-hidden="true"></lightning-icon>
```

Here, the yellow part is the unique name for the **`Archive`** icon of the **`Utility`** icon set. As we see in the documentation, each icon under each icon set has a unique name.

SLDS in Action

After learning all the theoretical information about SLDS, let's see them in action in an LWC.

Simple LWC with SLDS

We created a simple LWC that uses the **`Cards → Base Card Structure`** component blueprint. So, what we did is basically copy-pasting the HTML code from the SLDS documentation into our LWC's HTML file.

lwcSLDS.html

```
<template>
    <article class="slds-card">
        <div class="slds-card__header slds-grid my-header
slds-p-bottom_large">
            <header class="slds-media slds-media_center
slds-has-flexi-truncate">
                <div class="slds-media__figure">
                    <lightning-icon icon-name="standard:account"
alternative-text="account" title="account" size="small"
aria-hidden="true"></lightning-icon>
                </div>
                <div class="slds-media__body">
                    <h2 class="slds-card__header-title">
                        <a href="#" class="slds-card__header-link
slds-truncate" title="Accounts">
                            <span>Accounts</span>
                        </a>
                    </h2>
                </div>
                <div class="slds-no-flex">
                    <button class="slds-button slds-button_neutral"
onclick={newAccount}>New</button>
                </div>
            </header>
        </div>
        <div class="slds-card__body slds-card__body_inner">Anything can
go into the card body</div>
        <footer class="slds-card__footer">
            <a class="slds-card__footer-action" href="#"
onclick={openAllAccounts}>View All
```

```
                <span class="slds-assistive-text">Accounts</span>
            </a>
        </footer>
    </article>
</template>
```

After we copy-pasted the HTML blueprint, we added our custom **my-header** CSS class into the header part, and we also used the standard **slds-p-bottom_large** utility class to add some padding between the header and the body in this lightning card implementation.

Then, we easily added the **account** icon of the **standard** icon set by using the lightning-icon standard component, once again in the header part. Here, as you can see, we could add the assistive text by using the **alternate-text** attribute, and we could also define the size of the icon by using the **size** attribute.

As it is a blueprint, there is no JavaScript implementation; we should develop it according to our needs. So, here, in the New button, we added the **newAccount** call to the click event listener, and similarly, we added **openAllAccounts** call to the **click** event listener in the **View All** link. We implemented these actions in the JavaScript controller file:

lwcSLDS.js

```
import { LightningElement } from 'lwc';
import { NavigationMixin } from "lightning/navigation";

export default class LwcSLDS extends NavigationMixin(LightningElement) {

    newAccount(event) {
        event.preventDefault();
        this[NavigationMixin.Navigate]({
            type: "standard__objectPage",
            attributes: {
              objectApiName: "Account",
              actionName: "new",
            },
        });
```

```
    }

    openAllAccounts(event) {
        event.preventDefault();
        this[NavigationMixin.Navigate]({
            type: "standard__objectPage",
            attributes: {
              objectApiName: "Account",
              actionName: "list",
            },
            state: {
              filterName: "allAccounts"
            }
          });
    }
}
```

There is nothing fancy in this JavaScript controller; it is just using standard navigation functionalities in order to open the **New Account** modal and **All Accounts** list view in corresponding methods **newAccount(event)** and **openAllAccounts(event).**

Finally, we see how we defined our custom **my-header** CSS class in the LWC's CSS file:

lwcSLDS.css

```
div.my-header {
    background-color :  var(--lwc-brandBackgroundDark);
}
```

As seen here, instead of giving a hard-coded background-color value, we're using the **brandBackgroundDark** design token.

When we deploy our component, we see that everything is in place as expected: **background-color** is updated to dark blue, there is a padding between header and body, the **New** button and the **View All** link are working correctly:

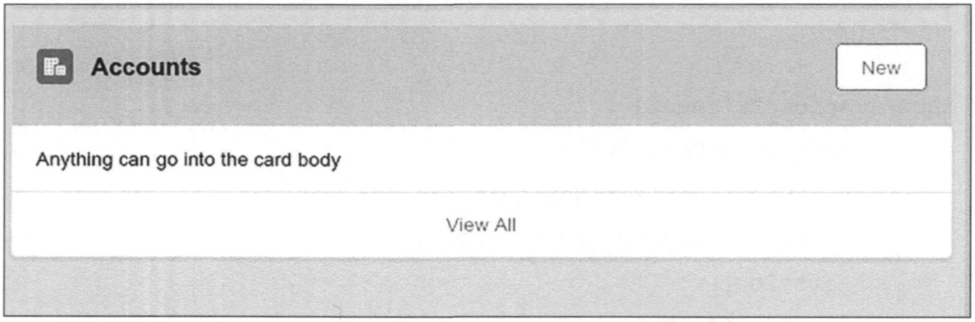

Figure 8.29: *lwcSLDS component is deployed*

Working with CSS libraries

It is possible to define separate CSS libraries and import them to multiple LWCs. This way, instead of writing repetitive duplicate CSS expressions in many LWCs (which would very quickly become a burden when one needs to update one common CSS expression in all the LWCs), we can just write once and use it in many LWCs.

To define a CSS library, the only thing we should do is to create a new LWC and remove the JavaScript controller and HTML view files. The remaining CSS file in the LWC will become our CSS library file.

Example:

Figure 8.30: *cssLibrary is created as a LWC in VS Code*

cssLibrary.css

```
p {
    font-weight: bold;
}

h3  {
    color: red;
}
```

Now, we import it into our previous **`lwcSLDS`** component's CSS file:

lwcSLDS.css

```
@import 'c/cssLibrary';

div.my-header {
    background-color :  var(--lwc-brandBackgroundDark);
}
```

Now, we can add the following lines into our **`lwcSLDS.html`** file to test whether it is working:

lwcSLDS.html

```
<template>
    <article class="slds-card">
        ...
    </article>
    <p>This paragraph is formatted via cssLibrary</p>
    <h3>This header is formatted via cssLibrary</h3>
</template>
```

When we deploy **`cssLibrary`** and the updated **`lwcSLDS`** components, we see that it is working!

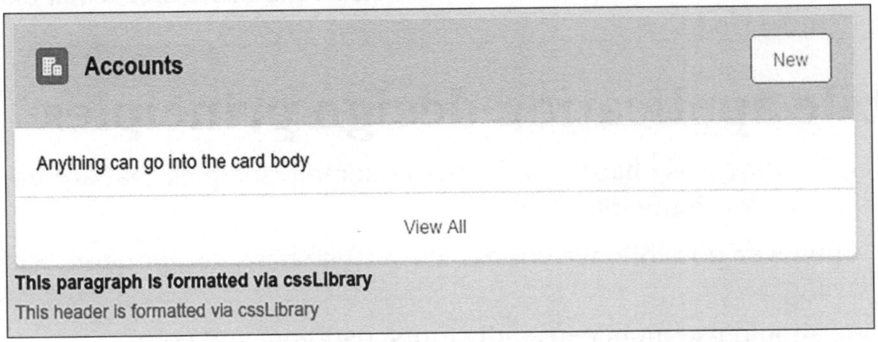

Figure 8.31: *The last two lines are formatted by cssLibrary*

Using SLDS in Visualforce Pages

SLDS is already ready-to-use in LWC and Aura components, so there is no need to manually import SLDS for those components.

However, if we need to use SLDS in Visualforce pages, we need to import it using a magical tag: **`<apex:slds />`**, and then when we simply add **`class="slds-scope"`** in the main **`<div>`**, our Visualforce page will start to use SLDS styling: a very convenient way to upgrade our existing Visualforce pages easily to use them in Lightning interface!

Example:

```
<apex:page showHeader="false" standardStylesheets="false"
sidebar="false" applyHtmlTag="false" applyBodyTag="false"
docType="html-5.0">

  <!-- Import the Design System style sheet -->
  <apex:slds />

    <!-- REQUIRED SLDS WRAPPER -->
    <div class="slds-scope">
```

Tip: While working with SLDS in Visual Studio Code, we need to be sure that **SLDS Validator** extension is active in our workplace. This is the extension interprets SLDS expressions.

SLDS Validator is already included in the **Salesforce Extension Pack** extension of Visual Studio Code.

Mobile application design principles

Before concluding this chapter, let's look at some principles that are important for mobile app development:

- Whenever possible, we should always use base components with SLDS styling.
- We should use mobile-friendly fonts, padding, and color.
- We shouldn't allow horizontal scrolling. Let's say, if we have a large table

with lots of columns, we should try to use **tiles** for presenting the data instead of a table.
- LWCs should be implemented with responsive layouts to support various mobile devices with different resolutions and screen sizes.
- To minimize bandwidth usage, we should avoid using large media files (for example, images, videos, and so on...) in mobile applications and mobile sites.
- Using pull-to-refresh functionality in a Salesforce mobile app may not always be a good idea, as it may cause the user to accidentally lose the data on the screen. (especially if (s)he tries to fill out a long form).
- We should follow the accessibility mobile design guidelines very carefully to cover all the users, including the disadvantageous ones.

Conclusion

It was another long chapter with lots of things to consume, but we should always keep in mind that we don't need to memorize everything. Instead, we should only remember the existing features and functionalities. Then, the only thing that matters is where to find them in the documentation when we need them. This is especially true for SLDS, as there are lots of minor details in its implementation.

Basically, SLDS is a very sophisticated design system in which almost every aspect of design and style implementation is considered. For Salesforce, it is very important that all non-technical Salesforce end users (all around the world) should always have the same look-and-feel and experience, whether or not they are using a custom application or a custom page. For this reason, the Salesforce Design team realized a very detailed work with guidelines, HTML blueprints, utility classes, resources, tools, tokens, and so on, along with very good documentation. As independent Salesforce developers, using the provided tools like SLDS as much as possible is also very beneficial for us because this way we can always be sure that we would not need to update many things every time a new Salesforce release is live.

From the beginning until this chapter, we obtained very good know-how about how to work with LWCs properly, except for one very important aspect: security! In the next chapter, we are going to focus on how to code securely, without having any flaws in LWCs.

References

- Lightning Design System Official Website - https://www.lightningdesignsystem.com/
- Lightning Design System Open Source Repository - https://github.com/salesforce-ux/design-system
- LWC Developer Guide - https://developer.salesforce.com/docs/component-library/documentation/en/lwc
- Lightning Design System Development for Designers - https://trailhead.salesforce.com/content/learn/modules/lightning-design-system-development-for-designers
- Salesforce UX Theo - https://github.com/salesforce-ux/theo
- Salesforce UX Design System Starter Kit - https://github.com/salesforce-ux/design-system-starter-kit#quick-start
- Figma UI Kit - https://www.figma.com/@salesforce
- Mobile and Offline Developer Guide - https://developer.salesforce.com/docs/atlas.en-us.mobile_offline.meta/mobile_offline/intro.htm
- Lightning Design System for React - https://react.lightningdesignsystem.com/
- Automated Accessibility Testing with sa11y - https://developer.salesforce.com/blogs/2020/10/automated-accessibility-testing-with-sa11y
- Salesforce sa11y GitHub project - https://github.com/salesforce/sa11y

CHAPTER 9

LWC Security

Introduction

Security was and is always the top priority for Salesforce. That's very understandable because as a "Software-as-a-Service" company, Salesforce's first offer for its clients is to allow them to work with their data in the cloud. That means the customers' data reside in third-party Internet servers, in a multi-tenant environment. So to convince the customers to work with Salesforce, it needs to be secure always. This is the main added value of the company.

So, things are not different at all for Lightning Interface: from the very beginning, Salesforce introduced **Lightning Locker** to enable automatic web security for the clients. Then it takes things further by developing a new brand security system, **Lightning Web Security (LWS)**. In this chapter, we're going to learn their details.

Despite Salesforce trying its best to provide security by default, it cannot fully assure that the custom applications' codebases are also 100% secure: here, the burden is on us, on the application developers. So, in this chapter, we'll also present best practices for developing secure applications. Finally, we'll conclude the chapter by looking briefly at the Salesforce Security Review, which is the main prerequisite for anyone who wants to publish a component, an application on the Salesforce AppExchange marketplace.

Structure

In this chapter, we will discuss the following topics:

- Lightning Locker
- Lightning Web Security (LWS)
- Developing secure LWC applications
- About Salesforce Security Review

Lightning Locker

Lightning Locker is the default security feature for Lightning Framework. It is automatically enabled for all LWCs. However, for Aura components, it is enabled if the component's API version is 40 or above.

Note: As we would remember, the component's API version can be updated manually in the component's configuration file:

For Aura components, it is the file which ends with "`.cmp-meta.xml`" suffix.

For LWCs, it is the file which ends with "`.js-meta.xml`" suffix.

Lightning Locker will automatically secure all requests within the component by:

- Enforcing the JavaScript strict mode
- Preventing the access to DOM elements of other components
- Restricting the use of JavaScript global objects (as "`window`", "`document`", "`element`" etc.) and Salesforce global variables (as `$A, Aura, Sfdc, sforce`, and so on)
- Limiting the usage of "`eval()`" JavaScript function
- Permitting only the secure MIME types to be used in Blob objects
- Blocking third-party web components

However, we should be aware that, Lightning Locker may not function as expected if the browser of the user is not supporting the prerequisites needed to run Lightning Locker. Nowadays, despite the fact that almost all modern browsers in standard users' laptops would be sufficiently recent to support Lightning Locker, this is something we should still keep in mind: we need to be always sure that our application checks the user's browser version before trying to load our components. If we notice that a browser is not supported instead of loading our components, we should show a warning message to guide the user to update its browser to a recent version.

Lightning Locker has also its own API versions: after all, with each release, Salesforce updated Lightning Locker to cover additional security vulnerabilities. To have a complete list of "which version of Lightning Locker covers which security vulnerabilities", we can visit the documentation page:

https://developer.salesforce.com/docs/platform/lwc/guide/security-locker-api-setting.html

---

Tip: It is possible to change the Salesforce org's Locker API version by visiting `Setup → Session Settings page.`

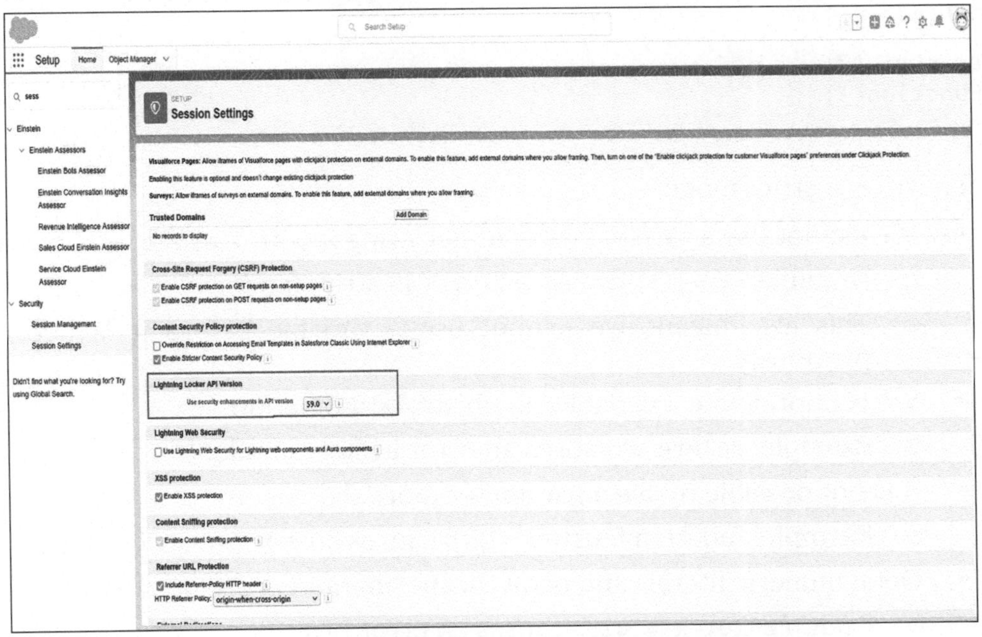

***Figure 9.1:** Setting for updating Locker API version*

Now, let's see in detail how Lightning Locker provides security for our components.

JavaScript strict mode enforcement

JavaScript is a language which promotes freedom (that comes with personal responsibility) instead of an enforced structure. That means, in its default mode, it is the developer's responsibility to write perfectly valid code expressions that would not break anything while the application is running.

Consequently, we can argue that the default mode of JavaScript is not completely suitable and secure for professional development teams which work in corporations. That's one of the reasons why "strict mode" was introduced with version 5 of ECMAScript. In "strict mode", previously accepted "bad syntaxes" are changed into real errors.

To use "strict mode", we just need to add a "`use strict`"; statement at the beginning of our JavaScript script for global scope or in a function for local scope.

Example:

```
"use strict";
myFunction();
```

When we're in strict mode:

- We cannot use a variable without declaring it with "`let`", "`const`" or "`var`".
  - Example: `x = 15;` causes an error in strict mode.
  - This also means we cannot use a variable before it is declared previously.
- We cannot delete a variable, an object, or a function.
  - Example: `delete x`; causes an error in strict mode.
- It is not possible to use a parameter more than once:
  - Example: function fcust(v1, v1) {}; causes an error in strict mode.
- Octal numeric literals and octal escape characters are not allowed.
  - Example: `let x = 015;` causes an error in strict mode.
  - Example2: `let y = "\015";` causes an error in strict mode.
- Keywords reserved for JavaScript cannot be used as variable names in strict mode:
  - this
  - arguments
  - eval
  - implements
  - interface
  - let
  - package
  - private
  - protected
  - public
  - static
  - yield

- `eval()` is more restricted in strict mode. We cannot use it to declare new variables, so the following causes an error:
    - `eval ("var x = 'hello, world!'");`
- Although the support for the "`with`" statement is being deprecated, it is worth mentioning that it is not already allowed in strict mode:
    - `with (['x', 'y', 'z']) { … }` causes an error in strict mode.

When Lightning Locker is enabled, components are automatically in "strict mode" without needing us to explicitly write the `"use strict";` statement in the JavaScript controller files of our components. So, all the previously mentioned rules are automatically valid for our components.

In addition, if we need to use third-party JavaScript libraries in our components, we need to pay attention to the following points (not only for **Lightning Locker** but also for **Lightning Web Security**):

- Before using a third-party JavaScript library, we need to be completely sure that there is no app (or component) in AppExchange or that there is no base component which provides the desired functionality.
- Third-party libraries should support strict mode.
- Third-party libraries shouldn't try to scan or manipulate DOM across namespaces.
- Due to the "Content Security Policy" requirement, it is forbidden to use third-party libraries from other domains. We can only use them from our Salesforce org. That means we need to upload them first as "static resources" into our Salesforce org. Then, by using the standard "`lightning/platformResourceLoader`" module, we import their methods.
    - We have already seen an example of how to use this "`lightning/platformResourceLoader`" module, in *Chapter* 3's "*Static resources and third-party* JS *libraries*" section.
- If a third-party library needs to manipulate DOM in our component, we need to add '`lwc:dom="manual"`' to the HTML element which needs to be manipulated by the library:

```
<template>
      <div lwc:dom="manual"></div>
</template>
```

- Third-party libraries' script tags cannot be used to load JavaScript and it is not possible to use inline JavaScript for event handlers.

- This security feature is provided by default via the "`Enable Stricter Content Security Policy`" setting in the `Setup → Session Settings` page.

- If a third-party library uses an external resource for "fonts", "images", and so on, they should also be uploaded into our Salesforce org as static resources. However, if this is not feasible (or possible), then we can add their hosting domains to our CSP directives by using the "`Setup → Trusted URLs`" page.
  - The connection to these external resources should always be "`https`". Salesforce will not allow insecure "`http`" connections to any external resource.

Note: As allowing "inline scripts" is a very critical vulnerability, in addition to Stricter CSP, LWC compiler also rejects attempts at including an inline script in Salesforce. (LWC Compiler error no = LWC1051)

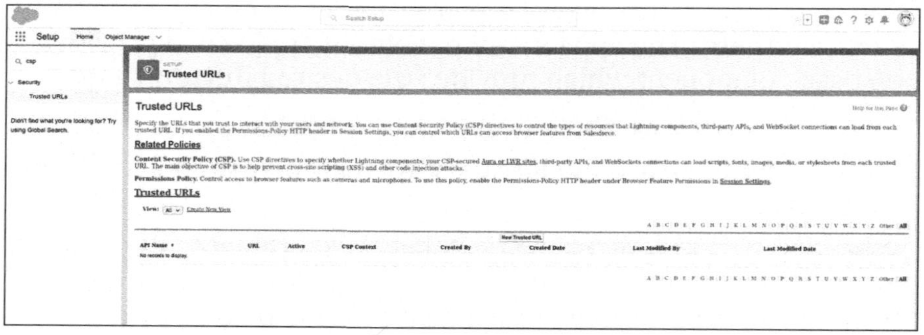

Figure 9.2: *Setup page for adding trusted URLs*

To understand whether or not a third-party library is Locker-compliant:

- We first need to create a simple component that uses the library.
- Initially, we need to be sure that the library loads without error when our component is connected to the DOM.
- We need to open the **Locker Console** in Lightning Component Library and check whether or not we have common issues like "declaring global variables, "CSP violations", "usage of unsupported DOM APIs", "DOM access violations" and so on.

Tip: It is possible to open the Locker Console specifically for our Salesforce org.

Let's say our "My Domain" is "abconlinelearning", then the Locker Console will be at this address:

https://abconlinelearning.lightning.force.com/docs/component-library/tools/locker-service-console

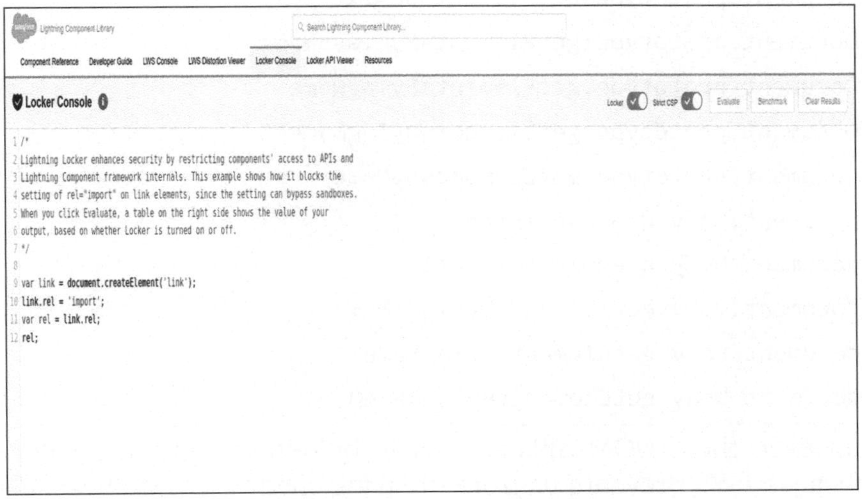

Figure 9.3: *Locker Console*

DOM access containment, secure wrappers, Salesforce global variables, third-party web components

When Lightning Locker is enabled, a component can only traverse and access elements that were created by itself. That's the reason why while working with LWCs, we cannot use "`document.querySelector()`" but instead we use "`this.template.querySelector()`".

Note: If the DOM tree is large, under Lightning Locker watch, components that use `this.template.querySelector` (or `this.template.querySelectorAll`) APIs can encounter performance problems as the garbage collection doesn't clear properly the browser memory. Even crashes may happen.

The best workaround to resolve this problem is to enable Lightning Web Security (LWS) because garbage collection works smoothly under LWS.

Under Lightning Locker restrictions, components cannot use global properties like "`window`", "`document`", and so on. As a result, the following DOM APIs are forbidden when Lightning Locker is enabled:

- `Document.prototype.getElementById`
- `Document.prototype.querySelector`
- `Document.prototype.querySelectorAll`
- `Document.prototype.getElementsByClassName`
- `Document.prototype.getElementsByTagName`
- `Document.prototype.getElementsByTagNameNS`
- `Document.prototype.getElementsByName`
- `document.body.querySelector`
- `document.body.querySelectorAll`
- `document.body.getElementsByClassName`
- `document.body.getElementsByTagName`
- `document.body.getElementsByTagNameNS`

Note: However, these DOM APIs are not forbidden in Lightning Web Security (LWS) because LWS prevents us from breaking shadow DOM encapsulation by enforcing a value of "`closed`" on the ShadowRoot's "`mode`" property, for all the components.

When Lightning Locker notices a call for "`window`", "`document`" or "`element`" global properties, it wraps them in a secure version: "`SecureWindow`" for "`window`", "`SecureDocument`" for "`document`" and "`SecureElement`" for "element". Although, these secure wrappers do not support all the APIs. For a complete list, we can visit the **Locker API Viewer** tool.

Tip: Similar to Locker Console, it is possible to open Locker API Viewer specifically for our Salesforce org.

Let's say our "My Domain" is "abconlinelearning", then it will be at this address:

https://abconlinelearning.lightning.force.com/docs/component-library/tools/locker-service-viewer

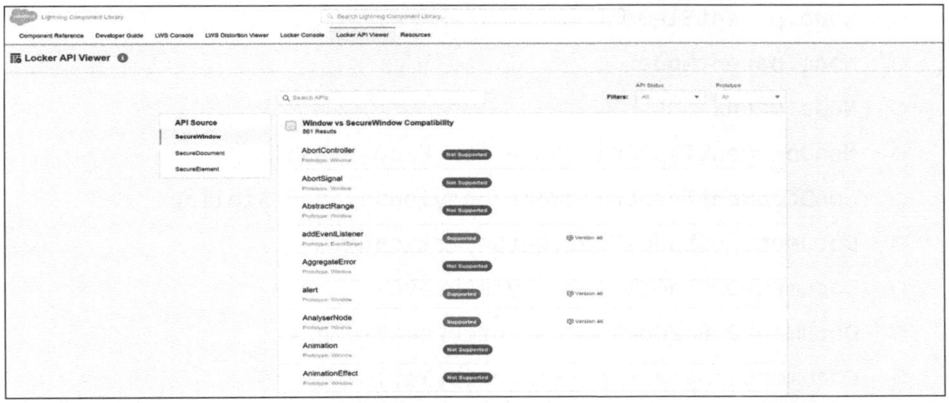

Figure 9.4: *Locker API Viewer*

`SecureWindow` wrapper blocks the `customElements` methods in order to prevent the creation of custom third-party web components. (For defining a custom web component, we need to use `customElements.define` API). Custom web components are security risks on the Salesforce platform because they allow the creation of an instance of any registered element, which as a result may potentially give access to sensitive information.

Note: Lightning Web Security (LWS) virtualizes `customElementRegistry` APIs to enable use of custom elements within the component namespace.

In addition to "`SecureWindow`", "`SecureDocument`" and "`SecureElement`", we have the following wrappers too:

- `SecureObject`: It is for wrapping an object that we don't have access to.
- `SecureLightningElement`: It is for wrapping the `LightningElement` base class. In our LWCs, we extend the `LightningElement` class, but in runtime, Lightning Locker switches the `LightningElement` class with `SecureLightningElement` directly. (So, we don't need to extend the `SecureLightningElement` class.)
- `SecureTemplate`: It is for wrapping the template object, the `shadowRoot` node. However, these APIs are not supported:
  - `Node.localName`
  - `Node.namespaceURI`
  - `Node.nodeValue`
  - `Node.nextSibling`
  - `Node.previousSibling`

  - `Node.parentElement`
  - `Node.parentNode`
  - `Node.prefix`
  - `NonDocumentTypeChildNode.nextElementSibling`
  - `NonDocumentTypeChildNode.previousElementSibling`
  - `DocumentOrShadowRoot.getSelection()`
  - `DocumentOrShadowRoot.styleSheets`
  - `DocumentOrShadowRoot.pointerLockElement`
  - `DocumentFragment.getElementById()`
  - `ParentNode.append`
  - `ParentNode.prepend`
  - `constructor`
  - `EventTarget.dispatchEvent`
  - `pictureInPictureElement`

Finally, Lightning Locker also blocks the following global JavaScript objects specific to Salesforce, which are available to other Salesforce features (or already deprecated):

- `$A`
- `Aura`
- `Sfdc`
- `sforce`

Note: In Lightning Web Security (LWS), instead of wrappers, API distortions are used to selectively modify APIs that enable non-secure.

Limiting eval() function

Lightning Locker permits the use of the `eval()` function only in the global scope, preventing its access to the local variables within the scope in which it's called.

However, LWS doesn't have this restriction because LWS runs the components in sandboxes where "global" means "global" of the sandbox.

Lightning Locker and MIME types

MIME (Multipurpose Internet Mail Extensions) types, also known as media types, indicate the nature and format of a document, file, and so on.

Files are processed as "blob" objects in web programming. The Salesforce platform processes the blob object according to its MIME type: if it is an audio file, then we see an audio player on the screen, but if it is a PDF file, then we see its preview. However, the attackers can send an executable malicious code under the disguise of a "pdf" file. So for security purposes, the contents of the files should be analyzed to detect their real MIME type. And that's what Lightning Locker does for us.

After it detects the file's MIME type, it allows or blocks it. The following MIME types are allowed under the Lightning Locker watch:

- `application/octet-stream – Default value for binary files`
- `application/json – JSON format`
- `application/pdf – Portable Document Format (.pdf)`
- `video/ – All video/* mime types`
- `audio/ – All audio/* mime types`
- `image/ – All image/* mime types`
- `font/ – All font/* mime types`
- `text/plain – Text (.txt)`
- `text/markdown – Markdown (.md)`
- `application/zip – Zip archive (.zip)`
- `application/x-bzip – Bzip archive (.bz)`
- `application/x-rar-compressed – RAR archive (.rar)`
- `application/x-tar – Tape archive (.tar)`

If the MIME type is `text/html`, `image/svg+xml` or `text/xml`, Lightning Locker does not directly block it but instead, it sanitizes the file by removing potential malicious code.

All other MIME types except the previously mentioned in this section are blocked by Lightning Locker.

Note: Lightning Web Security (LWS) requires that every blob object should be created by explicitly defining the MIME type. Thus, LWS interprets it accordingly.

If it is not possible to determine the MIME type (because it is a forbidden type), we can directly use `application/octet-stream` as its default MIME type.

The rest of the functionality and the supported MIME types are the same with Lightning Locker.

Lightning Web Security (LWS)

Lightning Web Security (LWS) is the recent security architecture for LWCs which started to replace Lightning Locker in the Spring '22 release. Currently (in the Winter '24 release), it is generally available for all Lightning components (LWCs and Aura components).

During the writing of this book (Winter '24 release), it can be enabled manually by using the `Setup → Session Settings` page:

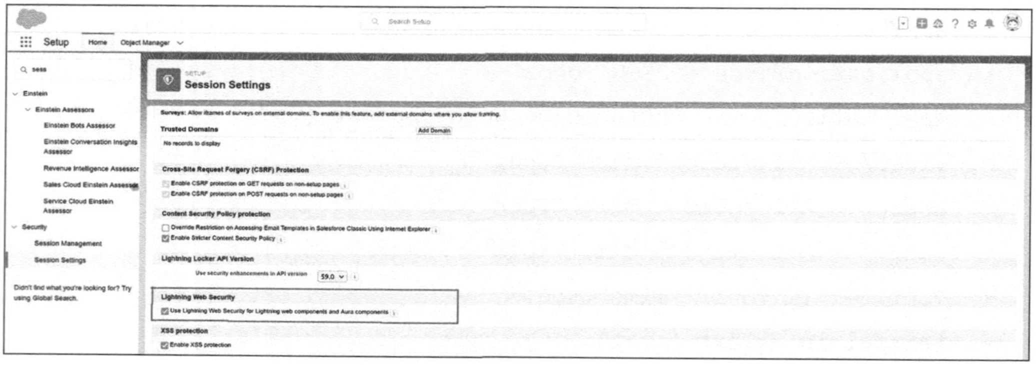

Figure 9.5: *Enabling Lightning Web Security*

When we enable LWS, Lightning Locker is automatically disabled. Besides, it wouldn't be wrong to expect that in the future, Lightning Locker will become obsolete and LWS will be the automatically enabled, default security architecture for Lightning components.

LWS vs Lightning Locker

Like Lightning Locker, JavaScript strict mode is also enforced in LWS. However, if a third-party JavaScript library uses an explicit `"use strict";` statement, the browser can throw errors while running the components under the LWS watch.

In LWS security architecture, every namespace in a page is confined to a sandbox where their correspondent components can access a virtual "global scope". LWS acts as the virtualization engine in the host environment (= browser) and the namespace JavaScript sandboxes are the virtual environments.

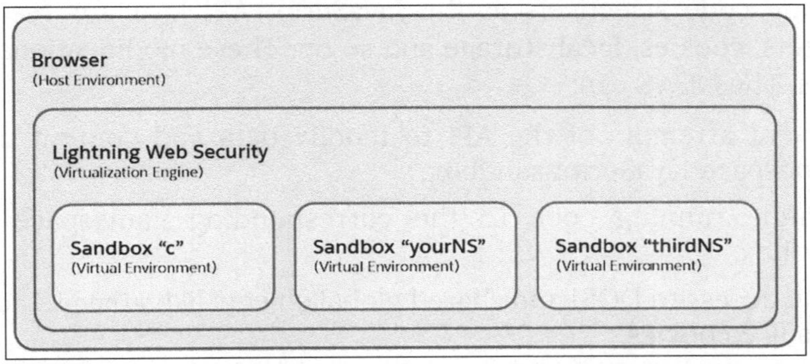

Figure 9.6: *Virtualization of the Browser (image from the official Salesforce documentation)*

Therefore, if a third-party library expects to be added to the global `window` object, LWS confines it to a virtual copy of the `window` object. So, to ensure that the third-party library does not attempt to access the actual global scope, we need to add the following code snippet into its script code:

```
(function (global) {
  global = global || self;
  global.myFunction = function () {};
})(this);
```

As `this` and `global` are undefined in LWS, this code ensures that **"`global`"** evaluates as the sandbox **"`global`"**. So, we have better support for third-party JavaScript libraries in LWS.

Lightning Locker has performance issues while filtering arrays between components. However, as LWS relies on shadow DOM instead of trying to filter DOM requests, this performance issue does not exist in LWS.

Another important feature of LWS is the ability for "cross-namespace component use" which means under LWS watch, as the components are isolated in their own namespace JavaScript sandbox, they can import components or modules easily from different namespaces and they can use them.

In LWS, it is possible to use iframe elements internally in each namespace JavaScript sandbox. This kind of development feature is being blocked by Lightning Locker.

We've already mentioned in the previous section of this chapter that, instead of using secure wrappers, LWS has the ability to update non-secure behaviors by modifying code selectively at the JavaScript API level for resources like global objects, cookies, local storage and so on. These modifications are called **distortions.** Thus, LWS can:

- Prevent attempts of the API to modify data and content outside the namespace JavaScript sandbox.
- Confine running code to the corresponding namespace JavaScript sandbox.
- Limit access to DOM and shared global objects like `window.location`, and data like cookies.

We can categorize LWS distortions as:

- `Content filtering` for filtering out attempts to access properties in other sandboxes.
- `Sanitization` for striping out malicious code.
- `Property accessor modification` for preventing reading and writing values of certain properties like `shadowRoot.mode`.

For a complete list of distortions, we can use the **LWS Distortion Viewer** tool.

Tip: Similar to Lightning Locker tools, it is possible to open the LWS Distortion Viewer specifically for our Salesforce org.

Let's say our "My Domain" is "abconlinelearning", then it will be at this address:

https://abconlinelearning.lightning.force.com/docs/component-library/tools/lws-distortion-viewer

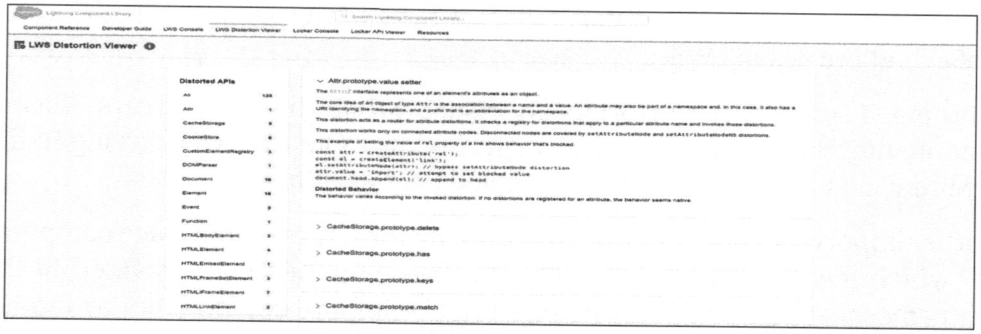

Figure 9.7: *LWS Distortion Viewer*

Because LWS does not use secure wrappers but distortions, it has an improved performance over Lightning Locker.

Likewise Locker Console, we have also a console for LWS in which we can check our JavaScript code to determine whether or not it has issues related to LWS.

Tip: It is also possible to open the LWS Console specifically for our Salesforce org.

Let's say our "My Domain" is "abconlinelearning", then it will be at this address:

https://abconlinelearning.lightning.force.com/docs/component-library/tools/lws-console

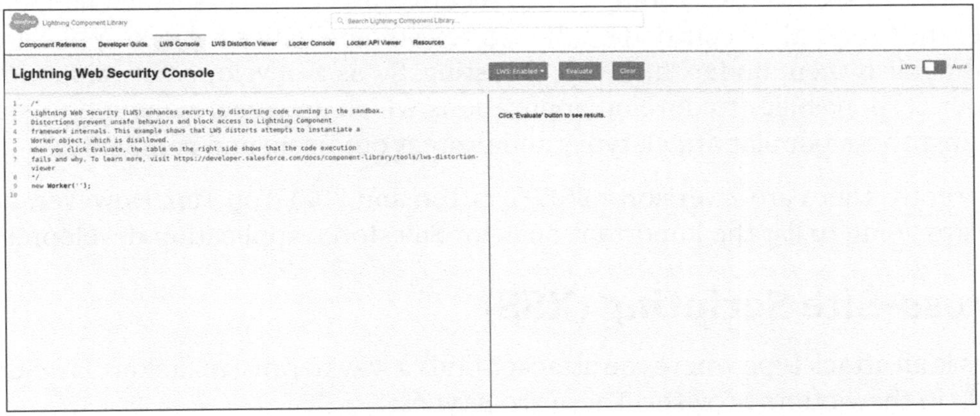

Figure 9.8: *LWS Console*

Briefly, we can think of Lightning Locker as Aura Component Framework regarding its destiny: namely, it is a temporary security solution while waiting for web standards to evolve. When we had web standards ready, Salesforce instantly passed to LWC Framework, as we've already discussed. Similarly, Lightning Web Security was already modeled after the latest TC39 standards and it will continue to evolve as browsers evolve. That's the reason, like Aura components are slowly outdating, Lightning Locker will also become obsolete sooner or later.

Developing secure LWC applications

We've seen the tools that Salesforce provides for security. And now, it is time to learn what we should do while developing our own components.

To be able to write secure codes, we first need to have a good understanding of the existing risks. So we start by learning them.

OWASP's top ten web application security risks

The Open Worldwide Application Security Project (OWASP) Foundation is a non-profit organization which works to improve the security of software. It is a very big organization with tens of thousands of members.

Their "Top 10" listing is a standard awareness document for developers and web application security. According to the security-breach events which happen all over the World, they consolidate the top ten vulnerabilities for web applications and publish them under this "Top 10" listing. So as a developer, at minimum, it is our responsibility to develop applications which are secure enough to stand against these popular attack types and protect our users and companies.

Currently, there are 2 versions: 2017-Top Ten and 2021-Top Ten. However, here we are going to list the important ones for Salesforce application development.

Cross-Site Scripting (XSS)

This is an attack type where the attacker finds a way to run a malicious JavaScript code in the victim's browser. There are 3 types:

Reflected XSS: If the website does not sanitize its query strings added to its URL and processes directly whatever exists in the address bar, then the only thing that the attacker needs to do is to create a link for this site and make the user click on it.

```
https://insecure-website.com/status?message=<script>/*+Bad+stuff+here...+*/</script>
```

```
<p>Status: <script>/* Bad stuff here... */</script></p>
```

Here, the attacker creates that link in which (s)he assigns an executable JavaScript code value for the "`message`" query-string parameter. So, when a victim clicks this link anywhere on the Internet, the attacker can obtain access to this site on behalf of the victim or directly obtain sensitive information about the victim according to what the executable JavaScript code is designed for.

Stored XSS: Let's say we have a forum site in which the users can reply with whatever messages they write and the forum site's code-base does not check or sanitize those inputs in any way. When an attacker notices this vulnerability, the only thing to do is just publish a "reply message" for one of the popular feeds by inserting a malicious JavaScript script like:

```
<p><script>/* Bad stuff here... */</script></p>
```

As the forum site directly publishes this message, whenever other users open that page with this message, the attacker's script will be executed automatically in their browsers. So the attacker would have the chance to victimize many users with just one script which is published continuously by the forum site to any user who visits that page...

DOM-based XSS: This type of XSS may happen if, on a website, an input from the user is directly used as HTML content for a DOM element on the page. That way, if the attacker has a way to control the value of the input field via an HTTP request, (s)he can easily inject a malicious JavaScript code into that HTTP request by constructing a URL similar to the one we say in **Reflected XSS**.

Briefly, XSS is an attack type which can be prevented by:

- Forbidding inline JavaScript code.
- Always sanitize user inputs and query string parameters before they are published on the site or before saving them to the database.
- Be extremely careful with dynamic DOM modifications on the page (if possible we should never permit any dynamic DOM modification on web pages which depends on the user input or somehow her/his involvement).
- We need to have strict CSP (Content Security Policies) on the websites to prevent any potential third-party URL calls.

Cross-Site Request Forgery(CSRF)

Let's assume we have a vulnerable website which updates emails via an HTTP request in which it explicitly discloses an important cookie (like a "`sessionId`") and the new email address while doing the request. Then the only thing for the attacker to do is to create a fake form in another site in which this request is sneakily done for replacing the user's email with the attacker's email address in that vulnerable website's database: the attack may be a success if the user has already opened the vulnerable website in another tab, so the browser would add automatically the "`sessionId`" to the hidden HTTP request.

This type of attack was extremely popular when users were surfing the web while their social media accounts were open in another tab of the browser.

This type of attack can be prevented by not storing any critical sensitive information like sessionId, username, and password in the user's browser or by encrypting them before making any requests to the server.

SOQL Injection

Originally, this type of attack is called **SQL injection** but as we look at vulnerabilities regarding Salesforce platform security, for us it is called **SOQL injection** (because Salesforce is using a variant of SQL which is SOQL).

This type of attack happens when we use the input of the users directly in SOQL queries without first escaping or sanitizing them. If we omit escaping the inputs of the user before using them in our queries, then malicious users would have the chance to exfiltrate data.

To prevent this type of attack, we should never use raw user input for directly querying our database.

Content Sniffing

This attack type involves tricking the browser into executing a script that is disguised as another file type.

To prevent this type of attack, we need to put a "`X-Content-Type-Options`" response header to "`nosniff`". In Salesforce, this is automatically done by enabling "`Enable Content Sniffing protection`" in the `Setup → Session Settings` page.

Salesforce-specific vulnerabilities

We've seen the most popular web application security vulnerabilities in the previous section. Now let's focus on Salesforce-specific vulnerabilities:

- **State changes on page loads:** While we're defining event handlers for "`init, body.onload, connectedCallback, renderedCallback`" lifecycle hooks, we need to be aware that we shouldn't allow any DML action in the backend. This may open doors for a type of CSRF attack.
- **Managing the navigation:** We shouldn't create dynamic URLs by using pure JavaScript. Despite Lightning Locker and/or Lightning Web Security preventing any malicious actions on the URLs, to be 100% safe, we need to use the standard `NavigationMixin` API for building our URLs.

- **Manual DOM manipulation:** Yes, Lightning Locker and Lightning Web Security have measures to prevent the exploitation of manual DOM manipulation but still in order to be 100% we shouldn't implement any manual DOM manipulation to our components unless it is 1000% the only way to resolve our specific business problem.
- If we have Aura components, we need to have their API versions at least 40 to be equipped with the default Lightning Locker security. Or we should enable Lightning Web Security in our org.
- While developing applications, for debugging purposes, all of us add statements like "`console.log(), console.error()`" in our code-base. When we go into Production, we should be sure that we remove as much as possible these statements because they may provide important know-how to external users about our application.
- **CRUD/FLS:** All Apex Classes with `@AuraEnabled` methods should be defined with the "`with sharing`" keyword and to enforce object-level/ field-level permissions "`WITH SECURITY_ENFORCED`" clause should be added to all SOQL queries. This way we can be sure that the users' data can only be seen by those who have permission to view it.

LWC Security Best Practices

Before concluding this section, let's look at some best practices which may guide us in our projects:

- Plan for enabling LWS if it is not enabled yet.
  - LWS provides more security than its predecessor Lightning Locker.
  - It offers built-in capabilities like HTML sanitization and blocks code that violates CSP (Content Security Policy).
  - It supports additional features like "cross-namespace component use": so, it is possible to use a LWC of a namespace in another LWC with a namespace different from the former.
- Minimize the usage of third-party libraries.
  - They may have vulnerabilities that we are not aware of.
  - If we must use a third-party library, then we need to add it to our LWC by using the "`platformResourceLoader`" module.
- Always keep in mind the "Adopt Principle of Least Privilege"
  - Every component, function, and event that we add should have the minimum access levels for accomplishing its main purpose.

- We should always try to keep our events "`composed: false`" and "`bubbles: false`" to be sure that they are restricted within the same shadow root. That way, we ensure that they don't propagate data outside and thus we prevent any unwanted data leakage.
    - If we need to define an event with "`composed: true`", then at least we should keep in mind to use the "`event.stopPropagation()`" method in one of the parents to stop the further propagation through the web page's DOM.
- Never implement custom raw JavaScript code to manipulate the component's DOM.
    - If we let LWC standard features (like `@api`, `@track` decorators, `for:each` iteration, `if:<property>` conditionals, and so on.) manage the state of the component's DOM, we reduce the risk of accidentally introducing XSS-style vulnerabilities that typically arise from improper DOM insertion.

About Salesforce Security Review

To publish our own applications and components in the Salesforce AppExchange Marketplace, we need to pass the security review done by Salesforce.

The security review is not free :), so we need to do our best to be ready to pass the security review on our first attempt. First, good news, if we apply what we've learnt in this chapter, we would very likely pass the security review!

Besides, Salesforce provides free-to-use scanners, and security tools to allow us to self-test our applications and components.

The complete list of scanners, which includes also licensed products, is below:

- **Salesforce Code Analyzer:** It scans Apex, JavaScript, Lightning, TypeScript and Visualforce code. It can be installed on a local computer for manually doing the scans in our local. It is also possible to integrate it into a continuous integration (CI) process. It is for scanning the internal code, it does not check external endpoints.
- **Source Code Scanner (Checkmarx):** It scans Apex, Visualforce and Lightning code. Checkmarx is not a free tool but Salesforce provides three scan limits which are included in the security review fee. We can only scan a code which is included in a security review submission.
- **PMD Source Code Analyzer:** It is a free, open-source tool but it can only scan Apex code. It is mentioned that it reports more false positives than the Source Code Scanner (Checkmarx).

- **Chimera:** It is for scanning external endpoints on domains we own. It can run from a Salesforce IP.
- **OWASP Zed Attack Proxy (ZAP):** It is a free, community-driven tool for scanning any external endpoints. It requires a download to local.
- **Burp Suite**: It is also for scanning external endpoints but it is not free and Salesforce does not provide any free scan. If we want to use it, we need to purchase a license.

For all the details to develop for Salesforce AppExchange, we need to visit the official ISVforce Guide at https://developer.salesforce.com/docs/atlas.en-us.packagingGuide.meta/packagingGuide/packaging_intro.htm.

Conclusion

Developing an application is not solely a function-oriented process, we also ensure that the users do not have any bad experiences, and do not have any losses due to potential cyber-attacks while using our application.

In this chapter, we summarized all the tools and the best practices for ensuring that our application ends up with a minimum number of vulnerabilities: after all, we need to recognize that no application can be 100% secure but this shouldn't prevent us from doing our best. Salesforce is a very big company, and it has numerous resources. That means as much as we stay with the standard features and do not try to re-discover America, we can be confident that our application will have state-of-the-art security features.

The next chapter is the last chapter of our book, in which we'll focus on how to debug and test our LWCs. The journey to becoming a LWC expert is about to conclude!

References

- LWC Developer Guide For Security - https://developer.salesforce.com/docs/platform/lwc/guide/security-intro.html
- TC39 Standards - https://tc39.es/
- Secure Client-Side Development - https://trailhead.salesforce.com/content/learn/modules/secure-clientside-development
- Lightning Web Security Basics - https://trailhead.salesforce.com/content/learn/modules/lightning-web-security-basics
- OWASP Top 10 Web Application Security Risks - https://owasp.org/www-project-top-ten/

- AppExchange Security Review - https://trailhead.salesforce.com/content/learn/modules/isv_security_review
- ISVforce Guide AppExchange Security Review - https://developer.salesforce.com/docs/atlas.en-us.packagingGuide.meta/packagingGuide/security_review_overview.htm
- Lightning Component Library - https://developer.salesforce.com/docs/component-library
- Debug Your Lightning Web Components - https://developer.salesforce.com/blogs/2019/02/debug-your-lightning-web-components
- Debug Components in an Org With LWS Enabled - https://developer.salesforce.com/docs/platform/lwc/guide/debug-lwsec.html

CHAPTER 10

LWC Debugging and Testing

Introduction

While doing software development, it is not unusual that sometimes things do not go as planned. As talented developers, we work hard and we code hard, but the moment of truth will always be when we run our application and see the result of its execution on the screen. As a matter of fact, most of the time our first execution of code will certainly throw exceptions, errors with red-colored annoying messages, or in the worst scenario, we will see that nothing happens, nothing even loads on the screen.

In order to decrease the number of those unwanted outputs and to shorten our development time, we need to add two additional approaches into our know-how bag. The first one is a **proactive** approach, which forces us to think of all the possible scenarios beforehand, which involves **writing tests** and then running them before deploying and executing our work. When the tests are successful, we can be more confident that our code is sufficiently stable. On the other hand, when even our tests miss some erroneous cases, then we need to be **reactive** this time and **debug the application** to understand what goes wrong.

LWC is a JavaScript framework, so debugging happens mostly in our browsers. Currently, writing tests for LWCs is not obligatory; however, as a best practice, we should always have good habits to write unit tests to cover the extreme cases.

Structure

In this chapter, we will discuss the following topics:

- LWC Debugging
- LWC Testing

LWC Debugging

As LWC is a JavaScript framework, it directly runs in browsers. So, the best way to debug an LWC is to deploy it to a Lightning page in a Salesforce org and then load the page via the internet browser. LWC is best compatible with the Google Chrome browser, so we will be using this browser while we debug our LWCs. Modern browsers already have very sophisticated **developer tools** to debug web applications, and Google Chrome browser is no different; that is why most of our debugging work will depend on Google Chrome developer tools.

Note: Debugging in a programming language involves mainly the following steps:

- Adding **breakpoints** will pause the code execution in a relevant manner to give us the ability to understand what is going on in the application at that point of time.
- Adding **watchers** to track the value changes of parameters, variables when the code is executed.
- If there are asynchronous calls (which are basically additional threads, like parallel execution paths in addition to the **main thread**), following their execution in parallel with the main thread.
- Intentionally logging the values of variables or printing messages (that help us understanding the execution flow) on the screen of the console by using the core functions of the programming language (`console.log()` is a good example for those types of standard functions in JavaScript)

In Salesforce, we have two execution modes for LWCs:

- Production mode
- Debug mode

Until now, we were always in **production mode**, which is the default mode for running LWCs in a Salesforce org. It is optimized for performance. It minimizes the JavaScript code by removing line breaks, spaces, tabs, and comments, and it shortens all the function and parameter names. The code that is loaded becomes humanly hard to read, but there is no encryption involved.

On the other hand, **debug mode** is a specific mode that is useful for developers and technical people to give them the chance to dive deeper while debugging the code. Here the code is loaded into the browser as it is written in the IDE. That is why it is 100% readable and easily comparable with the development code. However, we should note that in **debug mode**, Salesforce is functioning much slower.

Production Mode Debugging

To understand how to use the tools for debugging, let's use an LWC that we developed previously in this book:

lwcForLghtOutVFPage.js Controller:

```
import { LightningElement, wire } from 'lwc';
import getAccounts from '@salesforce/apex/simpleApexClass2.
getAllAccounts';

export default class LwcForLghtOutVFPage extends LightningElement {
    accounts;

    @wire(getAccounts, {}) wiredFunction({error, data}) {
        if(data) {
            this.accounts = data;
            console.log(this.accounts);
        }
        else if(error) {
            console.log("Error occurred while decorating the
'wiredFunction'.");
            console.log(error);
        }
    }
}
```

lwcForLghtOutVFPage.html Template:

```
<template>
    <h1><b>List of Accounts:</b></h1>
```

```
    <template for:each={accounts} for:item=”acc”>
        <p key={acc.Id}>{acc.Name}, {acc.Phone}</p>
    </template>
</template>
```

As seen, this LWC has a very basic function: it loads all the accounts of a Salesforce org. When we deploy it into our Salesforce org and run it:

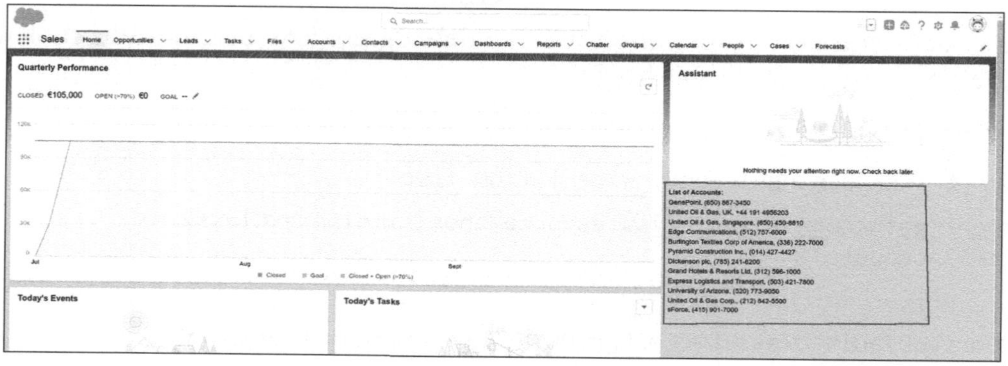

Figure 10.1: *Our LWC is active*

Now, we can open Google Chrome developer tools by pressing F12 or by using the menu:

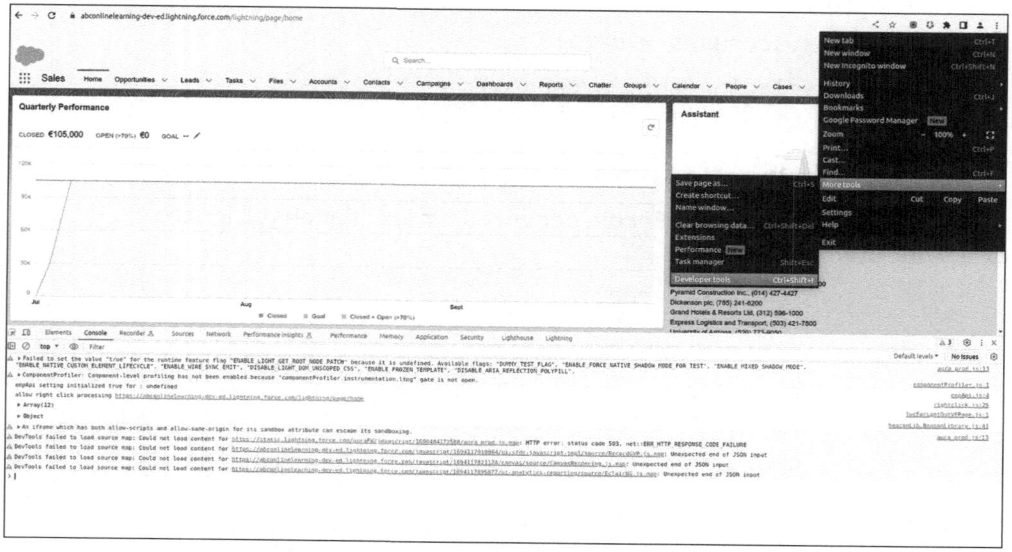

Figure 10.2: *Google Chrome's Developer Tools Window*

Initially, the `console` tab is open, and we see lots of warnings that are not related to us. We can filter them by using **`Default levels`** menu and do the filtering to see only the **`errors`** and the **`info`**:

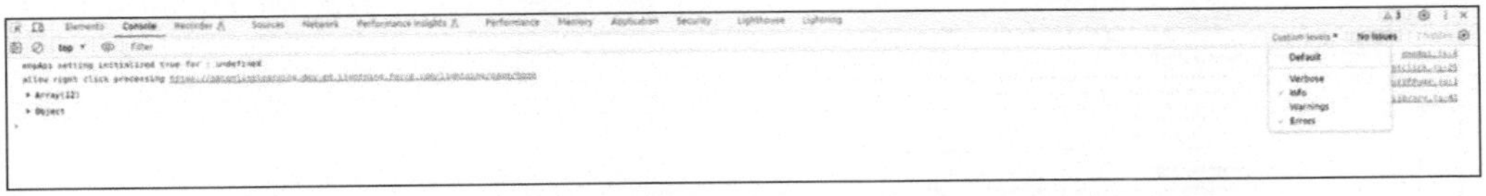

Figure 10.3: *Custom message levels for console are configured*

Tip: Our **`console.log()`**messages will be seen in the info level.

To see our JavaScript controller, we need to open **`Sources`** tab:

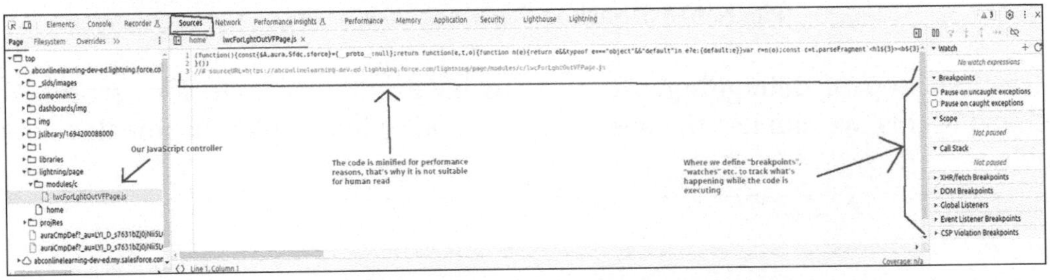

Figure 10.4: *Developer Tools Sources Tab*

Our JavaScript controller, **`lwcForLghtOutVFPage.js`**, can be found under **`lightning/page/modules/c`** folder on the left. When we click it, we see that its code is minified, and all the parameters' and functions' names are shortened. On the right panel, we see the accordion menu for tracking **Breakpoints**, **Listeners**, and so on.

Tip: When we are in **`Sources`** tab, if we cannot find our JavaScript controller on the left navigation menu, this means **Lightning Web Security** is enabled for our org. Then we need to disable it by using **`Setup → Session Settings`** menu:

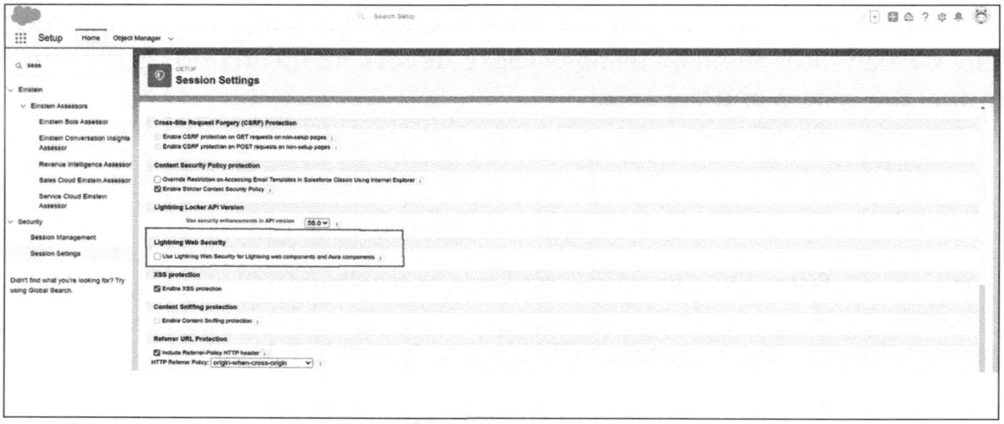

Figure 10.5: *Disabling "Lightning Web Security"*

As a first step of **debugging**, we need to have minimal code formatting. For achieving this, we can use the `pretty print` option in Google Chrome developer tools:

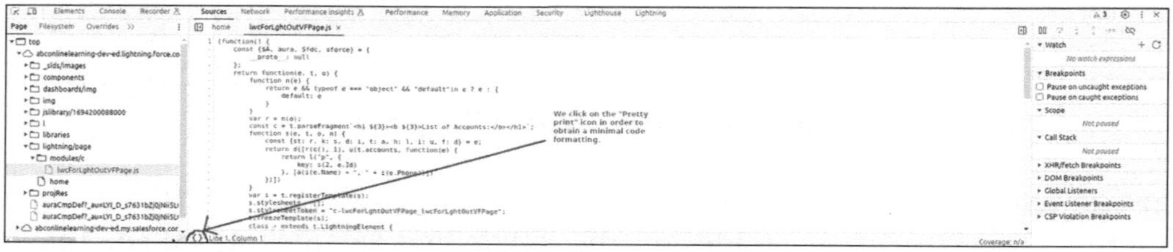

Figure 10.6: *Pretty print for code formatting*

Now, we have at least the spaces, the new lines and so on, which makes the code more readable. Although the parameter and function names are not the same as we determined them in our IDE (they continue to be replaced by shortened names), at least now we can more easily determine the part we wrote:

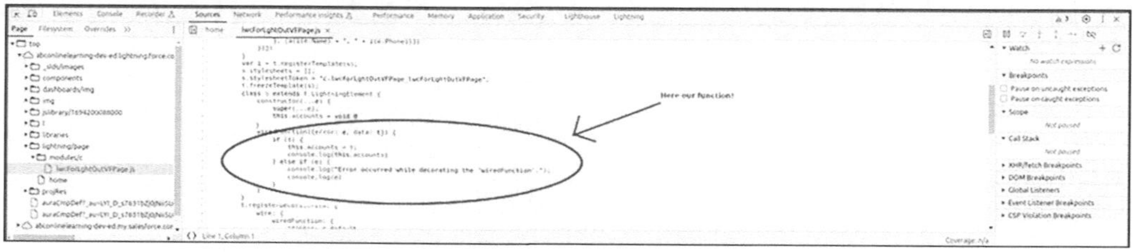

Figure 10.7: *Our main function*

At this point, we are ready to debug our code:

1. We can easily add **breakpoints** by clicking the **hyphens** that are at the beginning of the lines:

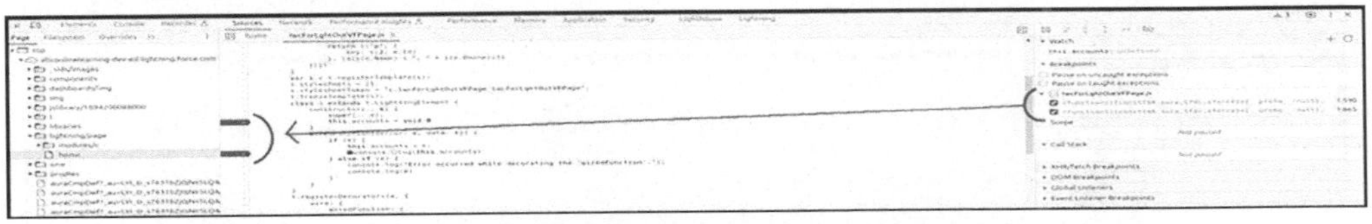

Figure 10.8: *We define two breakpoints*

2. We can track the main variables by clicking the **+** sign in the **Watch** tab.

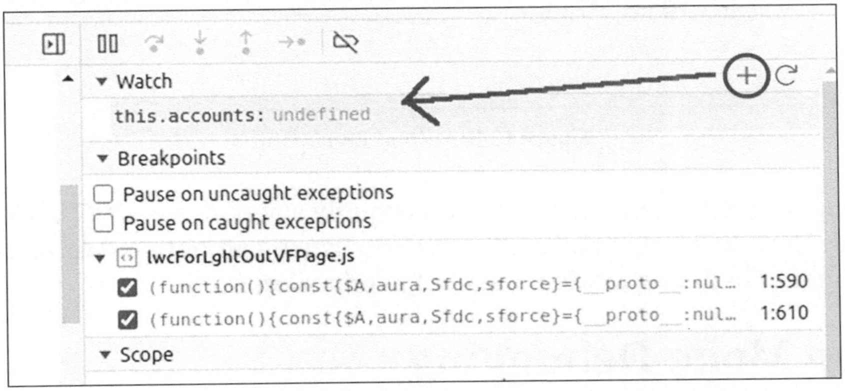

Figure 10.9: *We start to track this.accounts parameter in Watch*

3. When we reload the page, the execution stops at the first **breakpoint** as intended.

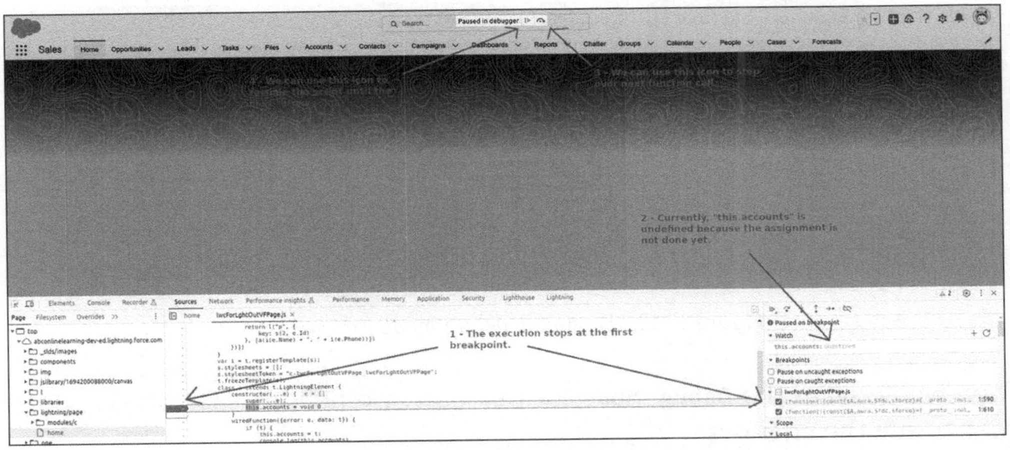

Figure 10.10: *First Breakpoint*

4. We execute the code until the second **breakpoint**, and now, in the **`Watch`** tab, we see that **`this.accounts`** is assigned to the correct array of 12 elements, which hold all the accounts of this org.

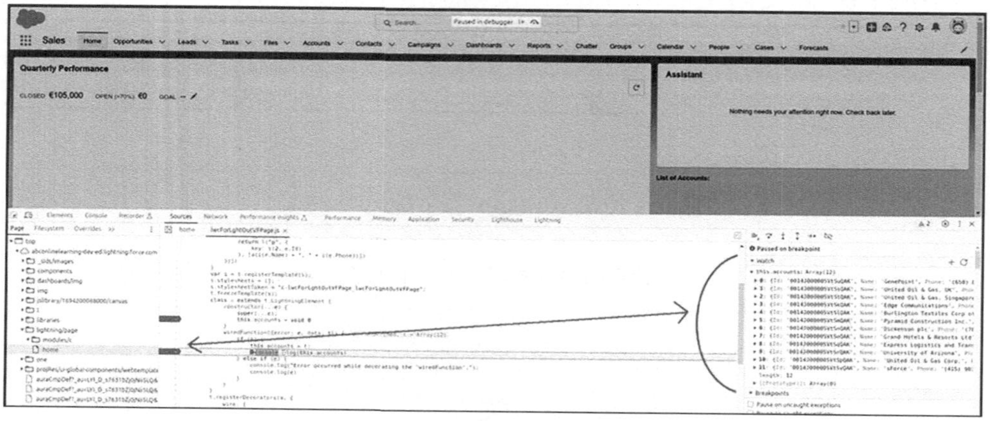

Figure 10.11: *Second Breakpoint*

The debugging is complete, and we can proudly say that our LWC is working as intended. Now, let's see what additional details we can obtain. We prefer to do the debugging in **debug mode** instead of **production mode**.

Debug Mode Debugging

In order to use **`Debug Mode`**, we need to activate it in Salesforce **`Setup`**. It can be activated not generally for every user, but instead, for specific selected users only.

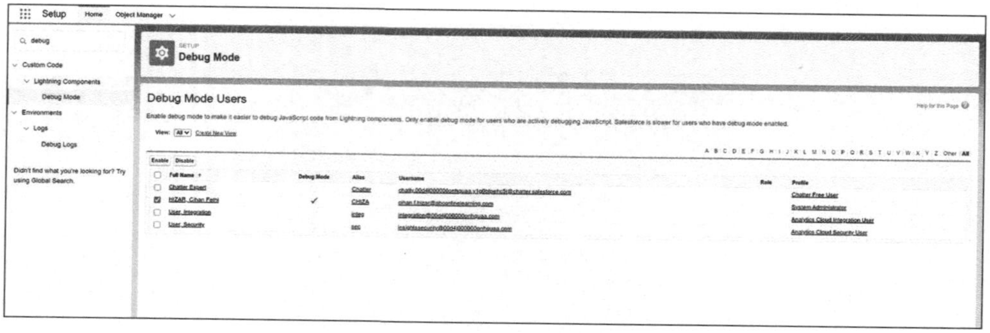

Figure 10.12: *We enable debug mode for our user*

When we activate the **`Debug Mode`** for our user, we need to refresh the page in order to see the changes:

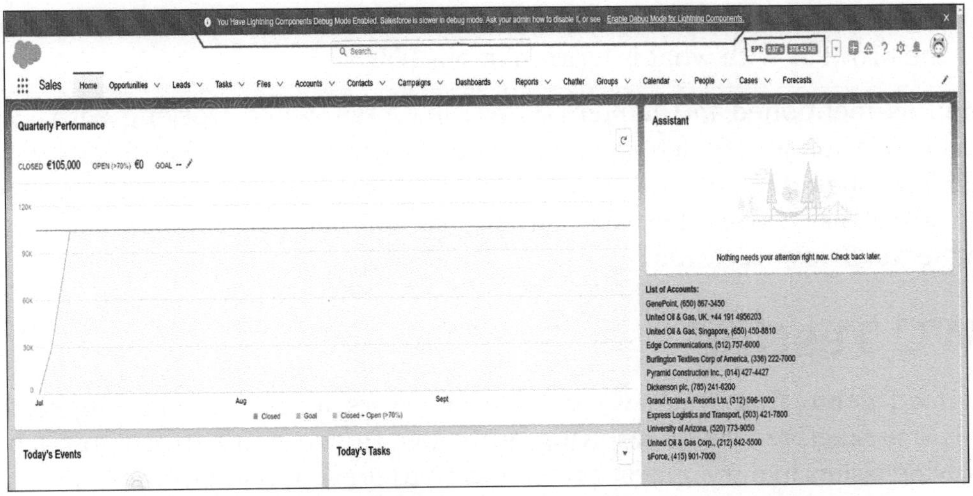

Figure 10.13: *Lightning Components Debug Mode Enabled*

Now, we have a banner at the top saying that ***we are in debug mode and in debug mode Salesforce will function slower than normal***. In addition, we have **EPT (Experience Page Time)** metrics. The first EPT metric is the page load time in seconds, and the second metric is the storage metric, which shows the memory usage of the page. Their colors indicate whether or not we have a performance issue: **Green** means we are without a problem, **Orange** means some optimizations are needed, and **Red** means we have a problem on the page performance that we should care about and fix.

When we open the Google Chrome developer tools, we notice that a good surprise is waiting for us: our code is loaded exactly the same as we wrote it in our IDE!

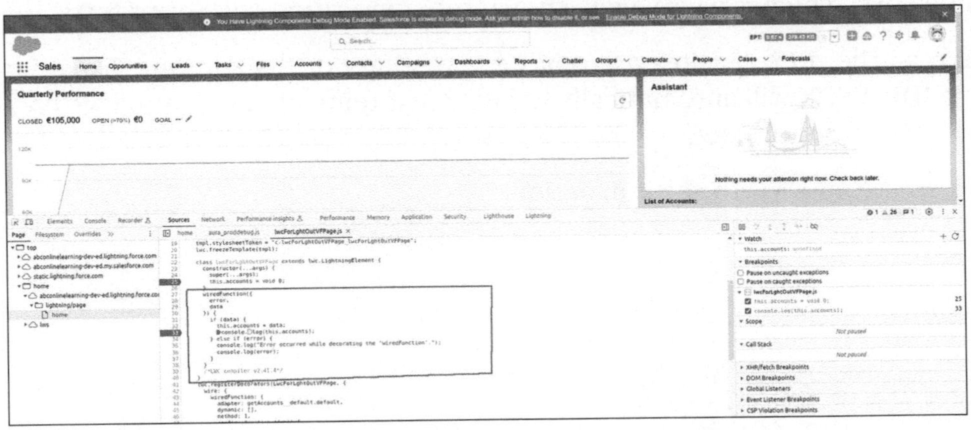

Figure 10.14: *Our code is loaded as it is while we are in debug mode*

So it is even easier to debug our code now as we can compare what is loaded into the browser with what is written in our IDE.

Note: As mentioned in *Chapter* 3, LWC in Detail, while working with LWCs, especially when we are debugging our code, in order to stop Salesforce hold the cache, we should open **`Setup → Session Settings`** page and uncheck the **`Enable secure and persistent browser caching to improve performance`** checkbox to disable the Salesforce caching.

LWC Testing

We need **debugging** when we encounter errors in our running application. So, it is a **reactive** way of resolving problems. However, a better approach for resolving issues in our applications would be to prevent them from happening in the first place. This is where **writing tests** come into the picture: it is a **proactive** approach in which we do our best to think of all the extreme scenarios where our application would fail and prepare the **tests** that will check for them.

Note: Before being able to write tests for our LWCs, we need to be sure that our SFDX project in Visual Studio Code has all the testing prerequisites like having the NPM package **`sfdx-lwc-jest`** installed, **`__tests__`** folders existing in the LWC, and so on.

We have already discussed how to fulfill those prerequisites in *Chapter* 2, *Creating Your First LWC*, so to remember how to be ready for writing tests, you can revisit that chapter.

As we can already guess from the name of the NPM package (which is **`sfdx-lwc-jest`**), for testing LWCs, we are going to use the JEST JavaScript Testing Framework, which is a very well-known tool for writing JavaScript tests.

When all the prerequisites are ready for writing our tests in our Visual Studio Code IDE, SFDX will automatically create a test template every time we create a new LWC in our project.

Let's create an LWC to see it in action:

lwcTestingExample.js:

```
import { LightningElement } from 'lwc';

export default class LwcTestingExample extends LightningElement {
    welcomeMessage = "Bienvenue!";

    handleClick() {
        this.welcomeMessage = "Welcome!";
    }
}
```

lwcTestingExample.html:

```
<template>
      <div>{welcomeMessage}</div>
      <lightning-button label="Translate to English" onclick=
{handleClick}>     </lightning-button>
</template>
```

This is a very simple LWC that shows a default **welcome message** in French on the screen when it is first loaded, and then when the user clicks the button it translates this message to English.

When we create this LWC in IDE, its test template is automatically created, as mentioned previously:

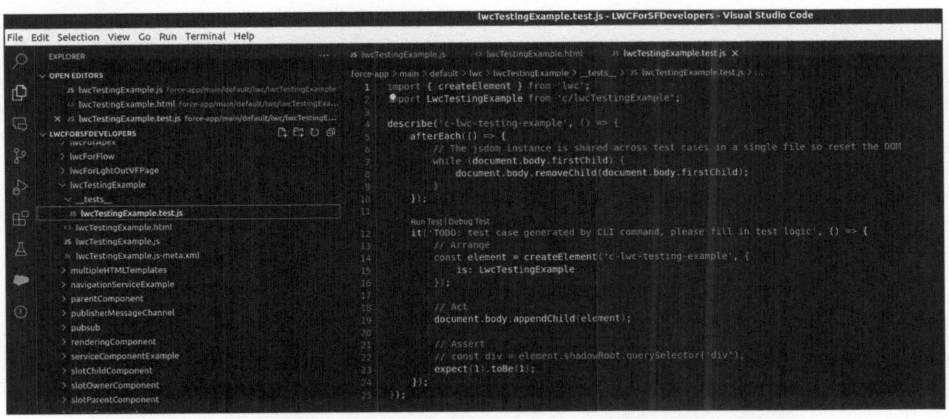

Figure 10.15: *Test template is created under `__tests__` folder*

Here is the code of the test template that is created automatically:

```
import { createElement } from 'lwc';
import LwcTestingExample from 'c/lwcTestingExample';

describe('c-lwc-testing-example', () => {
    afterEach(() => {
        // The jsdom instance is shared across test cases in a single
file so reset the DOM
        while (document.body.firstChild) {
            document.body.removeChild(document.body.firstChild);
        }
    });

    it('TODO: test case generated by CLI command, please fill in test
logic', () => {
        // Arrange
        const element = createElement('c-lwc-testing-example', {
            is: LwcTestingExample
        });

        // Act
        document.body.appendChild(element);

        // Assert
        // const div = element.shadowRoot.querySelector('div');
        expect(1).toBe(1);
    });
});
```

Initially, we import the **`createElement`** function from **`lwc`**, which will be used to create a copy of our component in the DOM. We need to have our component added to the DOM before we are able to test any test case.

Secondly, we import our current component from our LWC module: this assures the component we are going to test.

In the actual implementation, we have a **describe** block that consists of **afterEach** and **it** functions. All of them are the standard functions of the JEST JavaScript Testing Framework:

- **describe**: It is for creating a testing block that groups together several related tests.
- **afterEach**: It is the default method that is automatically called when a test function is run. It is mostly used to clear the DOM components that are created in the recent tests, before running other new tests. So, it gives us to have always a blank canvas before running a new test.
- **it**: It is the alias for **test()**. As the name implies, it is used to write a test case. So a **describe** block can have multiple **it()** functions, where each of them will be responsible for testing one of the cases for the component.

We can leave **afterEach** implementation as it is if we do not have any other requirements that should be executed every time we run a test. So, the actual work will be done under the **it** function.

As mentioned previously, we can have more than one test case, so we can have more than one **it** function under a **describe** block. Each **it** function should have the following initial part to create and add our component into the testing canvas:

```
// Arrange
const element = createElement('c-lwc-testing-example', {
     is: LwcTestingExample
 });

// Act
document.body.appendChild(element);
```

Consequently, thanks to this testing template that is automatically created for us, we can directly focus on writing the test code, which involves updating the following part:

```
    // Assert
    // const div = element.shadowRoot.querySelector('div');
    expect(1).toBe(1);
```

So, let us do it:

```
it('Testing the welcome message update after the user clicks on the button', () => {
        // Arrange
        const element = createElement('c-lwc-testing-example', {
            is: LwcTestingExample
        });

        // Act
        document.body.appendChild(element);

        element.shadowRoot.querySelector("lightning-button").click();

        // Assert
        return Promise.resolve().then(() => {
            const div = element.shadowRoot.querySelector('div');
            expect(div.textContent).toBe("Welcome!");
        });
    });
```

Initially, we update the definition of this test method to "*Testing the welcome message update after the user clicks on the button*". For each test method, we always need to have a proper definition to make our code more readable, as a best practice.

Our component has only one action: when the user clicks the button, it translates the text residing in the **`div`**. So, firstly, we need to imitate the button click:

```
element.shadowRoot.querySelector("lightning-button").click();
```

When running tests, all the user actions are imitated asynchronously; that is why we need to obtain their results by using **`Promise`** object:

```
return Promise.resolve().then(() => {
            const div = element.shadowRoot.querySelector('div');
            expect(div.textContent).toBe("Welcome!");
      });
```

Here, we are using **`return`** to terminate the test function as soon as the **`Promise`** is resolved. So, inside the **`Promise`**, we first obtain the updated inner text of the **`div`**, and then by using **`expert...toBe`** statement (which is one of the standard JEST statements for assertions), we check this text value to see whether or not it has the expected **`Welcome!`** value instead of the initial **`Bienvenue!`** value.

And that's it! Now we can run the test by using the **`Run Test`** link in Visual Studio Code:

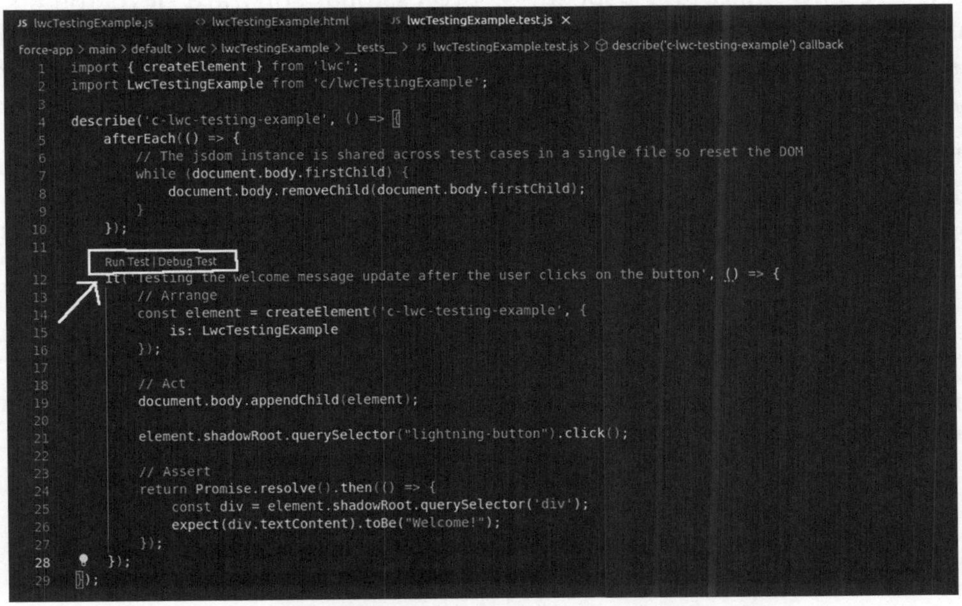

Figure 10.16: *We run tests by using Run Test link*

As expected, our test passed successfully:

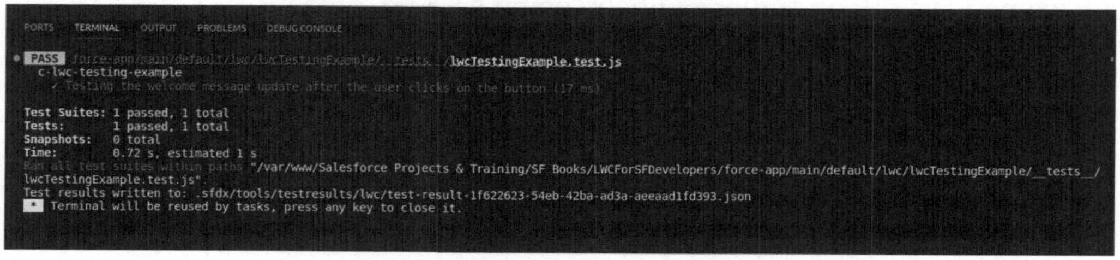

Figure 10.17: *Test is successful*

JavaScript testing via JEST Framework is a very large topic, which needs its own book to master it. We put the references for JEST documentation at the end of this chapter for guidance.

Conclusion

In this chapter, we learned how to debug and test our LWCs. Debugging and testing are two important aspects of professional software development. As mentioned, **debugging** is all about being **reactive** to the arisen problems after we deploy our application, but **testing** is all about being **proactive** and finding possible issues before doing any deployment.

As LWC is a JavaScript Framework, its debugging and testing are extremely similar to standard JavaScript debugging and testing: for debugging, we are mostly using browsers' tools, and for testing, we are benefiting from one of the popular JavaScript testing frameworks: JEST.

So, with this chapter, we are concluding our book. It was quite a journey! However, it is not the end; we have also added two appendices following this chapter to touch on two more topics that are surfacing LWC – Aura relations, which we believe are important.

Thank you!

References

- Debug Lightning Web Components - https://developer.salesforce.com/docs/platform/lwc/guide/debug-intro.html
- Troubleshoot Lightning Web Components - https://trailhead.salesforce.com/content/learn/trails/troubleshoot-lightning-web-components

- Test Lightning Web Components - https://developer.salesforce.com/docs/platform/lwc/guide/testing.html
- Lightning Web Components Tests - https://trailhead.salesforce.com/content/learn/modules/test-lightning-web-components
- JEST Docs - https://jestjs.io/docs/getting-started
- JEST API - https://jestjs.io/docs/api

Appendix 1

AURA-LWC Co-Existence

Before LWC came into the picture, Salesforce moved from one-page development (specifically, Visualforce pages) to component-based development via its Aura framework, as we know. So, there is a very good chance that, when we start a new project during these days, we would encounter lots of Aura components already running in the Salesforce org, with which we need our brand-new LWCs to co-exist. In this appendix, we will discuss how to achieve this.

Running an LWC under an Aura component is straightforward: we can put LWC just like any other HTML component in our Aura component's cmp file. Let's see this in action.

Here's our Aura component's cmp file:

auraForLWC.cmp:

```
<aura:component implements="flexipage:availableForAllPageTypes">
    <div class="slds-box slds-theme_info slds-theme_alert-texture">
        <span style="color:blue; font-weight:bold">This is Aura
component!</span>
        <c:lwcForAuraComponent />
    </div>
</aura:component>
```

As we can see, we simply add our LWC like an HTML component:

```
<c:lwcForAuraComponent>
```

And here is our LWC component's code:

lwcForAuraComponent LWC JavaScript Controller:

```
import { LightningElement, wire } from 'lwc';
import getAccounts from '@salesforce/apex/simpleApexClass2.
getAllAccounts';
export default class LwcForAuraComponent extends LightningElement {
    accounts;
    @wire(getAccounts, {}) wiredFunction({error, data}) {
        if(data) {
            this.accounts = data;
            console.log(this.accounts);
        }
        else if(error) {
            console.log("Error occurred while decorating the
'wiredFunction'.");
            console.log(error);
        }
    }
}
```

lwcForAuraComponent LWC HTML Template:

```
<template>
    <br/><br/>
    <div class="slds-box">
        <span style="color:green; font-weight:bold;">Now we're in our
LWC which resides in the Aura component...</span><br/><br/>
        <h1><b>List of Accounts:</b></h1>
```

```
        <template for:each={accounts} for:item="acc">
            <p key={acc.Id}>{acc.Name}, {acc.Phone}</p>
        </template>
    </div>
</template>
```

So, it is a simple LWC that lists all the accounts of a Salesforce org. When we deploy both components into our org, here is the result:

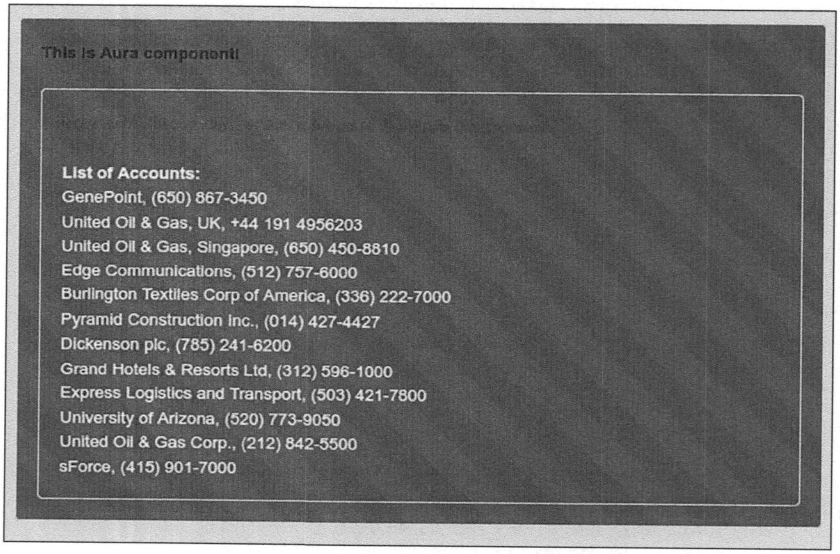

Figure A.1: *LWC inside Aura Component*

Tip: As there is a dependency between the Aura component and the LWC, we first deploy LWC and then Aura component.

Note: We can run a LWC under an Aura component but vice-versa is not possible: we cannot put an Aura component under an LWC.

If we need to transfer a message from an Aura component to an LWC, the only thing to do is to define the API for it in the LWC. So, our LWC becomes as follows:

lwcForAuraComponent LWC JavaScript Controller:

```
import { LightningElement, wire, api } from 'lwc';
import getAccounts from '@salesforce/apex/simpleApexClass2.
getAllAccounts';
```

```
export default class LwcForAuraComponent extends LightningElement {
    @api messageFromAura;
    accounts;
    @wire(getAccounts, {}) wiredFunction({error, data}) {
        if(data) {
            this.accounts = data;
            console.log(this.accounts);
        }
        else if(error) {
            console.log("Error occurred while decorating the
'wiredFunction'.");
            console.log(error);
        }
    }
}
```

lwcForAuraComponent LWC HTML Template:

```
<template>
    <br/><br/>
    <div class="slds-box">
        <span style="color:green; font-weight:bold;">Now we're in our
LWC which resides in the Aura component...</span><br/><br/>
        <h1><b>List of Accounts:</b></h1>
        <template for:each={accounts} for:item="acc">
            <p key={acc.Id}>{acc.Name}, {acc.Phone}</p>
        </template>
    </div>
    <br/>
    <p style="color:aqua; font-weight:bold;">{messageFromAura}</p>
</template>
```

Then, we update the Aura component as follows:

auraForLWC.cmp:

```
<aura:component implements="flexipage:availableForAllPageTypes">
    <div class="slds-box slds-theme_info slds-theme_alert-texture">
        <span style="color:blue; font-weight:bold">This is Aura
component!</span>
   <c:lwcForAuraComponent messageFromAura="This message is from Aura
component!"/>
    </div>
</aura:component>
```

As expected, the LWC obtains the message, as shown in *Figure A.2*:

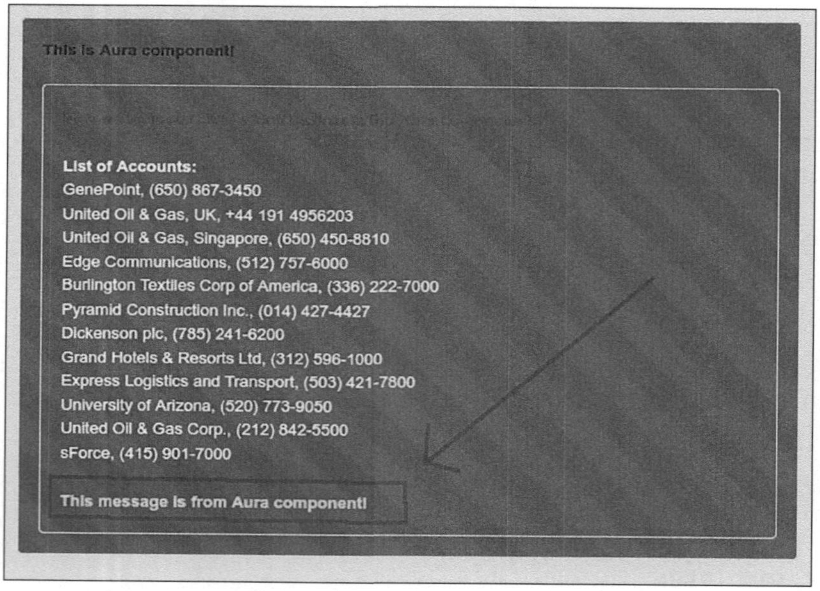

Figure A.2: *Message is transferred from Aura to LWC*

However, if we need to transfer a message from an LWC to an Aura component, we can do this by using events. Let's improve our components to support events:

lwcForAuraComponent LWC HTML Template:

```
<template>
```

```
    <br/><br/>
    <div class="slds-box">
        <span style="color:green; font-weight:bold;">Now we're in our
LWC which resides in the Aura component...</span><br/><br/>
        <h1><b>List of Accounts:</b></h1>
        <template for:each={accounts} for:item="acc">
            <p key={acc.Id}>{acc.Name}, {acc.Phone}</p>
        </template>
        <br/>
        <p style="color:aqua; font-weight:bold;">{messageFromAura}</p>
        <br/>
        <lightning-button label="Send Data to Aura" onclick={sendData}></
lightning-button>
        <br/>
    </div>
</template>
```

lwcForAuraComponent LWC JavaScript Controller:

```
import { LightningElement, wire, api } from 'lwc';
import getAccounts from '@salesforce/apex/simpleApexClass2.
getAllAccounts';
export default class LwcForAuraComponent extends LightningElement {
    @api messageFromAura;
    accounts;
    @wire(getAccounts, {}) wiredFunction({error, data}) {
        if(data) {
            this.accounts = data;
            console.log(this.accounts);
        }
        else if(error) {
            console.log("Error occurred while decorating the
'wiredFunction'.");
            console.log(error);
```

```
        }
    }
    sendData() {
        let lwcmessage = "This message is from LWC!";
        this.dispatchEvent(new CustomEvent("senddata", {detail :
{lwcmessage}}));
    }
}
```

auraForLWC.cmp:

```
<aura:component implements="flexipage:availableForAllPageTypes">
    <aura:attribute name="datalwc" type="String"></aura:attribute>
    <div class="slds-box slds-theme_info slds-theme_alert-texture">
        <span style="color:blue; font-weight:bold">This is Aura
component!</span>
        <c:lwcForAuraComponent onsenddata="{!c.printData}" message
FromAura="This message is from Aura component!"/>
        <br/>
        <p style="color:green; font-weight:bold;">{!v.datalwc}</p>
    </div>
</aura:component>
```

auraForLWCController.js:

```
({
    printData : function(component, event) {
        var dt = event.getParam("lwcmessage");
        component.set("v.datalwc", dt);
    }
})
```

First, we improve our LWC to dispatch a **`senddata`** event when the **`Send Data`** button is clicked. Then, we improve our Aura component to listen for this event and print the received message on the screen.

We re-deploy the components and click the **`Send Data`** button of LWC to trigger the **`senddata`** event. Here is the result:

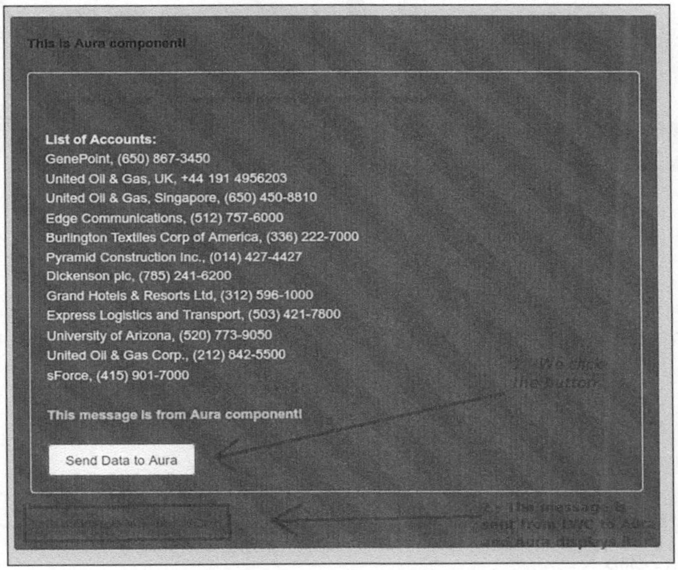

Figure A.3: *Message is transferred from LWC to Aura*

Apart from having a parent-child relationship, Aura components and LWCs can co-exist at the same time as standalone components on a Lightning page. So, when we need to send a message from an LWC to Aura (or vice-versa), we can use the Lightning Message Service (LMS). We already explored how to work with LMS from an LWC in *Chapter* 5, *Events in* LWC. For Aura components, the syntax for accessing LMS's message channels is much simpler than LWCs: it is done by just using the **`<lightning:messageChannel>`** component.

LMS is a global messaging service to which all components of a page, whether LWCs or Aura components, can publish and/or subscribe to its message channels. So, all components are messaging from and to the message channels of LMS, which provides us a way to transfer data from one component to another regardless of their type.

APPENDIX 2

Migrate Aura Components to LWCs

In *Appendix 1*, we explored how Aura components and LWCs can co-exist on a Lightning page. However, sometimes in a project, we would need to replace existing Aura components with LWCs.

To migrate an Aura component to an LWC, there are several steps to consider. Here, we list the important ones:

- **Migration of bundle files**
  - `aura.cmp` ↔ `lwc.html`
  - `auraController.js`, `auraHelper.js`, `auraRenderer.js` ↔ `lwc.js`
  - `aura.css` ↔ `lwc.css`
  - `aura.design` ↔ `lwc.js-meta.xml`
- **Migration of lifecycle hooks**
  - `Aura init event` ↔ `connectedCallback()`
  - `Aura render event` ↔ `constructor()`, `connectedCallback()`,`errorCallback()`
  - `Aura reRender event` ↔ `renderedCallback()`
  - `Aura afterRender event` ↔ `renderedCallback()`
  - `Aura unRender event` ↔ `disconnectedCallback()`
- **Migration of markup**
  - **Migration of Aura attributes to LWC JS Controller properties**
    - `access = "global" Aura attribute` ↔ `@api lwcProperty;`

- access = “public” Aura attribute ↔ @api lwcProperty;
- access = “private” Aura attribute ↔ lwcProperty;

- **Migration of conditional expressions**
  - **Aura version**:

```
<aura:if isTrue="{!v.something}">
        <div>Conditional Code</div>
        <aura:set attribute="else">
                <div>Conditional Code</div>
        </aura:set>
</aura:if>
```

  - **LWC version**:

```
<template>
        <div lwc:if={something}>Conditional Code</div>
        <div lwc:elseif={something}>Conditional Code</div>
</template>
```

- **Migration of iterations**
  - **Aura version**:

```
<aura:iteration items="{!v.items}" itemVar="item"> {!item}
</aura:iteration>
```

  - **LWC version**:

```
<template for:each={items} for:item="item">
        <p key={item.id}>{item}</p>
</template>
```

- **Migration of global value providers**
  - $Browser ↔@salesforce/client/formFactor

- `$ContentAsset` ↔`@salesforce/contentAssetUrl`
- `$Label` ↔`@salesforce/label`
- `$Locale` ↔`@salesforce/i18n`
- `$Resource` ↔`@salesforce/resourceUrl`

- **Migration of base components**
  - **Aura version**:

```
<aura:component>
<lightning:formattedText linkify="true" value="I like
salesforce" />
</aura:component
```

  - **LWC version**:

```
<template>
<lightning-formatted-text linkify value="I like
salesforce"></lightning-formatted-text>
</template>
```

  - Here, we have shared only one example of a **`base component`**, which is **`formatted-text`**. To see all base components, please refer to the Lightning Component Reference at https://developer.salesforce.com/docs/component-library/overview/components

- **Migration of Aura facets**
  - Facets are **`slots`** in LWC.
- **Migration of Apex**
  - For each Aura component, there is only one Apex controller that should be defined as:

```
<aura:component controller="ApexControllerClassName" ...>
```

- However, LWCs can work with multiple Apex classes and can import as many individual methods from as many Apex classes as they need:

```
import method1 from "@salesforce/apex/namespace1.class1.
method1";
import method2 from "@salesforce/apex/namespace1.class2.
method2";
so on...
```

- Then, in the Aura component, we define an action and a **`callback()`** to be able to call the Apex class method. However, in an LWC, the imported method is already a promise object.

These were the important steps. For all the details, please refer to the official documentation at https://developer.salesforce.com/docs/platform/lwc/guide/migrate-introduction.html.

Index

Symbols

A

C

S

T

U

V